REGULATED CHILDREN/ LIBERATED CHILDREN:

Education in Psychohistorical Perspective

Barbara Finkelstein, Editor

Psychohistory Press, Publishers
New York, New York, U.S.A.

REGULATED CHILDREN/LIBERATED CHILDREN:
Education in Psychohistorical Perspective

Library of Congress Cataloging in Publication Data

Main entry under title:

REGULATED CHILDREN/LIBERATED CHILDREN:
Education in Psychohistorical Perspective

   Includes bibliographical references and index.
   1. Education—United States—History—Addresses, essays, lectures. 2. Education—Europe—History—Addresses, essays, lectures. 3. Educational psychology—History—Addresses, essays, lectures. I. Finkelstein, Barbara, 1937-
LA209.R45   370'.973   79-14905
ISBN 0-914434-08-X

Table of Contents

Introduction

— BARBARA FINKELSTEIN

INTRODUCTION

The essays in this volume constitute an effort to incorporate an awareness of children into our understanding of modern educational history. As several of the authors whose essays appear in this book have written previously, the traditional history of education advances a remarkable bias: If historians of education study what people *teach* and *write*, they will somehow discover what is *learned*. Whether they define the history of education narrowly, as the history of schooling, or more broadly, as a wider range of efforts to transmit knowledge, attitudes, or sensibilities; whether they define the history of education as role training —a process of political, economic, and sexual socialization—historians of education have visualized learners as essentially passive. They have treated them as though they were helpless assignees of social status, recipients of shared culture, unwitting creations of political and economic arrangements—as uncritically absorbent recipients of roles, responsibilities, duties and skills. Their histories proceed as though children were cavernous holes into which are poured status, skills, books, and curricula, and out of which emerge formed human beings. Unwittingly asserting that human beings become only what others intend them to become, they have relegated learners and learning to the back seat of the historical bus. While most historians of education recognize that what is taught is not always what is learned, that what is intended is not necessarily what occurs in the process of cultural transmission, they have not as yet found ways to incorporate live learners into their histories.

This book is devoted to the task of introducing learners and learning into educational history. It is offered not as an introduction to an established order of knowledge, but as an introduction to the potentiality of new forms of inquiry into the history of education. Proceeding on the assumption that the processes of cultural transmission will be incompletely understood and unnecessarily narrowed by a single-minded preoccupation with educational ideas and structures, these ten essays focus on educational processes and consequences. They provide examples of educational history in which learning is explicitly emphasized. It is a history which is necessarily focused on the substance of adult-child relationships as they have been visually represented, institutionally enclosed and advanced, and philosophically and scientifically imagined. It is a history in which the substance of human relationships, i.e., the emotional and social as well as the political and economic dimensions of human experience, is considered to be important. It is a history in which careful attention is paid to relationships between the transmission of culture and the acquisition of identity.

Using hitherto ignored sources of data—autobiographies, diaries, art, and poetry—exploring the meaning of educational environments as they focus, advance, and extend relationships between adults and children, incorporating psychological, literary and anthropological as well as sociological and economic frameworks into the analyses of educational development, the essays provide a wide range of unusual approaches to the history of education.

The very sensibility that has inspired the creation of this book—a deeply felt conviction that educational effort is important insofar as it helps to illuminate the ways people come to comprehend who they are, what they wish to be, how they learn to believe, how they come to behave—is itself relatively new in presentations of educational history. So complete has been the disposition to relate the history of education to political, economic, or intellectual history that historians of education have not as yet connected the development of education to the development of the human capacity to create, to learn, and to love, as well as to work and vote and philosophize.

The work of two bold and original family historians has illuminated previously unexplored connections between the history of education and the history of the human capacity to love, to feel, and to think. Both Lloyd deMause and Phillippe Aries (in a rare instance of agreement) have emphasized the simultaneity in time of the discovery of childhood innocence and vulnerability and the emergence of protective institutions for the young. Describing the modern family in psychological rather than in economic terms, both have documented the emergence in mid-seventeenth century Europe of a new quality and possibility in child-rearing—that of an over-controlling, carefully planned regimen of protection and supervision. The modern family, as deMause has brilliantly documented and as Edmund Shorter and Lawrence Stone have confirmed and extended, can be described as a psychological environment in which parents are attentive to and preoccupied with children in the early stages of their development, eschewing infanticide, neglect, and indifference as acceptable courses of conduct toward young children. Understood in this way, the emergence of the modern family coincides with the emergence of parents as conscious educators as well as reproducers of their offspring. It corresponds also with a view of children as learners, vulnerable to outside influence and in need of protection and restraint.

The modern school, like the modern family, can also be understood as a psychological and cognitive as well as an economic and political environment, in which and through which human impulse and imagination, as well as intellect and reason, can be formed and informed.

Nowhere is the relationship between education and restraint more clearly articulated and graphically illustrated than in the minds and imaginations of America's first generation of Puritans. Heir to a tradition of intrusive child-rearing, nurtured in the bosom of law and prescription instructing parents and teachers to attach the development of reason to the moulding of sentiment, the first generation of Puritans seems to have tied affection and restraint inextricably together, to have envisioned loving relationships as those that were forged by reason and advanced through education. Both Ray Hiner's essay on Cotton Mather and Ross Beales' on Anne Bradstreet reveal the presence of an overwhelming and conscious commitment to the restraining possibilities of education, and to the role of education in the development of human consciousness. They locate the source of Mather's and Bradstreet's educational sensibility not only in Puritan theology and the rigors of the frontier, but in the daily psychological reality of growing up and becoming parents as well. They illuminate the existence of a virtual identification of love and learning in the consciousness of colonial American parents.

Enjoining himself as well as other parents to educate—to catechize children, to teach them to read and write at an early age, to entertain them with scripture, to offer them tid-bits of wisdom on every occasion—Cotton Mather was a pre-eminent expositor of tutorial parenthood. As Hiner observes in his essay, the model parent, the parent of his public utterance, was "a persistent, intrusive, but compassionate person who never missed an opportunity to educate." The objects of tutorial vigor were children, "narrow-mouthed vessels into which things must be drop after drop enstilled."

If Cotton Mather tended to regard children as passive vessels into which wisdom, knowledge, civility, and piety were to be poured, Anne Bradstreet most assuredly did not. Ross Beales' essay documents the remarkable fact that Puritan theology was not so harsh as to completely preclude the recognition of children as active learners who were fundamentally different from one another. Rather than compelling her to be unrelentingly severe... "her religion provided a framework for understanding the complex emotions and actions of children and for patiently rearing them." Beales is suggesting that Puritan consciousness, though by no means child-oriented or empathic, nonetheless enclosed an exquisite educational sensibility—the basis for a deep and meaningful, if somewhat distanced and formal, relationship between parents and children.

The college experiences of colonial youth also reflected a commitment to the restraining possibilities of formal education. Phyllis Vine's essay explores the cognitive, emotional and social ambience through which the political sensibilities of America's first generation of male Republican leaders was being nurtured. In its strict attention to public behavior, in its elaboration of shaming techniques of pedagogy and discipline, in its emphasis on communal rather than individual uses of intellect, and in its commitment to honor and withdrawal from the company of women, the eighteenth-century college extended and refined the commitment to restrained nurture and tutorial parenthood. In the process, students were learning to become politically sensitive, socially oriented, hierarchically inclined directors of an emerging body politic.

If this seventeenth and early eighteenth century generation of American colonials elaborated the commitment to tutorial parenthood in its educational arrangements and practices, their European counterparts were apparently proceeding on less child-oriented assumptions. Even in literary and artistic renderings of children prior to the eighteenth century, children, to use Judith Plotz's words, were treated as "projections of adult sins and desires, as symbolic emblems of moral frailty," or, in the Puritan mode, "as volatile human beings in need of correction." Extending the observations of deMause and Stone, the essays of Sterling Fishman and Judith Plotz document the emergence in nineteenth-century Western Europe of a new educational sensibility. Incorporated into the artistic consciousness was a fundamental re-imagination of relations between loving and learning.

Artists and writers began to dissociate learning from corporal punishment, to symbolize it as something more than a process of stuffing children with knowledge. As Fishman observes, "education [came to be] depicted as a gentle and affectionate activity rather than a violent or potentially violent one. Teachers no longer appeared with their omnipresent instruments of violence. Students were no longer universally sullen....Children came to be portrayed as eager and cheerful, teachers as loving and caring." Traditional treatments of educational settings—as harsh and unrelenting school environments in which children stood cowering in the presences of books, cudgels and taskmasters—re-emerged as an art of the grotesque, a caricature as well as a simple representation of real life.

The transformation in visual renderings of educational effort appears to have signalled a revolution in European educational consciousness. Judith Plotz's essay elaborates the substance of an extraordinary corpus of Romantic poetry which appears to constitute nothing less than a revolution in the capacity of human beings to imagine new educational possibilities. In its empathic language, its emphasis on the importance of early childhood experiences, its concern with growth and maturation, and its recognition of what Plotz calls activated self-consciousness, Romantic poetry defined education as a process of individual growth and development. Envisioning the child in isolation from the requirements of convention and tradition, imagining the teacher as a sort of intellectual and emotional midwife, the Romantic poets tied individuality and education inextricably together. And, in the process, they elaborated a compelling vision of educational possibility that has attracted and confounded, if it has not seduced, subsequent generations of thoughtful educators.

By the early decades of the nineteenth century, the commitment to careful nurture had been translated into two different visions of educational possibility for the lives of the young and the very young. Inherent in the educational consciousness of both European Romantics and American Puritans was a view that children benefited from being enclosed within self-conscious educational settings in which their cognitive and moral capacities would be carefully and particularly attended.

But they differed profoundly about the substance and meaning of tutorial environments. For the Puritans, books, sermons, and prayers constituted the ideal focus of adult-child relationships, particularly those of parents and children. Ambivalent if not downright hostile toward physical expressions of affection between parent and child, they envisioned loving relationships as those in which the commitment to reason was extended. The tasks of formal education—learning to read and write, to recite the catechism, to reproduce portions of the Bible—importantly moulded the substance of adult-child relationships. And in the process children were learning to govern their own passions, not only by being whipped or otherwise beaten into submission, but by constantly attending to the tasks of formal learning, seeking approval through intellectual expression, finding a vocabulary with which to order the world from educational artifacts—the Bible, books, sermons—and using their minds to direct their emotions. The education environment of the Puritan imagination nurtured close but formalized relationships between adults and children.

The sensibility of European Romantic poets proceeded from different assumptions. In their view, a too-early preoccupation with the tasks of formal education would doom a child to a premature atrophy of the mental and imaginative powers. Celebrating the creative impulse, cherishing the unwillingness of children to accept the force of circumstance, the tutorial environment of the Romantic imagination was one in which books and the acquisition of literacy existed only to activate children's minds, rather than to mould them in particular directions. Their tutorial environment involved adults intimately in the lives of children, not primarily as instruments of cultural transmission but as midwives to creative possibility and sentimental affection.

The double-vision of educational possibility, to use Sterling Fishman's apt phrase, comprised two distinct and opposing understandings of the role of systematic and deliberate education in the organization of childhood experience. The first mobilized an educational process in the service of collective harmony. The second defined a process in which the growth of individual power and creativity constituted its principal purpose. The publicly oriented process enclosed children in closely regulated environments which required children to suspend their impulses, eschew subjectivity, suppress imaginative expression, and otherwise refrain from spontaneous, informal expressive human discourse. Children were asked to imitate and repeat, to memorize, recall, declaim and reproduce the order of things. Rewarded when they recited the discouraged from interpreting or re-creating, children were enclosed in a materials, punished if subjective elements entered into their recitations, discouraged from interpreting or recreating, children were enclosed in a process of depersonalization and social re-orientation. Required to discover rather than invent, to imitate rather than create, to mimic rather than transform culture, children were committed by the requirements of communal harmony to highly structured and controlled environments.

The second process of tutorial enclosure defined the child as a social participant in which his or her differences would be cherished and nurtured. Surrounding children with a variety of materials, soliciting their observations, engaging them in collaborative dialogue, rewarding expressions of curiosity and imagination, this sort of environment muted the instrumental quality of an insistent preoccupation with structured intellectual expression.

Throughout the nineteenth and twentieth centuries, various forms of tutorial environments were extended, elaborated, and formalized, and with particular vigor in the United States. Over the course of these two centuries, childhood came to be idealized as a stage in the life-cycle when children ought to be in school. Children themselves were entering schools in ever-increasing numbers. Over these two centuries teachers as well as parents became important agents of cultural transmission. And in the process, the political, moral, psychological, and cognitive functions of schools were consciously and vehemently debated, elaborated, and extended.

My own essay illustrates the variability of educational processes and arrangements which enclosed and informed children as they learned to read, write, and reckon in the seventy years from 1790 to 1860 in the United States. Exploring a multiplicity of social networks in which formal learning proceeded, analyzing the ways in which the processes of acquiring literacy informed the minds and imaginations of children, the essay inadvertently suggests that American educational practice was distinguished by its diverse effects on the development of children and by the multiple orientations of its pedagogies.

The essays of Deborah Fitts and Dominic Cavallo explore changes in tutorial environments as they began to advance a conscious awareness of the psychological and moral possibilities of school attendance. Interpreting both the feminization of teaching and the emergence of the kindergarten as attempts to reorganize the substance of tutorial environments, Fitts and Cavallo document an emerging preference in the mid-nineteenth century for personal, domestic, moral enclosures for children, as over and against the more impersonal cognitive and public processes that were becoming the rule in cities. Using the tutorial family as a model, and projecting women as the proper guardians of the hearts and minds of young children in the early stages of their development, the advocates of feminization sought to transform the ambience of early education to incorporate softer modes of discipline and to appeal to conscience instead of fear. As women were projected as keepers of sensibility, the schools over which they presided were coming to symbolize, if not to completely extend, the substance of domestic education as it was practiced in settings where the claims of childhood and the claims of community were somehow balanced.

Kindergarten educators, too, favored educational environments in which the moral and psychological development of each child was particularly attended. Viewing themselves as pedagogical midwives rather than drillmasters, engaging each child as a separate moral entity, preferring moral persuasion to corporal punishment or peer pressure as a mode of discipline, kindergartners institutionalized a new kind of tutorial environment for children. Neither wholly domestic nor fully public, the kindergarten was a specialized educational institution drawing children out of the private and idiosyncratic realm of the family into a tutorial environment that was moral and psychological rather than cognitive and impersonal in its deliberate emphases.

The debate within the ranks of kindergarten advocates in the half-century from 1870-1930 is the subject of Dominic Cavallo's essay. No simple academic argument, the debate involved nothing less than a fundamental reassessment of the proper psychological and social functions of schools. On the one side were educators such as Elizabeth Peabody, for whom schools represented a simple extension of domestic nurture, a child's garden that would ultimately help to produce a morally autonomous human being—self-governed, self-motivated, self-controlled, and self-disciplined. On the other side were progressive kindergartners—Susan Blow, William Torrey Harris, G. Stanley Hall, John Dewey—who envisioned schools as institutions in which re-socialization could occur. Through a pedagogical process in which shame and peer pressure rather than guilt and moral persuasion predominated, the new kindergarten educators mobilized the schools in the cause of social adjustment. Defining the schools as important instruments of socialization and teachers as expert interveners and readjusters, progressive educators consciously envisioned schools as transitional institutions, as psychological and cognitive bridges between the increasingly differentiated worlds of family and work place, men and women, children and adults.

An inherent tension between the needs of children and the requirements of society was brilliantly articulated by Sigmund Freud in 1909: "[H]itherto education has set itself the task of controlling, or it would often be more proper to say, of suppressing the instincts. The results have been by no means gratifying....Nor has anyone enquired by what means and at what cost the suppression of the inconvenient instincts has been achieved." Sol Cohen's essay explores the emergence of a psychoanalytic pedagogy in which the claims of childhood were understood to be in opposition to the claims of society. Like the Romantic poets to whose educational sensibility they were heir, psychoanalytic pedagogues launched an assault on the debilitating effects of cultural imposition. In theory and in practice, they elaborated and institutionalized a radically new educational reality for children. Anna Freud, August Aichorn, Eric Hoffer, Erik Erikson, Siegfried Bernfeld, Lilli Roubiczed-Peller, Peter Blos (a small group—Anna Freud estimated it at 25 or 30)— all participated, advancing a compelling vision of education which, although they ultimately rejected it, has nonetheless captured adherents in the United States.

Extending what Cohen describes as a liberationist or permissivist trend in the work of Sigmund Freud, his daughter Anna projected an educational setting designed to liberate children from restraint and imposition. Cherishing the child's shrewdness and originality, and seeing danger in education, psychoanalytically informed pedagogues created educational environments which were distinctly untutorial. Within this environment, adults behaved as observers and supporters rather than as drillmasters and midwives. Their disillusionment with the effects of unrestrained education constitutes an important chapter in the history of pedagogical possibility.

The immersion of children into educational environments in which emotional and imaginative, as well as intellectual and cognitive, expression was rewarded and encouraged only rarely occurred in practice. Existing primarily in the minds and imaginations of a very few European theorists—Romantic poets and artists—and as occasional radical experiments conducted by psychoanalytic pedagogues and practitioners such as A. S. Neill, Caroline Pratt, and a few alternative-school advocates in the United States, the Romantic educational tradition appears to have been European rather than American in its formulation.

The genius of American education appears to reside in the dazzling array of tutorial environments which have enclosed children in increasingly larger numbers, culminating in the 1920s and 1930s when schools came to form a principal substance of daily reality for almost every American child. Neither wholly cognitive in orientation, nor, as some historians have asserted, anti-intellectual in form and function, American education has been diverse in substance, complex in effect, and social and psychological in orientation. Not infrequently subversive in its consequences, it has been liberating for the oppressed and oppressive to the well-born. It has set children against the traditions and customs of their families, and it has also strengthened and refined their ties. It has muted the severity of relationships between adults and children, and has introduced severity and regulation where none had existed before. It has structured a period of childhood dependency as one in which cognitive and social development are inextricably related—creating mobility for some children, alienation for others, isolation for still others, and communalism for a very few.

Tutorial American environments have turned Americans to bridge-building, to outer space, and to scientific discovery, rather than to poetry, art, or philosophical or psychological speculation—but it has foreclosed none of these orientations for talented and idiosyncratic young people.

I

Anne Bradstreet and her Children

— ROSS W. BEALES

Since the publication of Bernard Bailyn's *Education in the Forming of American Society* (1960), it has become commonplace, indeed almost obligatory, for historians to cite Bailyn's definition of education as "the entire process by which a culture transmits itself across the generations." Whether one is satisfied with this definition or chooses a more elaborate conceptualization such as Lawrence A. Cremin's, we may exhibit the same myopia which Bailyn discerned in earlier historians. Certainly there have been substantial contributions toward understanding the varied aspects of education outside formal classrooms and schools,[1] but the current broader understanding of education is hardly new. Indeed, the New England Puritans probably would have understood and sympathized with Bailyn's concern to interpret education in its broadest cultural context.

The Puritans' idea of education outside the classroom had much to do with their hope to encourage the development and perpetuation of desirable traits of character, including, of course, piety. In their efforts to achieve their goals, they placed primary responsibility on parents. Thus, for Eleazar Mather, families were "the Seminaries of Church and Common-wealth," and "the Generation to come will reap the fruit of Family-Education; such Children as you bring up, such Parents will they be, when you are gone, to their Children, and such Children shall they have who are Parents in the next Generation." Israel Loring admonished parents: "Begin betimes to teach your Children. You have the advantage early to teach them, before their young and tender minds receive ill impressions from others." Benjamin Lord reminded his parishioners that "if children, and very youth, are well educated and governed at first, and rightly principled, with just notions of important things; are well disposed, and of an orderly behaviour, this is not only so far well in them, for the present, but, this looks forward to some thing still better; it has some smiling, hopeful aspect on their future days."[2]

Not only was early childhood education, in its broadest sense, important, but the role of the mother in that process was seen as special. According to John Robinson, pastor of the Puritan separatists in Leyden, "Children, in their first days, have the greater benefit of good mothers, not only because they suck their milk, but in a sort, their manners also, by being continually with them, and receiving their first impressions from them."[3] In eulogizing his wife, John Saffin wrote:

She was well versed in Domastick cares
Did prudently Order her house Affaires
The Education of her Children young,
She knew full well, did unto her belong;
And O how Loveingly with awefull heed,
She did her Children, and her Maidens Breed.
That with a look, a nod, in silence Beckt,
She could command Obedience, due Respect.

Unfortunately, relatively little information about mother-infant and mother-child relationships survives from the colonial period. Indeed, those relationships were probably taken for granted, and were, therefore, unrecorded. Usually without considerable detail, diarists (often male) might note the birth and death of infants, the mother's period of confinement following childbirth, difficulties in nursing, occasional information about weaning, the development of a child's ability to sit, crawl, or walk, and the child's first attendance at school. These events in an infant's or a child's life thus serve to delineate the broad contours of development, but relatively little evidence survives about the affective relationships between mother and child or between father and child, particularly in the seventeenth century.[4]

The writings of Anne Bradstreet (c. 1612-1672) provide important insights into a mother's relationship with her children. Although Bradstreet has long had an important place in the literary history of early America,[5] historians of family life have paid relatively little attention to her poetry and prose for information about seventeenth-century attitudes concerning parenthood and childrearing.[6] While women bore the principal, if not exclusive, responsibility of caring for infants and small children, thereby greatly influencing their moral and psychological development, few seventeenth-century New England women left written accounts of their lives. An examination of Bradstreet's ideas about parents and children provides an important perspective on family life from a woman's experience. In addition, such an examination is a useful corrective to a major theme in much of the literature about childrearing in early America: namely, that certain parental attitudes and child-rearing practices had psychologically harmful effects on children.[7]

As a Puritan, as a woman, as an adult who recalled her own relationship with her parents, and as a mother, Anne Bradstreet viewed the meaning of childhood and parenthood from several perspectives. Her ideas can be understood by examining several major aspects of her experience and concern: her sometimes ambivalent attitude toward parenthood and a parent's relationship with children; her imputation of innocence as well as sin to children's behavior; her strong emotional ties to children; and her recognition of individual character and temperament.

Anne Bradstreet was born in England in about 1612, the first daughter and second child of Thomas and Dorothy Dudley. Her father, later the second governor of the Massachusetts Bay Colony, was clerk or secretary to Judge Augustine Nicolls at Faxton manor in Northamptonshire. At the age of 16, Anne married 25-year-old Simon Bradstreet, who would also become a governor of Massachusetts. In 1630 she and her husband accompanied her parents to New England aboard the *Arbella,* which also carried Governor John Winthrop to Massachusetts. Simon Bradstreet was associated with John Winthrop, Jr., in the founding of Ipswich, Massachusetts, and during the 1640s the Bradstreets moved to the area which was later incorporated as Andover, where Anne Bradstreet died in 1672.[8]

Although Simon Bradstreet was the most prominent layman among the settlers of Andover, in demographic terms the Bradstreets were a fairly typical family. As portrayed by Philip J. Greven, Jr., the average first-generation woman in Andover married at the age of nineteen, while her husband was about twenty-seven. Although a few women bore as many as twelve or thirteen children, the average completed family had slightly more than eight children. During the first generation in Andover, most children survived the risks of infancy and childhood, with about seven of every eight reaching the age of 21. The risk of death for women during their childbearing years was slightly less than the risk of death for men in those same years, and persons who attained adulthood were likely to live to relatively advanced ages.[9] The Bradstreets reflected this pattern. They had married young and had eight children, all of whom lived to adulthood. Both Anne and Simon died at old ages, she at 60 when their youngest child was 20 years old, and he at 94.[10]

Anne Bradstreet wrote throughout her married life. While it is difficult to date precisely some of her works, she wrote not merely about and for her husband and children but also about her grandchildren and her own parents, thereby providing at least some information about four generations of her family. She had much to say about her parents. Her strong-willed and sometimes contentious father, who was both colleague and rival to Governor Winthrop, made the sharpest conscious impression upon her. He was probably the model for Old Age in her poem, "Of the Four Ages of Man," and upon his death in 1653 she composed a poetic eulogy "To the Memory of My Dear and Ever Honoured Father." Although her eulogy dealt largely with Dudley's public character, Bradstreet also acknowledged the close relationship between father and daughter:

> Nor is't relation near my hand shall tie;
> For who more cause to boast his worth than I?
> Who heard or saw, observed or knew him better?
> Or who alive than I a greater debtor?
> Let malice bite and envy gnaw its fill,
> He was my father, and I'll praise him still.

Dudley had been the "guide" and "instructor" who had introduced her to the world of books and learning; he was "a prizer of good company," a man whose manners were at once "pleasant and severe."[11]

Despite Thomas Dudley's forceful character and crucial importance for his daughter's intellectual development, Dorothy Dudley is both more elusive and more interesting for an understanding of family life. When she died in 1643, her daughter wrote a fourteen-line epitaph summarizing her virtues as wife, mother, and neighbor. Critics have noted that this poem portrays Dorothy Dudley as the embodiment of all the wifely duties and piety which Puritan ministers prescribed for the ideal woman. In her daughter's words, she was "a worthy matron of unspotted life."[12]

Bradstreet may have revealed more about her mother than she intended or realized. In "Of the Four Ages of Man," Childhood's monologue offers suggestive evidence about the relationship between mothers and daughters. Bradstreet's observations may have reflected her childhood relationship with her mother as well as her own experience as a mother. Through Childhood's words, Bradstreet decribed the difficulties of pregnancy, the pains of birth, and the draining demands of motherhood:

> My mother's breeding sickness I will spare,

Her nine months weary burthen not declare.
To show her bearing pains, I should do wrong,
To tell those pangs which can't be told by tongue:
With tears into the world I did arrive;
My mother still did waste as I did thrive,
Who yet with love and all alacrity,
Spending, was willing to be spent for me.

In alluding to the pain of childbirth and to a mother's sacrifices, was Bradstreet merely reporting her own experience, or was she writing not only as a mother but about her own mother, recalling what she knew of her mother's experience?

With wayward cries I did disturb her rest,
Who sought still to appease me with the breast:
With weary arms she danced and "By By" sung,
When wretched I, ingrate, had done the wrong.[13]

Bradstreet wrote her poem on the ages of man after she had borne five children, the eldest of whom was probably no more than ten, so she could speak directly from the experience of childbirth, nursing, and childrearing. But her knowledge would also have derived from her mother's experience, for Bradstreet was the eldest daughter in a growing family and was about nine years old when her youngest sister was born. As a result, she may have written, through Childhood, about both her mother and herself, acknowledging the special relationship and understanding that could exist only between a mother and her daughter.

There is a basic ambivalence in Bradstreet's relationship with children. The infant, after all, is an "ingrate" with an inborn propensity to inflict pain and choose wrong over right. Thus, Childhood confesses:

Stained from birth with Adam's sinful fact,
Thence I began to sin as soon as act:
A perverse will, a love to what's forbid,
A serpent's tongue in pleasing face lay hid:
A lying sting as soon as it could speak,
And fifth commandment do daily break.

Both John F. Walzer and Peter Gregg Slater have explored aspects of parental ambivalence. It should be emphasized that while parental hostility and possibly violence today may express a frustrated inability to deal with a complex world, colonial New England society may have differed significantly in the relatively harmless consequences of such ambivalence. Within the Puritan world view, the child's "perverse will" was but one manifestation of the flawed character which all mankind, parents and children alike, shared. Thus a parent might recognize his or her own limitations and pray, with Deacon John Paine after the birth of his second child, "O that God would please to bless me indeed and keep me and mine from Sin that god would please So to indow me with wisdom and grace that I may bring up these littel Lambs that he hath commited to my charge in the fear of the lord." Furthermore, Puritan society offered ideological support for parenthood and clearly defined the familial roles of parents and children.[14]

In expressing ambivalence about parenthood, was Bradstreet suggesting that children should feel guilty for the trouble which they caused their parents? The child, the source of a nine-month burden and labor pains, thrived while the mother wasted away. The child disturbed the mother's rest and was the "wretched I," the "ingrate," who "had done the wrong." Bradstreet's older children—indeed, many children in an era before family limitation and institutionalized childbirth—would have witnessed the "breeding sickness," the "bearing pains," and the "weary arms" of their mothers. Whether children were not merely witnesses, but guilty witnesses as well, can only be hypothesized, but if children did feel guilt for the pain they caused their mothers, such guilt could have been reinforced by, and in turn strengthened, Puritanism's emphasis on human depravity, unworthiness, and deserved liability for punishment.[15]

While Bradstreet was ambivalent about children, she also appreciated the complexity of childhood. Although critics have stressed her acknowledgment that childhood was "Stained from birth with Adam's sinful fact," Bradstreet also presented a picture of childish innocence. Thus, Childhood speaks:

> When infancy was past, my childishness
> Did act all folly that it could express,
> My silliness did only take delight
> In that which riper age did scorn and slight.

Children's ambitions were low, for they delighted "in rattles, baubles, and such toyish stuff." Ignorant of adult concerns, the child was free of envy and arrogance. The child did not seek riches, buy favor, or covet offices for self-aggrandizement. Nor did the child vex its neighbors with lawsuits, or fear the loss of cargoes at sea and the destruction of crops by drought or flood. Protected by its innocence and ignorance, the child's quarrels and ambitions wrought little harm:

> Where e'er I went, mine innocence was shield.
> My quarrels not for diadems did rise,

But for an apple, plum, or some such prize:
My strokes did cause no blood, no wounds or scars,
My little wrath did end soon as my wars.

Thus, just as Michael Wigglesworth could search for "the easiest room
in Hell" for dying infants, parents could view their children with a
measure of sentimentality, seeing in them an innocence that was special
to childhood. This innocence would end with youth, however, for "the
seeds/Lay raked up of all the cursed weeds/Which sprouted forth in
mine ensuing age."[16]

In addition to childhood's innocent ignorance, as well as the " 'sins' and
'dangers' " to which the child was subject, Bradstreet portrayed the complexity of children, which lay as much in the child's helpless inability to
understand its own moods as in the fact that "mine innocence" was
"stained from birth." Thus, Childhood acknowledges:

Oft stubborn, peevish, sullen, pout and cry,
Then nought can please, and yet I know not why.

In her empathy with children's kaleidoscopic and often seemingly
perverse moods, Bradstreet rose above a parent's frustrated efforts to
understand children. She knew that a child could not help itself, for it
could not comprehend its own nature. A modern psychologist might not
attribute children's behavior to original sin, but such an interpretation
provided an intellectual foundation upon which a parent's patience
might rest.[17] Certainly, in the Puritan view, a child was a sinful
creature, but that was not a personal or individual defect of character;
rather, it was the common and pervasive condition of mankind.

Bradstreet also examined the strong emotional attachments between
parent and child. In her autobiography, she recalled the pain which the
early childless years of her marriage had caused: "It pleased God to keep
me a long time without a child, which was a great grief to me and cost me
many prayers and tears before I obtained one." Thankful for the "many
more" children she bore, she was also fortunate and grateful that all of
them survived to adulthood. Like all parents, she was aware of the
dangers of illness and accident to which children were exposed; as
Childhood exclaims, "That wonder 'tis, my glass till now doth hold."
She was also acutely sensitive to her own risks at childbirth, bidding
poetic farewell to her husband during one of her pregnancies and asking
him to protect her "little babes" from "step-dame's injury."[18]

In her late forties, with only three children remaining at home (the
youngest nearly seven years old), her concern for her children was, if
anything, more intense. She had bred her children with great pain, fed

them with great care, but:

> My cares are more and fears than ever,
> My throbs such now as 'fore were never.
> Alas, my birds, you wisdom want,
> Of perils you are ignorant.

She acknowledged but did not regret her own mortality and contrasted her age with her children's youthfulness and beauty:

> Once young and pleasant, as are you,
> But former toys (no joys) adieu.
> My age I will not once lament,
> But sing, my time so near is spent.

Although she anticipated a restful heaven, angelic song, and eternal spring, she also wished that her children would remember her and thus wrote her own epitaph, asking them to tell their own children:

> You had a dam that loved you well,
> That did what could be done for young,
> And nursed you up till you were strong,
> And 'fore she once would let you fly,
> She showed you joy and misery;
> Taught what was good, and what was ill,
> What would save life, and what would kill.
> Thus gone, amongst you I may live,
> And dead, yet speak, and counsel give:
> Farewell, my birds, farewell adieu,
> I happy am, if well with you.

Thus, as a parent, Bradstreet was a teacher, expressing her love in the lessons of life. If her children learned those lessons well, then she would be like Abel, who "being dead yet speaketh."[19]

Reconciled to her own mortality and anticipating immortality, she could bid farewell to her children. It was more difficult, however, to accept the deaths of three grandchildren. Elizabeth Bradstreet, whom she called her "dear babe," her "sweet babe, the pleasure of mine eye," died in 1665 at the age of a year and a half. Bradstreet consoled herself that Elizabeth was in heaven, for she knew that God's hand guides both nature and fate, eradicating newly set plants and buds.[20]

The death of a second grandchild, her own namesake, at the age of three years and seven months, turned the poet, "with troubled heart and trembling hand," to a realization that she had prized earthly things too much. Experience should have made her wise enough to know that there was no "stable joy" on earth. The child was, she knew,

> ...but as a withering flower,
> That's here today, perhaps gone in an hour;
> Like as a bubble, or the brittle glass,
> Or like a shadow turning as it was.

Again, however, Bradstreet's "throbbing heart" found solace in the knowledge that the child was in heaven.[21]

Several months later, the death of yet a third grandchild, barely one month old, brought Bradstreet to an almost fierce resignation before God's will:

> With dreadful awe before Him let's be mute,
> Such was His will, but why, let's not dispute,
> With humble hearts and mouths put in the dust,
> Let's say He's merciful as well as just.
> He will return and make up all our losses,
> And smile again after our bitter crosses.

Here Bradstreet came close to cynicism and blasphemy, depending on how she would have us read the line "Let's say He's merciful as well as just."[22]

Bradstreet was thus not only a dutiful mother but, more importantly, one who loved her children and grandchildren with a strength and depth of feeling not usually associated with Puritanism. She knew that she should not place too much importance on mere earthly things. What prevented grief from turning into despair was her faith in an all-knowing if impenetrable Providence.

Her strong emotional attachment to children and grandchildren did not blind her to a parent's responsibility in rearing children. Her love was not uncritical, indiscriminate, or self-indulgent. As she reminded her children, she had shown them "joy and misery;/Taught what was good, and what was ill,/What would save life, and what would kill." Furthermore, just as she acknowledged that in her own spiritual life she could "no more live without correction than without food," she knew that "some children (like sour land) are of so tough and morose a disposition that the plough of correction must make long furrows on their back and the harrow of discipline go often over them before they be fit soil to sow the seed of morality much less of grace in them." A "prudent nature" would bring them to a "fit capacity" for "good instruction and exhortation" in their early youth.[23] If her own children had tough, morose dispositions, her writings gave no hint of it.

In one of her most felicitous contemplations, she observed that "diverse children have their different natures: some are like flesh which nothing but salt will keep from putrefaction, some again like tender fruits that are best preserved with sugar." She concluded that "those parents are wise that can fit their nurture according to their nature." Parental authority must not be blind, for "authority without wisdom is like a heavy axe without an edge: fitter to bruise than polish." If the "plough of correction" or the use of "salt" implied physical punishment, she also knew that the prospect as much as the reality of punishment could make a child mindful. "I have been with God like an untoward child, that no longer than the rod has been on my back (or at least in sight) but I have been apt to forget Him and myself, too."[24]

Bradstreet's writings portray her close and enduring relationship with her children. Her love for them was deep, and her concern, especially for their spiritual well-being, was constant. While Puritan theology set forth the reality of man's depravity—the stain from "Adam's sinful fact"—it did not preclude a recognition of the variety of human temperament and character. Nor did Puritanism ignore differences between children and adults.[25] Just as a wise father would not expect a young child to perform tasks appropriate for a child twice as strong,[26] a parent would recognize the intellectual and emotional capacities of different ages. It was the parent's responsibility to nurse up—that is, to educate—children until they were strong and wise enough to be on their own. If, as a mother, Bradstreet had her patience tried by the "perverse will," the "serpent's sting," and the "lying tongue" of her children, she could also see an innocence in childish behavior. Furthermore, her religion provided a framework for understanding the emotions and actions of children and for patiently rearing them with "great pains, weakness, cares, and fears."[27]

Bradstreet was probably an effective parent. She loved both her husband[28] and the children for whom she had yearned. She recognized the differences among her children and the need to apply various disciplinary techniques to them. Her Puritan world view permitted an empathic tolerance of childhood's complexities. And despite or, indeed, because of her love, she could allow her children to grow to maturity and leave the parental nest.

How representative was she of more general Puritan attitudes about the experience of childhood? Her social position, but particularly the fact that she wrote—and wrote in a disciplined, self-conscious way—set her apart from most people of her era, male or female. Although aware of her uniqueness as a writer, she wrote for her family, not for publication.[29] Since this intimate audience could criticize her work within the context of their relationships with her, her writings probably accurately reflect her family life. Furthermore, some of her writings, the "Meditations Divine and Moral," may embody an element of folk wisdom. She wrote to her 30-year-old son, for whom the meditations were composed, that she had "avoided encroaching upon others' conceptions because I would leave you nothing but mine own."[30]

Finally, one should also note that the theme of childhood's innocence was also set forth by Puritan theologians. In expounding upon the doctrine that *"the Children of God. . .must be as little Children,"* the Reverend John Cotton used language very similar to Bradstreet's in her discussion of childhood. According to Cotton, all persons who wanted their sins forgiven were to be of "Child-like dispositions, free from ambition, and malice, and revenge." Like children, they were "to frame themselves to humility and innocency, and meekness, and simplicity, and contentment, and resting on promise and hopes...."[31] Clearly the idea of mankind's depravity was softened in its application to children.

"Parents perpetuate their lives in their posterity and their manners," wrote Bradstreet to her son Simon.[32] Interestingly, her writings give no hint that young Simon's father had played a role in rearing the Bradstreet children.[33] It was Anne Bradstreet who bore the responsibility of child-rearing and could thus, as a writer, most completely articulate the ideas and the reality of parenthood. An abiding sense of responsibility, a love that was deep but not blind, and a sensitivity to individual personality, ability, and maturity reflected her child-rearing ideas and, one suspects, her experience.

Ross W. Beales, Jr. is a member of the Department of History, College of the Holy Cross, Worcester, Mass. Research for this essay was made possible by a National Endowment for the Humanities Fellowship at the American Antiquarian Society, 1977-78. The author wishes to thank N. Ray Hiner and Peter Gregg Slater for their comments on an earlier version which was presented at the Missouri Valley History Conference, Omaha, March 10, 1978. He is also grateful to Barbara Finkelstein for her many suggestions.

FOOTNOTES

1. Bernard Bailyn, *Education in the Forming of American Society: Needs and Opportunities for Study* (Chapel Hill: University of North Carolina Press, 1960), p. 14; Lawrence A. Cremin, *American Education: The Colonial Experience, 1607-1783* (New York: Harper & Row, 1970), p. xiii; *idem,* "The Family as Educator: Some Comments on Recent Historiography," *Teachers College Record* 76 (1974): 250-265; Sol Cohen, "The History of the History of American Education, 1900-1976: The Uses of the Past," *Harvard Educational Review* 46 (1976):298-330.

2. Eleazar Mather, *A Serious Exhortation to the Present and Succeeding Generation in New-England.* . .(Cambridge, Mass.: S. G. and M. J., 1671), p. 20; Israel Loring, *The Duty and Interest of Young Persons to Remember their Creator.* . .(Boston: printed for Daniel Henchman, 1718), p. 21; Benjamin Lord, *Sober-Mindedness, an Excellent Character of Young Men.* . .(Providence: William Goddard, 1763), p. 18.

3. Citing Aristotle as the authority for his observations, Robinson continues: "But afterwards, when they come to riper years, good fathers are more behoveful for their forming in virtue and good manners, by their greater wisdom and authority: and oft-times also, by correcting the fruits of their mother's indulgence, by their severity." *The Works of John Robinson, Pastor of the Pilgrim Fathers, with a Memoir and Annotations,* ed. Robert Ashton, 3 vols. (London: John Snow, 1851), 1:244.

4. John Saffin, *John Saffin His Book (1665-1708): A Collection of Various Matters of Divinity Law & State Affairs Epitomiz'd Both in Verse and Prose,* intro. Caroline Hazard (New York: Harbor Press, 1928), p. 84.Information on such practices as nursing and weaning may be found in James Axtell, *The School upon a Hill: Education and Society in Colonial New England* (New Haven: Yale University Press, 1974), pp. 75-88, and Joseph E. Illick, "Child-Rearing in Seventeenth-Century England and America," in Lloyd deMause, ed., *The History of Childhood* (New York: The Psychohistory Press, 1974), pp. 325-327. There is as yet no systematic or detailed treatment of these and other aspects of the early development of children and their parents' treatment of them.

5. For materials on Anne Bradstreet published by early 1969, see Ann Stanford, "Anne Bradstreet: An Annotated Checklist," *Bulletin of Bibliography* 27 (1970):34-37. See also Kenneth R. Ball, "Puritan Humility in Anne Bradstreet's Poetry," *Cithara* 13 (1973):29-41; Jane Donahue Eberwein, "The 'Unrefined Ore' of Anne Bradstreet's Quaternions," *Early American Literature* 9 (1974):19-26; Anne Hildebrand, "Anne Bradstreet's Quaternions and 'Contemplations,' " *Early American Literature* 8 (1973):117-125; Rosemary M. Laughlin, "Anne Bradstreet: Poet in Search of Form," *American Literature* 42 (1970):1-17; Kenneth A. Requa, "Anne Bradstreet's Poetic Voices," *Early American Literature* 9 (1974):3-18; Alvin H. Rosenfeld, "Anne Bradstreet's 'Contemplations': Patterns of Form and Meaning," *New England Quarterly* 43 (1970): 79-96; Ann Stanford, "Anne Bradstreet," in Everett Emerson, ed., *Major Writers of Early American Literature* (Madison, Wisconsin: University of Wisconsin Press, 1972), pp. 33-58; *idem, Anne Bradstreet, The Worldly Puritan: An Introduction to Her Poetry* (New York: Burt Franklin and Co., 1974); Elizabeth Wade White, *Anne Bradstreet: "The Tenth Muse"* (New York: Oxford University Press, 1971).

6. See, for example, Axtell, *School upon a Hill,* pp. 87, 89-90 n.61; Philip Greven, *The Protestant Temperament: Patterns of Child-Rearing, Religious Experience, and the Self in Early America* (New York: Alfred A. Knopf, 1977), pp. 29-30, 49; Illick, "Child-Rearing in Seventeenth-Century England and America," pp. 326, 346 n.101, 346-345 n.105, 349 n.123, 350 n.130; Edmund S. Morgan, *The Puritan Family: Religion and Domestic Relations in Seventeenth-Century New England,* rev. ed. (New York: Harper & Row, Torchbook, 1966), pp. 92-93, 107-108; Peter Gregg Slater, *Children in the New England Mind: In Death and in Life* (Hamden, Connecticut: Archon Books, 1977) pp. 15, 22, 34, 71; David E. Stannard, *The Puritan Way of Death: A Study in Religion, Culture, and Social Change* (New York: Oxford University Press, 1977), pp. 57, 154-155.

7. For a discussion of this perspective on childrearing, see Ross W. Beales, Jr., "In Search of the Historical Child: Miniature Adulthood and Youth in Colonial New England," *American Quarterly* 27 (1975):380-383. Frequently quoted is John Robinson's advice that "surely there is in all children, though not alike, a stubbornness, and

stoutness of mind arising from natural pride, which must, in the first place, be broken and beaten down; that so the foundation of their education being laid in humility and tractableness, other virtues may, in their time, be built thereon. . . .For the beating, and keeping down of this stubbornness parents must provide carefully. . .that children's wills and wilfulness be restrained and repressed, and that, in time; lest sooner than they imagine, the tender sprigs grow to that stiffness, that they will rather break than bow. Children should not know, if it could be kept from them, that they have a will in their own, but in their parents' keeping: neither should these words be heard from them, save by way of consent, 'I will' or 'I will not.' " Robinson, *Works*, 1:246-247. For historians' use of Robinson, see John Demos, *A Little Commonwealth: Family Life in Plymouth Colony* (New York: Oxford University Press, 1970), pp. 134-135; *idem*, "Demography and Psychology in the Historical Study of Family-Life: A Personal Report," in Peter Laslett and Richard Wall, eds., *Household and Family in Past Time*. . .(Cambridge: Cambridge University Press, 1972), p. 566; *idem*, "The American Family in Past Time," *American Scholar* 43 (1974): 427; Axtell, *School upon a Hill*, pp. 147-148; Greven, *Protestant Temperament*, p. 37. Both Demos and Axtell ignore Robinson's qualifying phrase, "though not alike." Robinson's advice raises a host of problems for historians of early American family life, not the least of which is the fact that Robinson was a Puritan separatist who never came to America. On the pitfalls of using prescriptive advice, see Jay Mechling, "Advice to Historians on Advice to Mothers," *Journal of Social History* 9 (1975):44-63.

8. The best biography of Anne Bradstreet is White, *Anne Bradstreet: "The Tenth Muse."*

9. Philip J. Greven, Jr., *Four Generations: Population, Land, and Family in Colonial Andover, Massachusetts* (Ithaca, New York: Cornell University Press, 1970), pp. 21-40. A completed family was one in which the first wife survived to age 45. Greven's data on the risk of death for women during their childbearing years are not completely persuasive, for he includes only ages 20-39, thereby ignoring deaths of women aged 40-45.

10. Historians need to examine more closely the ages which were regarded as "old" in colonial America. Bradstreet herself certainly felt old. See Anne Bradstreet, *The Works of Anne Bradstreet*, ed. Jeannine Hensley (Cambridge, Mass.: Harvard University Press, 1967), pp. 294-295.

11. Harold S. Jantz, "The First Century of New England Verse," *Proceedings of the American Antiquarian Society*, n.s. 53 (1943):253; Bradstreet, *Works*, pp. 201-203.

12. Bradstreet, *Works*, p. 204, line 7. Daniel Denison, one of the Dudleys' sons-in-law, described Dorothy Dudley as "a fine vertuous woman." See the "Autobiography of Major-General Daniel Denison," *New-England Historical and Genealogical Register* 46 (1892):128-129.

13. Bradstreet, *Works*, p. 53, lines 68-75, 76-79. The idea that her mother "still did waste as I did thrive" and "Spending, was willing to be spent for me" may have reflected a popular belief and perception, based on a mother's nutritional needs while nursing, that mothers could literally "waste" if food supplies were limited.

14. *Ibid.*, p. 54, lines 122-127; John F. Walzer, "A Period of Ambivalence: Eighteenth-Century American Childhood," in deMause, ed., *History of Childhood*, pp. 351-382; Slater, *Children in the New England Mind*, pp. 21-23; "Deacon John Paine's Journal," *Mayflower Descendant* 8 (1906):227. The most sympathetic portrayal of childrearing ideas and parent-child relationships in seventeenth-century New England is Morgan, *Puritan Family*.

15. Thomas Shepard informed his son that the latter's mother "did lose her life by being careful to preserve thine, for in the ship [which carried the Shepards to New England in 1635] thou wert so feeble and froward both in the day and night that hereby she lost

her strength and at last her life." Thomas Shepard, *God's Plot: The Paradoxes of Puritan Piety, Being the Autobiography and Journal of Thomas Shepard,* ed. Michael McGiffert ([Amherst, Mass.]: University of Massachusetts Press, 1972), p. 36. During the spiritual crisis leading to his conversion in the 1740s, Nathan Cole asked his parents to forgive him "every think [*sic*] they had against me concerning my disobedience or whatsoever else it might be; they said they had not any thing against me, and both fell aweeping like Children for Joy to see me so concerned for my Soul." It is interesting that Cole, then married and about thirty years old, should have felt a generalized sense of guilt for sins against his parents which neither he nor they could specify. Michael J. Crawford, ed., "The Spiritual Travels of Nathan Cole," *William and Mary Quarterly,* 3d ser. 33 (1976):94.

16. Bradstreet, *Works,* pp. 53, lines 80-83, 84; 54, lines 103-107; Gerhard T. Alexis, "Wigglesworth's 'Easiest Room,' " *New England Quarterly* 42 (1969):573-583; Bradstreet, *Works,* p. 54, lines 116-118. On adolescence, see Beales, "In Search of the Historical Child," pp. 391-398; N. Ray Hiner, "Adolescence in Eighteenth-Century America," *History of Childhood Quarterly* 3 (1975):253-280; Vivian C. Fox, "Is Adolescence a Phenomenon of Modern Times?" *Journal of Psychohistory* 5 (1977):271-290; and John Demos and Virginia Demos, "Adolescence in Historical Perspective," *Journal of Marriage and the Family* 31 (1969):632-638.

17. Bradstreet, *Works,* p. 54, lines 128-129. Slater makes the same point in *Children in the New England Mind,* p. 22.

18. Bradstreet, *Works,* pp. 241; 258, lines 5-6; 55, line 143; 224, lines 24, 26.

19. *Ibid.,* pp. 233, lines 61-64; 234, lines 73-76, 86-96; Heb. 11:4. If Bradstreet had Abel in mind when she wrote "And dead, yet speak," did she see her Cain in the "serpent's sting" which lay hidden in the "pleasing face" of her children?

20. Bradstreet, *Works,* p. 235.

21. *Ibid.,* p. 236.

22. *Ibid.,* p. 237, lines 9-14; Stanford, "Anne Bradstreet," in Emerson, ed., *Major Writers,* p. 56.

23. Bradstreet, *Works,* pp. 257; 285, No. 61.

24. *Ibid.,* pp. 273-274, No. 10; 274, No. 12; 242.

25. See Beales, "In Search of the Historical Child," pp. 383-391.

26. Bradstreet, *Works,* p. 280, No. 41.

27. *Ibid.,* p. 241.

28. On Bradstreet's love for her husband, see *ibid.,* pp. 224-230.

29. *The Tenth Muse. . .*(London, 1650) was published without her knowledge; see Adrienne Rich, "Anne Bradstreet and her Poetry," in Bradstreet, *Works,* p. xv.

30. Bradstreet, *Works,* p. 271.

31. John Cotton, *A Practical Commentary, or an Exposition with Observations, Reasons, and Uses Upon the First Epistle Generall of John* (London, 1656), pp. 85, 87.

32. Bradstreet, *Works,* p. 271.

33. Nor do her writings suggest the presence of servants and their assistance in caring for children. The Bradstreet household may be presumed to have had servants; it was reported, for example, that a maid was responsible for the fire which destroyed their house in 1666; see "Rev. Samuel Danforth's Records of the First Church in Roxbury, Mass.," *New-England Historical and Genealogical Register* 34 (1880):165. For Bradstreet's reaction to the fire, see Bradstreet, *Works,* pp. 292-293.

II

Cotton Mather and his Children: The Evolution of a Parent Educator, 1686-1728

— N. RAY HINER

In 1709 Cotton Mather sat in his study reflecting on his children, and, filled with the spirit of joy and thanksgiving, he exclaimed unto God, "How can I hear my children sing, and not sing unto thee."[1] Fifteen years later, in a dark and bitter mood, Mather could only lament, "How little comfort, yea, how much contrary to it, have I seen in my children."[2] Surely, most parents, even today, can empathize with Mather's ambivalent feelings about parenthood and children. Parents can find both profound satisfaction and exquisite suffering, a sense of generativity and fulfillment and an awareness of sterility and defeat in their relations with their children. Why are parents so susceptible, so vulnerable, to the influence of their children? What is the source of this enormous power?

Historians of education should study the entire process by which human beings acquire their identities and transmit their culture from generation to generation, but they have habitually concentrated on only one aspect of this comprehensive psycho-cultural process—on how parents and other adults educate children—while generally ignoring how children influence adults. This omission is curious since the research of modern psychologists and social psychologists shows that all human relationships, from the mother-infant dyad to the most complex human group, are inevitably reciprocal and dynamic. The human infant in its mother's (or father's) arms is not just a passive *tabula rasa* on which adults inscribe their wishes and commands. It is also an active organism which seeks constantly to manipulate its social and cultural environment to satisfy its unique developmental needs, whether through the search for the immediate necessities of food, physical warmth and psychological security, or in the less immediate but critical quest for stimulation and autonomy. The baby cries, it coos, it kicks, it even smiles—and adults respond.[3] This much seems obvious, but much less obvious is why adults respond and how and to what extent their responses to their children shape their own development.

Although there are many ways to approach this question, Therese Benedek, a child psychoanalyst, offers one of the most promising. According to Benedek, parents are influenced by their children because they consciously and unconsciously identify with them. They look at their children, they interact with them, and they are confronted with themselves—either as they think they were when they were children, or, through a process of projecting onto the child their own ideals or aspirations, as they hope to become through their children's development. This process of identification and interaction normally enhances the self-esteem of healthy parents, but Benedek argues further that as children pass through each critical stage of development, they may revive (usually unconsciously) their parents' own unresolved developmental conflicts. If these conflicts are severe, the process can produce pathologic manifestations in the parents, which lead to bad parenting and almost guarantee that the children will not become more fully integrated persons than their parents. On the other hand, Benedek believes that this fresh awakening of unresolved conflicts also provides new opportunities for parents to work through their problems, achieve a higher level of integration, and thus provide their children with better care and nurturance than they themselves received. In this sense, then, children can and do educate their parents.[4]

Modern psychologists are not the only source of insight into the educational relationships between parents and children. Although Cotton Mather lived more than two hundred years ago and wrote in a now antiquated religious idiom, he was a profoundly introspective man and an obsessively conscientious parent who probed deeply into this question. In 1721 he asked himself why his children were important to him. First, Mather recognized that he was bound by the requisites of his religion and culture to show concern for his children. "These are *my children;*" he wrote, "I am therefore from nature and duty to *love* them." But Mather knew it was not just nature or duty which made his children important. His children were also dear to him because, as he put it, "I see my image on my children." He had identified so strongly with his children, they were so "nearly related" to him, that he compared this relationship with his oneness with Christ. Finally, he admitted that he valued his children because they provided immediate, reciprocal satisfactions. "The affection which my children have and show to me causes me to delight in them," he said, and "my children in their conversation with me entertain me with many things that are delectable." For Mather, then, nature, duty, identification, and reciprocity constituted the basic sources of children's importance to parents.[5]

Mather's insight into the nature of parenthood did not come easily. It was the product of forty-one years of sometimes rewarding, often painful parenthood. His first two wives suffered fatal physical illnesses, and his third wife became mentally ill. His eldest son was a delinquent, six of his sixteen children died young, and only two survived him.[6] Even so, parenthood stimulated Mather's development and permitted him to resolve many of the conflicts he had experienced as a child and young adult. There was also a creative interaction between Mather's responses to the joys and vicissitudes of parenthood and his public statements concerning child-rearing. One of the most prolific writers in American history, he left more than four hundred published works, an extensive diary, and numerous unpublished sermons and letters. He often used his sermons and essays, both consciously and unconsciously, as opportunities to explore the dimensions of problems he was facing as a parent, and at times he was able to work out solutions to these problems, at least on a conscious, theoretical level. When Mather wrote of children and families, he wrote from life, and many of those who heard him or read his works were themselves parents who confronted issues very similar to those discussed by Mather. Thus, Mather's experience as a parent had wider educational implications because he occupied a position of leadership in the culture.

At first glance, Mather is a rather unlikely source of knowledge about parenthood. His reputation among American historians is hardly a sterling one. He is sometimes depicted as a pompous, superprig, an ambitious, hypocritical, and neurotic defender of an archaic religious and social order—hardly a person who could be expected to contribute to the solution of the educational problems of his day.[7] Although his unsavory reputation is by no means entirely deserved, it is accurate in one respect. Mather was pathologically troubled, at least during his adolescence and early adulthood. From his earliest years, he was forced to carry the enormous burden of two generations of high expectations and achievement. Grandson of the Reverend Richard Mather, a patriarchcal figure among New England Puritans, and son of the Reverend Increase Mather, a prominent and influential Boston minister, Cotton was marked very early to carry on the distinguished ministerial tradition of his family. His father wrote in his autobiography that "if ever a father had a particular faith for a child, then I had so for that child, of whom I could with assurance say, God had blessed him, yea and he shall be blessed."[8]

Cotton evidently had little opportunity or conscious inclination to challenge the plan for his life that had been laid out by his father. Samuel Mather, Cotton's son, explained in his biography of his father that Cotton always expected to be great, "for he believed he should be so, he expected it; and therefore . . . he bore and did many things and disregarded all the difficulties that would encompass him." If we are to believe Samuel, Cotton was indeed a precocious child who took eagerly to his books, who prayed as soon as he could speak, and even as a child composed prayers for his schoolmates and reproved his "playmates for their wicked words and practices."[9] Even though this may have made him unpopular with his peers, it no doubt endeared him to his father.

However, there were early signals that Cotton might not be capable of realizing his father's high aspirations. As early as 1672, when Cotton was nine years old, Increase noted in his diary:

> [I am much] exercised in my spirit about my son Cotton, lest the hesitancy in his speech should make him incapable of improvement in the worke of the ministry whereunto I had designed him.[10]

Two years later Increase was still troubled, and wrote on October 7, 1674:

> I fasted and prayed before the Lord because of my son Cotton's impediment in his speech. At the close of the day, I called him and his mother into my study. Wee prayed together and with many tears beweyled our sinfulness, and begged of God mercy in this particular, and solemnly gave the child to God upon our knees, begging the lord to accept him.[11]

We can understand the anguish of both parent and child in this situation, but Increase's approach to his son's problem may not have helped. Apparently, Cotton had so completely internalized his father's perfectionistic standards that he could not face the possibility of failing as a minister and the deep humiliation it would bring. From Cotton's point of view, it must have seemed better not to try at all than to try and fail. If he stammered he would not have to try, and therefore he would never fail. In any event, when Cotton entered Harvard the following year at the age of twelve, he took his speech impediment with him, and apparently he kept it throughout his stay there. Convinced that this problem effectively closed the ministry as a calling, he chose to study medicine. If he could not heal men's souls, he would heal their bodies.[12]

But his father's hopes retained a strong hold on Cotton, and a timely visit from his old schoolmaster, John Corlet, led him to reconsider his career choice. Corlet went directly to the point:

> I have come to talk with you about the infirmity in your speech,

and offer you my advice about it. What I advise you to do, is seek a cure for it, in the method of deliberation. Did you ever know anyone to stammer in singing of the Psalms? . . . But first use yourself to a very deliberate way of speaking; a drawling that shall be a little short of singing. Even this drawling will be better than stammering, especially if what you speak, be well worth our waiting for. This deliberate way of speaking will also give you a great command of pertinent thoughts; yea and if you find a word likely to be too hard for you, there will be time for you to think of substituting another that won't be so.[13]

Corlet's advice worked so effectively that Cotton decided to study for the ministry. In August 1680, at the age of seventeen, he preached his first public sermon at his grandfather's church at Dorcester, and six months later he accepted a unanimous invitation to serve as his father's assistant at the Second Church in Boston.[14]

Cotton's impediment recurred periodically for several years, and, according to contemporaries, he retained a very deliberate manner of public speaking throughout his life.[15] Paradoxically, once Mather had learned the technique of slowed speech, he seemed most secure in his public speaking behavior only when his father was present. Even the threat of his absence would produce such anxiety and fears of abandonment that the impediment would often reappear.

Cotton was successful enough during his first year at his father's church that several churches became interested in calling him to pastor their flocks. The congregation at New Haven issued a formal invitation in November, 1681, which was renewed in February, 1682.[16] No doubt at the urging of Increase, the Second Church also voted unanimously in December 1682 to ask him to continue on a permanent basis there.[17] Cotton equivocated, and his impediemnt returned with such force that, in Cotton's words, it threatened "to render me unserviceable." The New Haven call represented a real opportunity for Cotton to set out on his own and establish a separate professional identity, but apparently neither he nor his father really wanted this. Cotton chose to remain in his father's church, eventually receiving ordination there on May 13, 1685.[18] Deciding not to strike out on his own, Cotton's speech improved again, and he began to perform his ministerial duties with greater self-assurance. Nonetheless, he lacked confidence in his ability to function effectively as a minister outside the framework of security and protection his father seemed to provide. Cotton had identified so completely with his father's power and authority that as long as he remained in his father's church as his assistant he felt he was in friendly territory and could exercise his own verbal abilities without undue fear of impediment. He remained within the paternal orbit until his own death in 1728, five years after his father had died at the age of eighty-four.

Although our understanding of the etiology of stammering is inadequate, it is widely held that the personality structure of the stammerer and the obsessive-compulsive neurotic are highly similar if not synonymous, and that the onset of stammering as a symptom represents the failure of obsessive defenses. According to Leon Salzman, the "consistent theme of all obsessionals is the presence of anxieties about being in danger because of an incapacity to fulfill the requirements of others and to feel certain of one's acceptance." The obsessive deals with this fear and anxiety by equivocation, efforts at omniscience and control through pedantic intellectuality, and, if the anxiety is severe, through phobias, obsessional thoughts, and compulsive rituals and behaviors.[19] Similarly, stammerers often have demanding, perfectionistic parents who place great emphasis on intellectual pursuits and the power of language, who render their children "basically helpless, insecure, and afraid," and drive them eventually "toward safety and some degree of psuedo-harmony by developing neurotic trends." Both stammerers and obsessionals are doomed throughout their lives to compare their behavior to the idealized standards they have acquired from their parents.[20] Stammerers, especially, are at the mercy of what Domonick Barbara calls the "tyranny of the should." They believe they "should be able to endure everything, to understand everything, to like everybody, to always be productive." They feel they "should be the epitome of understanding, generosity, blind faith, courage, dignity." They feel they "should be perfect lovers, parents, and marriage partners." They "should be completely self-sufficient, reliable at all times, and always productive" in their work.[21] Cotton Mather eventually ceased stammering, but obsessive-compulsive defenses persisted as his preferred style of dealing with stress, and he never escaped the tyranny of the should. It was in this psychological context that Mather's development as a parent began.

As early as 1683 Cotton reported in his diary that he began to have "a strange persuasion" that "there would a time come, when I should have my bed blessed with such a consort given unto me, as Isaac, the servant of the Lord was favored withal." The consort not forthcoming, Mather complained that Satan was "buffeting" him with "unclean temptations," and he resolved to pluck out his right eye and cut off his right hand, if he did not lay aside his sins and "pollutions." Finally, after many intense bouts with Satan and his temptations, Cotton married sixteen-year-old Abigail Phillips in May, 1686, about a year after his ordination.[22]

Mather's first marriage was a fruitful one. (See Chart, p. 30.) During their almost seventeen years of marriage, Abigail gave birth to ten children, or one child every 19-20 months on the average, although only four of them reached maturity. Unfortunately for him and his children, Mather began his family at a psychologically inopportune time. In April, 1688,

COTTON MATHER AND HIS CHILDREN, 1686-1728*

Year	Cotton Mather	Abigail Phillips	Abigal	Katherine	Mary	Joseph	Abigal	Methetabel	Hannah	Increase	Samuel	Unnamed	Elizabeth Hubbard	Elizabeth	Samuel	Nathaniel	Jerusha	Martha	Eleazar	Lydia George	Father	Mother
1686	M	M																			47	45
87	24	17	B																		48	46
88	25	18	1																		49	47
89	26	19	2	B																	50	48
1690	27	20	3	1																	51	49
91	28	21	4	2	B																52	50
92	29	22	+?	3	1																53	51
93	30	23		4	+	B+															54	52
94	31	24		5			B														55	53
95	32	25		6			1	B													56	54
96	33	26		7			2	+													57	55
97	34	27		8			3		B												58	56
98	35	28		9			4		1												59	57
99	36	29		10			5		2	B			Second wife								60	58
1700	37	30		11			6		3	1	B										61	59
01	38	31		12			7		4	2	+										62	60
02	39	+		13			8		5	3		B+									63	61
03	M			14			9		6	4			M								64	62
04	41			15			10		7	5				B							65	63
05	42			16			11		8	6				1							66	64
06	43			17			12		9	7				2	B						67	65
07	44			18			13		10	8				3	1						68	66
08	45			19			14		11	9				4	2					Third wife	69	67
09	46			20			15		12	10				5	3	B+					70	68
1710	47			21			16		13	11				6	4						71	69
11	48			22			17		14	12				7	5	B					72	70
12	49			23			18		15	13			↓	8	6	1					73	71
13	50			24			19		16	14			+	9	7	+	B+	B+			74	72
14	51			25			20		17	15				10	8						75	+
15	M			26			21		18	16				11	9					M	76	
16	53			+			N22		19	17				12	10						77	
17	54						23		20	18				13	11						78	
18	55						24		21	19				14	12						79	
19	56						25		22	20				15	13						80	
1720	57						26		23	21				16	14						81	
21	58						+		24	22				17	15						82	
22	59								25	23				18	16						83	
23	60								26	24				19	17						+	
24	61								27	+				20	18							
25	62								28					21	19							
26	63								29					+	20							
27	64								30						21							
1728	+								31						22					↓		

B = Born
+ = Died
M = Married

* Please note that as all births do not fall on the first day of the year, the ages provided for any given year on this chart are accurate within a range of plus or minus one year.

barely seven months after the birth of his first child, Mather's father, Increase, left for England to attempt to restore the colonial charter that had been nullified in 1684. Cotton, then twenty-five years old, was thus left with total responsibility for a large congregation in a period of political and social crisis. During the more than three years in which his father was absent, Cotton became deeply involved in the colony's political affairs and the witchcraft controversy at Salem.[23]

Cotton was too busy with political and religious affairs and much too preoccupied with dealing with his father's absence to become very introspective about his children during this period. In May, 1690, he complained in a letter to his father: "I am sorry for myself, who am left alone, in the midst of more cares, fears, anxieties, than, I believe any one person in these territories; and who have just now been within a few minutes of death, by a very dangerous fever . . . " Later, when he heard, after some reports to the contrary, that his father was safely on his way home, he dreamed:

> that being left alone, I was putt upon preaching a sermon publickly, for which I had no time to prepare aforehand. I dream'd, that being driven to this extemporaneous extremity, I preached upon these words, I will never leave thee nor forsake thee. The thoughts, which I had upon this text, in my sleep were so proper and lively, and I could after I woke, remember so many of them, that indeed I preached the Lord's-Day following upon that very text.[24]

Even the promise of his father's return enhanced his sense of security and competence.

Preoccupied and anxious during his father's absence, he fathered two more daughters, making his wife pregnant for the fourth time before his father returned in 1692. Joseph, his fourth child, was born with a malformed colon and died shortly after birth (1693).[25] He also lost three other children during the early years of his marriage: Abigail sometime before 1693, Mary in 1693, and Methetabel in 1696. The death of Methetabel, who was "overlaid by her nurse," seems to have affected Cotton very deeply, in part because he had inadvertently omitted her name from his morning prayers on the day she died. In his characteristically neurotic manner, Mather attributed so much power to his own speech that he feared, at least on an unconscious level, that his omission of a word may have caused his daughter's death. There is also some evidence that Methetabel's untimely death aroused Mather's fears about his own death, fears which were accompanied by a mild recurrence of his speech impediment and an intensive period of compulsive fasting and praying.[26]

Although his children appear regularly in his diary during the first eight or nine years of Mather's parenthood, they do not seem to have influenced his published work in a direct way. He did publish two major works on educational topics, *Addresses to Old Men, Young Men, and Little Children* (1690), and *Early Religion Urged* (1694), but they concentrated almost entirely on youth and were based more on Mather's observation of the current scene and his own experience as an adolescent than on any actual interaction with or reflection on his young children.[27] Beyond the intense press of immediate affairs, there are two possible explanations for Cotton's lack of public discussion of young children during this period. First, he may not have separated from his father sufficiently to develop the secure identity which would have allowed him to forget his own problems and identify with his children in a consistent, mature manner. Second, because most of Mather's unresolved conflicts were rooted in his relationship with his father, and because all of his surviving children before 1699 were female, he probably identified with them less directly, and they therefore revived fewer unresolved conflicts than would have male children.

In 1698 and 1699 a rather strange series of events jarred Cotton into a more conscious and systematic recognition of his parental duties. During this period, Mather became concerned that his lack of vigor in resisting the judges in the Salem witchcraft trials would bring some "marks of the Divine Displeasure" on his family.[28] On January 30, he reported that "my little daughter Nibby, (about two years old) fell directly upon the fire, and yett by a wonderful providence of heaven, was pull'd out without the least scorch upon hands or face to damnify her." Almost a year later he recorded that his "little daughter Nanny" (almost two years old),

> being in my study, with her two sisters, when I was not there, fell into the fire. The right side of her face especially and her right hand and arm, were sorely burned in this fall . . . Alas for my Sin, the Just God throwes my child into the fire![29]

Approximately two months later, on February 22, 1699, his elder daughter Katy (then ten years old) was severely burned after the candle she was carrying ignited her loose shoulder garments and headgear.[30] Nanny and Katy lay ill for several weeks and Mather was understandably horrified. He immediately began a series of lectures and sermons on parents and children which culminated in the publication of *A Family Well-Ordered, or An Essay to Render Parents and Children Happy in One Another* (1699), one of the most comprehensive works on parenting published in the seventeenth century. The model parent depicted by Mather in this essay is a persistent, intrusive, but compassionate person who never misses an opportunity to teach his children piety, civility, and basic intellectual skills. To Mather, children were "narrow-mouth'd vessels, and things must be drop after drop instilled into them." Mather also told parents that their authority should not be harsh, but "sweet" and "so tempered with kindness, and meekness, and loving tenderness," that their children may fear them "with delight," and see that they "love them, with as much delight." Parents, Mather warned, should never give their children a blow in passion.[31] Mather was no doubt unable to live up to his own high standards, but he had come to a more complete acceptance of his complex role as parent-educator and he had shared this awareness with his community.

Shortly after he completed the manuscript for *A Family Well-Ordered*, his sense of parenthood was stimulated even further. On July 8, 1699, Cotton was overjoyed by the birth of his son Increase, who he believed had been destined to serve the Lord Jesus Christ "throughout eternal ages." But his joy became concern when the infant became ill in February, 1700 and suffered convulsions which continued intermittently for more than three months. Once, Increase nearly choked to death on "a pin, which he suck'd out of the silver nipple of his bottle, tho' wee know not how it came there." Increase eventually recovered, and Mather, extremely relieved and elated, resolved to leave his personal meditations as a memorial for his son. Here, finally, was a child with whom Cotton could identify closely and for whom he could have great hopes for the future.[32]

However, during the next two years Cotton was subjected to considerable stress which threatened to undermine the developmental progress he had achieved. In July, 1700, his father was forced to move to Cambridge to maintain his position as President of Harvard. Cotton, then 37, lamented in his diary that he was thus "left alone in the care of a vast congregation, the largest in all these parts of the world." He feared his enemies, his health was poor, and he doubted his ability to hold the congregation together. His father soon resigned his office and returned to Boston, but the affair reveals the extent to which Cotton still leaned on his father for support and suggests how fragile his psychological defenses were in some areas. These defenses would be severely tested during the next two years.[33]

In October Mather almost lost his six-year-old daughter, the second Abigail, who caught her headdress afire while alone in the home. Cotton was convinced she would have been consumed had not a passer-by seen the flames through a window and rescued her.[34] In December his wife gave birth to another son, Samuel, who died in February during a convulsion. Katy and Hannah were also quite ill during this period, although they had recovered by late spring.[35] In May, 1702, his wife, four or five months pregnant, suffered a miscarriage, and the dead infant, a boy, was apparently buried without a name.[36] His wife was slow to recover and remained seriously ill during the next five months. In October, 1702, his daughter Abigail contracted smallpox, which soon infected Hannah, Increase, and a young maidservant. Only his teenage daughter Katherine escaped the illness. Cotton turned his study into a hospital for his sick children and divided his time between his languishing wife and his "little creatures," who, he said, "keep calling me so often to pray with them, that I can scarce do it less than ten or a dozen times a day; besides what I do with my neighbors."[37] Mather continued his frenetic ministering to family and neighbors until December 1, the "black day" when, as he said, "The desire of my eyes was taken from me."[38]

Mather's children survived the smallpox, but his wife's death left him profoundly shaken. Abigail was a strong, intelligent, and discreet woman on whom Cotton had come to depend for companionship and support. At one point during her illness, he developed "a particular faith" that God would spare her. After Abigail's death, he resolved in the future to approach such particular faiths with "exquisite caution." He includes in his diary a long and somewhat pathetic statement in which he tries to convince himself that her death was a blessing to her, if obviously a tragedy to him and his family.[39] Mather's first efforts to mourn the loss of his wife of sixteen years contained an element of unhealthy denial, but this soon passed and he began the more healthy process of replacing this lost "object" whom he had valued so highly. After a nearly disastrous relationship with Kate Maccarty, an aggressive young woman of mixed reputation, had driven him to obsessive fantasies of impurity, blasphemy, atheism, and even suicide, Mather finally married Elizabeth Hubbard, a respectable widow from his own neighborhood, on August 18, 1703.[40]

Mather continued to publish at an astonishing rate, even when his family was threatened by illness and ravished by death. Several of these essays and sermons treated parents, children and youth, and one, *Cares About Nurseries*, included detailed instructions for catechising both children and youth, although none was as comprehensive or as perceptive as his earlier *A Family Well-Ordered*.[41] Mather used his writing as both an escape from and a means of working through his problems, and in times of great stress he worked even harder. The evidence from both his published writings and his diary during this period suggests that he kept his psychological balance and maintained his earlier commitment to his role as parent-educator, especially in the face of great personal loss.

Mather's second marriage was highly successful. He and Elizabeth were very compatible and the new family settled rather quickly into a comfortable routine. In fact, the years of his marriage to Elizabeth, from 1703 to 1713, were probably the happiest years of Mather's tragedy-filled life. These years were not without trial, but the crucible of suffering through which he had passed seemed to have mellowed him. He became less obsessive, less compulsive in some areas, less grandiose, less inclined toward magical thinking, more relaxed, more self-accepting, more realistic about his own capacities, more creative in his work, more effective as a parent, and, in general, grew in his capacity to enjoy life. Although he felt a bit guilty about it, he found that he could sleep longer —not arising sometimes until 7 or 8 a.m.! He also found time to appreciate the beauty of nature. In March, 1706, he wrote in his diary:

> I see all creatures every where full of their delights. The birds are singing; the fish are sporting; the four-footed are glad of what they meet withal; the very insects have their satisfactions. Tis a marvellous display of infinite goodness. The good God has made his creatures capable of delights; He accommodates them with continual delights. Their delights are the delicious entertainments of his infinite goodness. His goodness takes pleasure, and is delighted, in the delights of his creatures.[42]

For a person who had often been obsessed with fears of his own death and who had experienced the death of many of those closest to him, this celebration of life represented real progress.

Mather felt more loved and he became more loving. His relationship with his father, who had reached old age, became less dependent and more tender. He initiated an extraordinarily energetic program to promote social benevolence and community action, and, although his numerous projects for doing good sometimes had a compulsive quality, they were often effective and gave him a deeper sense of meaning and purpose.[43] His willingness to initiate community action, to reach out to other people, through more direct, concrete acts, constituted an important change from his earlier obsessive tendencies toward morbid introspection and sterile, hair-splitting intellectuality.

Mather also seemed to gain greater satisfaction from his children during this period, and he continued to reflect upon his role as a parent and educator. In February, 1706, he recorded the basic principles and practices he followed in the education of his children. He began teaching them to read and write at an early age. He prayed regularly for each of them by name; he entertained them at the table "with delightful stories, especially scriptural ones," and when his children "accidentally" came into his presence, he tried to offer them a short sentence "that may be monitory and profitable to them." He offered them guidance for their private devotion and taught them to have a benign temper by asking them to do "services and kindness for one another" and cautioning them against taking revenge against others. He considered "the slavish way of education, carried on with raving and kicking and scourging" to be "abominable; and a dreadful judgement of God upon the world." He would, he said, "never come to give a child a blow; except in the case of obstinacy: or some gross enormity." He preferred to punish his children by chasing them out of his presence, "the sorest punishment in the family," or by denying them the privilege of being taught or other less significant rewards.[44] Mather no doubt failed to mention his practices which he deemed less admirable, but Samuel confirms that Cotton generally practiced what he preached, at least during his second marriage.[45] Mather had clearly identified with the role of parent and had gained enough distance from his father that he continued to grow in his ability to relate to his children in a consistent and objective manner.

Of all his children, only his son Increase seemed to revive deep conflicts in Mather. By 1712, near the end of Cotton's second marriage, "Creasy" had reached the beginning of adolescence (see chart on page 30) and Cotton began to express his deep concern about the company his son had been keeping. When Cotton observed Creasy's emerging sexuality and his growing willfulness, he was overwhelmed by memories of the sins of his own youth, and he became extremely fearful that Creasy would succumb to the temptations which had buffeted him so strongly when he was young. Paradoxically, because he was so tense and so anticipatory in his relationship with Creasy, Cotton may have actually helped to produce the behavior he feared most.[46] As Therese Benedek has observed, "It seems that parents and children, like paranoids, achieve what they anticipate with anxiety and intend to avoid."[47]

Creasy's problems had not yet become so severe that they interfered with Cotton's ability to be an effective parent to his other children or to carry on his work and writing. Between 1703 and 1713, Cotton devoted a significant portion of his published work to a consideration of the education of children and youth; and, unlike some of his earlier work, it contains relatively less emphasis on their natural depravity and more recognition of their great potential. To Mather, there was "no melody more delightful" than the prayers of the "lovely young people" who pray to God and seek him early. Mather's growing acceptance of himself had made it easier for him to develop a more balanced and complete assessment of the characteristics of children and young people, and they in turn reinforced his sense of efficacy as a "good" parent.[48]

The pleasant melodies of Mather's happy years soon came to an abrupt end. Between November 9, 1713, and April 4, 1714, he lost his wife, his mother, his infant twins, Martha and Eleazor, and his two-year-old daughter Jerusha.[49] The impact of these enormous losses left him deeply conscious of the transitory, ephemeral character of life and turned his mind once more to a preoccupation with his own death. In a speech before the General Assembly in 1715, he described "a dying world." "So quickly, so nimbly, so swiftly, a generation passes," he observed. "A generation," he declared,

is like the spark, that rises from our fires. The sparks fly upwards

and some shine brighter, some last longer than others. They all go
out! Some sooner, some later; all quickly; and they all fall down into the common heap of ashes. This is the trouble, which all the
generations are born into.[50]

Mather made a valiant effort to recover from the troubles death had
brought him. He married Lydia George in July, 1715, and for a brief
period it seemed that some semblance of order and normality would
return to his life.[51] His writing and preaching continued unabated; he
had placed Creasy on a ship bound to London to learn navigation; his
daughter Abigail was married to a promising young merchant; his second
son Sammy was a healthy, playful boy; and Hannah and Elizabeth were
safely at home. But even then, his eldest daughter Katy was suffering
from consumption and eventually succumbed to the illness in December,
1716. In a sermon preached as a memorial to Katy, Cotton lamented that
losing a daughter was "a killing thing unto a parent."[52]

From the end of 1716 until his death in 1728, Mather's affairs continued a downward spiral which afforded him few of the opportunities
for satisfaction or development which had come to him during the hap-
pier years of his second marriage. His financial condition became so
precarious that he almost had to sell his precious library; and his involve-
ment in the smallpox controversy alienated many of his fellow Bosto-
nians, leading eventually to an abortive attempt to bomb his home.[53]
Furthermore, his marriage to Lydia proved unfruitful and unhappy. Her
mental health began to deteriorate; she became suspicious and hostile,
stole some of his private papers, and at one point, after a loud and bitter
argument, left the house in the middle of the night to stay with a
neighbor.[54] Although Mather managed to keep the marriage officially
intact, their problems were so serious that Mather arranged for Hannah
and Elizabeth to leave home to escape Lydia's persecutions.[55]

Cotton also continued to have problems with Creasy. When Creasy
returned from England, Cotton negotiated a position for him with a
relative as a bookkeeper, but he did not stick to his books and Cotton's
earlier fears became a reality. On November 5, 1717, Cotton wrote in his
diary:

The evil that I greatly feared, is come upon me. I am within these
few hours, astonished with information, that an harlot big with
bastard, accuses my son Creasy, and layes her belly to him. Oh!
Dreadful Case! Oh sorrow beyond any that I have met withal!
What shall I do now for the foolish youth! What for my afflicted
and abased family? . . . The most sensible judges upon the strictest
inquiry, believe the youth to be innocent. But yett, oh! ye humiliations![56]

There were more humiliations to come. On April 4, 1721, Cotton tells us that his "miserable, miserable, miserable son Increase" had "brought himself under public trouble and infamy by bearing a part in a night-riot with some detestable rakes in the town."[57] Mather was completely disgusted with Creasy, yet he could never bring himself to reject him completely, and when Creasy was drowned at sea in 1724 he was thrown into deep mourning for his son. "Ah! vain world!" he wrote, "how little is to be expected in thee and from thee!" "Ah, disappointed harvests, how frequent are you?" "Now we see that this world will afford unto us no substantial happiness." Mather's suffering was so intense because he suspected that his son's failures were in part reflections of his own weaknesses and unresolved conflicts. In his mind, at least, his son's failures and transgressions were his own.[58]

It is perhaps not surprising that Cotton's writing on children and young people during the last ten to twelve years of his life concentrated on the meaning of death, the need for early piety, and the vicissitudes of adolescence and young adulthood. One of his most important publications during this period was *The Pure Nazarite* (1723), one of the first essays ever published on the subject of masturbation. Although Mather voiced the then commonplace fears that masturbation would produce impotence, sterility, or deformed offspring, the general tone of the essay is remarkably tolerant and empathic. He warns the young people who engage in this libidinal practice against making rash vows and tells them that if they are patient in their struggle their adversary will eventually flee. The autobiographical element in this essay is patent, and it is a perfect illustration of the relationship between Mather's private life and public work.[59]

The last years of Cotton's life were not without compensations. Mather necessarily took on a more active, caretaking role in his relationship with his aging father, who died in 1723 at the age of eighty-four. He spent considerable time with his father, reading to him and talking with him, and in general gave his father great comfort, a fact which Increase acknowledged in his last years. Cotton seems to have handled this reversal of roles with considerable grace and dignity.[60]

Cotton received his greatest satisfaction as a parent from the development and achievements of his youngest son Samuel (or Samachi, as he sometimes called him). Samuel never worked as hard as Cotton would have liked, but he did not fall into Creasy's errors, as Cotton obviously feared he might. In 1723 Samuel graduated from Harvard, and on October 25, 1724, Cotton proudly recorded in his diary:

This day my son Samuel, (which yet short of eighteen) appeared in the pulpit where his father and grandfather before him, have served our glorious Lord; and preached on Exod. XV. 2. 'He is my

Father's God and I will exalt him.'[61]

Through Samuel, Cotton gained some sense of generativity and a degree of fulfillment as a parent. While Creasy's life and death left Cotton frustrated and depressed, Samuel's promising future lifted his spirits and gave him some hope that his work and his father's would be continued.

In spite of the almost overwhelming problems Cotton faced during the last ten years of his life, he apparently did not lose the capacity for healthy parenting that he had developed during his second marriage. Samuel said that in his later years Cotton never kept

> a morose carriage toward his children, nor a haughty distance from them; but forever when they came into his presence, he would condescend to the familiarity of an acquaintance; and thus he would instruct and edify, thus allure and charm us, thus make us love his society, ever come into it with delight and never leave it but with sorrow . . . .

Samuel declared that his father's approach to children was more likely to cause them "to love their parents and incline them to be good and virtuous than any crabbed looks, austere orders, or surly demands whatsoever."[62] Cotton certainly loved his children and he seems to have made it possible for them to return that love.

One of the most important tests of a mature love for children is a parent's ability to provide the child with some degree of autonomy as a separate being within the context of consistent concern and nurture, and a willingness to accept and even encourage the child's growing independence. Mather never found it easy to respect the autonomy of his children, and he sometimes identified with his children too closely. It had been very difficult for him to separate from his own father, and at times he seemed unwilling or unable to respect the psychological boundaries of his children, especially his boys.[63] In the case of his errant son Increase, Mather's intrusiveness produced the opposite of what he consciously wanted. If he had been able to maintain a greater emotional distance from his children, his love would have been less narcissistic and he would have, even by his own standards, been a more successful parent.

Yet we should not judge Mather by his own obsessively perfectionistic standards. He was definitely not the stereotypically punitive, severe, and threatening Puritan parent whose primary concern was to deprive children of the innocent joys of childhood. Cotton was not an abusing parent; he was not blindly dedicated to breaking his children's wills; he was not insensitive to the special individual needs of his children; and he was not incapable of appreciating his children as children. He sincerely wanted to be a good parent; he devoted considerable time and energy to thinking and writing about parent-child relationships; and he showed a remarkable ability to use each difficult stage of parenthood as a source of further insight and a foundation for continued development as a person. Cotton Mather was never a perfect parent or completely healthy psychologically, but he learned from his mistakes, and in a most profound sense he grew with his children.[64]

FOOTNOTES

*The research for this essay was funded in part by grants from the Menninger Foundation, the National Endowment for the Humanities, and the University of Kansas General Research Fund. I also wish to acknowledge the helpful suggestions offered by Ross Beales, John Clark, Barbara Finkelstein, John Fitzpatrick, Clifford Griffin, Joseph Hawes, and Paul Pruyser.

1. Cotton Mather, *Family Religion Urged* (Boston: n.p., 1709), p. 17.

2. Worthington Chauncey Ford (ed.), *The Diary of Cotton Mather* (reprinted in New York: Frederick Unger Publishing Co., n.d.), Vol. II, p. 706.

3. John Bowlby, *Attachment and Loss* (New York: Basic Books, 1969), Vol. I, pp. 200-204, 216-234; Rene Spitz, *The First Year of Life* (New York: International Universities Press, 1965), pp. 117-120, 160-164, 180-190; Phyllis Greenacre, "Considerations Regarding the Parent-Infant Relationship," *The International Journal of Psychoanalysis*, XLI (1960), 571-584; Donald W. Winnicott, "The Mother-Infant Experience of Mutuality," *Parenthood: Its Psychology and Psychopathology*, E. James Anthony and Therese Benedek, editors (Boston: Little, Brown, and Co., 1970), pp. 245-256; Therese Benedek, "Parenthood as a Developmental Phase," *Psychoanalytic Investigations: Selected Papers* (New York: Quadrangle, 1973), 377-407; and Kurt Danziger, *Socialization* (Middlesex, England: Penguin Books, 1971), pp. 58-70.

4. See Therese Benedek, "Parenthood as a Developmental Phase" and her three essays in *Parenthood: Its Psychology and Psychopathology*: "The Family as a Psychologic Field" (pp. 109-136); "Fatherhood and Providing" (pp. 167-183); and "Parenthood During the Life Cycle" (pp. 185-206). Lloyd deMause has also emphasized the importance of children as a source of psychic development for parents. See his "The Evolution of Childhood," *History of Childhood Quarterly*, I (Spring, 1974), 503-575; "The Psychogenic Theory of History," *Journal of Psychohistory*, IV (Winter, 1977), 253-267; and "The Formation of the American Personality Through Psychospeciation," *Journal of Psychohistory*, IV (Summer, 1976), 1-15.

5. *Diary*, II, p. 642. For a sympathetic, but brief and essentially static description of Mather as a parent, see Elizabeth Bancroft Schlesinger, "Cotton Mather and His Children," *William and Mary Quarterly*, X (April, 1953), 181-189.

6. Most of the standard biographical sources list only fifteen children for Cotton, but they fail to include a boy (apparently unnamed) who was born four to five months premature on May 25, 1702. See *Diary*, I, p. 430.

7. See Samuel Eliot Morison, *Harvard College in the Seventeenth Century* (Cambridge: Harvard University Press, 1936), I, pp. 82-83, II, p. 417; Perry Miller, *The New England Mind: From Colony to Province* (Boston: Beacon Press, edition, 1961), pp. 357, 476, *et passim*. For less critical views, see Robert Middlekauff, *The Mathers: Three Generations of Puritan Intellectuals* (New York:

Oxford University Press, 1971), pp. 191-367; David Levin, "The Hazing of Cotton Mather: The Creation of a Biographical Personality," *In Defense of Historical Literature* (New York: Hill and Wang, 1967), pp. 34-57; and Kenneth Silverman (comp.). *Selected Letters of Cotton Mather* (Baton Rouge: Louisiana State University Press, 1971), pp. IX-XVII. Also see Barrett Wendell, *Cotton Mather: The Puritan Priest*, (Cambridge, Mass.: Harvard University Press, 1926; and Ralph and Louise Boas, *Cotton Mather: Keeper of the Puritan Conscience*, (New York: Harper and Brothers, 1928).

8. Michael G. Hall (ed.), "The Autobiography of Increase Mather," *Proceedings of the American Antiquarian Society*, LXXI, Part 2 (1961), 314.

9. Samuel Mather, *The Life of the Very Reverend and Learned Cotton Mather* (Boston: Samuel Gerrish, 1729), pp. 6-7.

10. "Autobiography of Increase Mather," p. 301.

11. *Ibid*.

12. Samuel Mather, *op. cit.*, pp. 26-27.

13. Cotton Mather, *The Angel of Bethesda*, Gordon W. Jones, editor (Barre, Massachusetts: American Antiquarian Society and Barre Publishers, 1972), pp. 230-231.

14. Samuel Mather, *op. cit.*, pp. 27-28.

15. See Thomas Prince's preface to *Ibid.*, p. 5; and Carol Gay, "The Fettered Tongue: A Study of the Speech Defect of Cotton Mather," *American Literature*, XLVI (January, 1975), 461-464.

16. *Diary*, I, p. 42.

17. *Ibid.*, pp. 47-53; and Samuel Mather, *op. cit.*, p. 27.

18. *Ibid.*, p. 28; and *Diary*, I, pp. 91-99.

19. Leon Salzman, *The Obsessive Personality: Origins, Dynamics, and Therapy* (New York: Science House, 1968), p. 90. Also see David Shapiro, *Neurotic Styles* (New York: Basic Books, 1965), pp. 23-48; Wilhelm Reich, *Character Analysis* (third edition. New York: Noonday Press, 1949), pp. 193-199; and Otto Fenichel, *The Psychoanalytic Theory of Neuroses* (New York: W.W. Norton, 1945), 268-308.

20. Dominick A. Barbara, *Stuttering: A Psychodynamic Approach to Its Understanding and Treatment* (New York: Julian Press, 1954), pp. 74-77, 90, 94. Also Harold Kolansky, "Some Psychoanalytic Considerations on Speech in Normal Development and Psychopathology," *Psychoanalytic Study of the Child* XXII (1967), 274-295; and Peter I. Glauger, "Freud's Contribution on Stuttering: Their Relation to Some Current Insights," *Journal of the American Psychoanalytic Association*, VI (April, 1958), 326-347.

21. Barbara, *op. cit.*, pp. 126-127. Also see Fenichel, *op. cit.*, pp. 311-317; and Shapiro, *op. cit.*, p. 32.

22. *Diary*, I, pp. 68-69, 78-79, 126-127.

23. Barrett, *Cotton Mather*, pp. 73-123.

24. *Diary*, I, pp. XXI-XXII, 140.

25. *Ibid.*, pp. 136-163-164, 174, 185-186, 240; Wendall, *op. cit.*, pp. 116, 119, 154-156; and *Sibley's Harvard Graduates*, III, p. 41.

26. *Diary*, I, pp. 185-195.

27. *Addresses to Old Men, Young Men, and Little Children* (Boston: R. Pierce, 1690); and *Early Religion Urged* (Boston: n.p., 1694). Also see *Help for Distressed Parents* (Boston: John Allen, 1695).

28. *Diary*, I, p. 216.

29. *Ibid.*, pp. 217, 282-284.

30. *Ibid.*, pp. 293-295.

31. *A Family Well-Ordered, or An Essay to Render Parents and Children Happy in One Another* (Boston: B. Green and J. Allen, 1699), pp. 20-25.
32. *Diary*, I, pp. 307, 340.
33. *Ibid.*, p. 360.
34. *Ibid.*, p. 369.
35. *Ibid.*, p. 382.
36. *Ibid.*, p. 430.
37. *Ibid.*, pp. 445-447
38. *Ibid.*, p. 448.
39. *Ibid.*, pp. 449-454
40. *Ibid.*, pp. 457-496. For recent discussions of the character and dynamics of grief, see David K. Switzer, *The Dynamics of Grief* (Nashville: Abingdon Press, 1970); Bert Schoenberg, *et al.* (eds.), *Loss and Grief: Psychological Management in Medical Practice* (New York: Columbia University Press, 1970); and Colin M. Parkes, *Bereavement: Studies of Grief in Adult Life* (New York: International Universities Press, 1972). Also see Peter Slater's valuable essay, "From the *Cradle* to the *Coffin*: Parental Bereavement and the Shadow of Infant Damnation in Puritan Society," *The Psychohistory Review*, VI (Fall-Winter, 1977-78), 4-24.
41. *Cares About Nurseries* (Boston: n.p., 1702).
42. *Diary*, I, pp. 545, 553.
43. *Ibid.*, p. 560. Also see his *Bonifacius: An Essay Upon the Good* (Boston: B. Green for Samuel Gerrish, 1710).
44. *Diary*, I, 534-536.
45. Samuel Mather, *op. cit.*, pp. 15-19, 140.
46. *Diary*, II, p. 22, 33-34, 49, 92, 106-107, 151, 199, 203-204, 216-218, 224, 234.
47. Benedek, "Parenthood as a Developmental Phase," p. 392.
48. [Cotton Mather], *Agreeable Admonitions for Old and Young* (Boston: B. Green, 1703), p. 13. Also see his *Youth Under Good Conduct* (Boston: Timothy Green, 1707); *The Best Ornaments of Youth* (Boston: Timothy Green, 1707); *Family Religion Urged; Youth in Its Brightest Glory* (Boston: T. Green, 1709); *Bonifacius; The Wages and Joys of Early Piety* (Boston: B. Green for Samuel Gerrish, 1712); *Memorials of Early Piety* (Boston: T. Green, 1711).
49. *Diary*, II, pp. 255-261; Cotton Mather, *Maternal Consolations* (Boston: T. Fleet for Samuel Gerrish, 1714), pp. 1-5, 39-40; and Increase Mather, *A Sermon Concerning Obedience* (Boston: T. Green, 1714).
50. *Successive Generations* (Boston: B. Green for Samuel Gerrish, 1715), pp. 9-10.
51. *Diary*, II, p. 337.
52. *Diary*, II, pp. 298, 372-374; and *Victorina* (Boston: B. Green for Daniel Henchman, 1717), p. i.
53. Silverman, *Selected Letters of Cotton Mather*, pp. 284-285, 294-296, 308-309.
54. *Diary*, II, pp. 657-658.
55. *Ibid.*, pp. 583-586, 590-591, 712, 750-752, and Silverman, *op. cit.*, p. 284.
56. *Diary*, II, p. 484.
57. *Ibid.*, pp. 611-612.
58. [Cotton Mather], *The Words of Understanding* (Boston: S. Kneeland for Edwards, 1724), pp. 54-55.
59. [Cotton Mather], *The Pure Nazarite* (Boston: T. Fleet for John Phillips, 1723), pp. 10-15. Also see *Onania; or the Heinous Sin* (Tenth Edition; Boston: 1724); E.H. Hare, "Masturbatory Insanity: The History of an Idea," *The Journal of Mental Science*, CVIII (January 1962), 1-25; R.P. Neuman, "Masturbation, Madness, and the Modern Concepts of Childhood and Adolescence," *Journal*

of Social History (Spring, 1975), 1-27; and Steve M. Dranoff, "Masturbation and the Male Adolescent," *Adolescence*, IX (Summer, 1974), 169-176.

60. *Diary*, II, pp. 343, 450-451, 461, 505, 519-520, 530, 539, 619, 652-653; and "The Autobiography of Increase Mather," p. 357.

61. *Diary*, II, pp. 769-770.

62. Samuel Mather, *op. cit.*, p. 140.

63. According to Peter Slater, Cotton's children "possessed no sphere of personal privacy, no psychological space which their father felt bound to honor." See his "Cotton Mather and His Children," unpublished paper (1978), p. 12.

64. For a more detailed description of Mather's early life and ministry, see David Levin's *Cotton Mather: The Young Life of the Lord's Remembrances* (Cambridge: Harvard University Press, 1978). This excellent work came to my attention too late to include in earlier references.

III

Preparation for Republicanism: Honor and Shame in the Eighteenth-Century College

— PHYLLIS VINE

By 1823, when Thomas Jefferson noted that "the insubordination of our youth is now the greatest obstacle to their education," he could have been referring to the series of student revolts which had erupted in American colleges in the early nineteenth century. Unlike the misdemeanors which were sprinkled through the eighteenth-century colleges, the behavior of students in the nineteenth century actually led educators to expel them in large numbers.[1] Asking students to leave the institution because their behavior threatened its purpose reflects a change in American higher education between the eighteenth and nineteenth centuries. In the eighteenth century discipline was an integral part of the collegiate system. Students were punished, educated, and supervised within the confines of the institution. This was based on educators' intentions to teach students to behave with republican virtue, a quality which embodied the passionate fusion of public and private good. To accomplish this eighteenth-century goal, educators relied on shaming techniques in the presence of a public audience to build character.

At a time in American society when higher education was not required for success, students who attended college were among the sponsored elite. Their families recognized the necessity of planning for their futures by sending them to institutions which would help arrange future marriage and business associations. The fluidity of eighteenth-century America undermined the family's ability to guarantee a place for its children. It also generated the desire and energy needed to invigorate the fifteen institutions of higher education. By placing their sons in colleges, parents could draw on a larger group of individuals who might be of assistance when beset with the problems of providing training for their children.[2] Parents expected the colleges to teach students how to distinguish themselves in a public role and draw on its circle of patronage for help.[3]

Once they arrived at school, students in the eighteenth century participated in a culture which was every bit as important in guiding their transition to adulthood as the conjugation of Latin verbs or the correct translation of *Ovid*. For the education of this select group of males between the ages of 16 and 25, part of the transition involved a series of rites through which they could acquire "good manners, a virtuous conduct, a steady regard to the rights of others, and to the public."[4] The attributes that Dickinson College President Charles Nisbet described above did not evolve without design, and the structure of higher education contained the mechanisms to mold that very individual. The rites and rituals began upon admission, when a student first copied the rules of his particular college; they ended when he underwent the initiation ceremony of graduation. The combination of these and other rituals during the college years taught students how to behave in accordance with the values educators deemed appropriate for public responsibility and leadership— hardly a small task for those who lamented the increasing barbarism of Britain's colonies or the precarious nature of republican government.

Though the particular features of any rite of passage differ from culture to culture, they follow a more or less standard pattern.[5] Rites of passage begin with a separation of the subject from the environment or social setting in which he is normally found. Boys in the eighteenth-century colleges were removed from the home, segregated from members of the opposite sex, and introduced into an all male environment. Once in school, they were guided by a number of mechanisms through successive stages of their education. The components of this process included the adoption of definitions of self which had significance and status only within that particular system. For example, categories such as Freshman, Sophomore, Junior and Senior represented a hierarchy of distinction or achievement. These classes conveyed a set of meanings and prerogatives otherwise insignificant. Moreover, particular obligations and expectations characterized social intercourse, such as the regular hazing of Freshmen, the adoption of academic gowns, or the practice of removing one's hat at an appropriate distance from another who also shared the culture. (At Yale a student had to remove his hat at least 10 rods from the President, and 5 rods from a tutor.[6]) When the individual complied with the various parts of the ritual, it became a "means of divesting [him] of his status as a child in the domestic domain and of investing him with the status of actual or potential citizen in the political-jural domain."[7]

One of the mechanisms of utmost importance in the rite of passage was the ritualistic exercise of discipline which was designed around values of shame and honor. Just as the Renaissance study of the Latin language was one of the puberty rites young males had to undergo,[8] being shamed among one's social group was an aspect of the rite for the eighteenth-century college male. This paper will discuss that pattern of shaming through an examination of discipline. As we examine the manner in which educators sought to inculcate a sense of shame and the quest for honor among students, we may begin to understand how education was designed to mold an archetypical personality who embodied republican culture.

This study grew out of an examination of theories of discipline and patterns of correction in five schools located in the Middle Atlantic region: Princeton University, Columbia College, The University of Pennsylvania, Dickinson College, and Union College. Though infractions abound in the records of these institutions of higher learning, very few errant students were expelled from school, and certainly none for academic reasons. Extant records suggest that with few exceptions the main reason a student was asked to leave (no matter how serious the original transgression) was due to his unwillingness to apologize appropriately. It became clear that educators preferred to reform students rather than expel them. Guilt was of secondary importance to penitence, and teachers wanted to bring their charges into the fold of well-defined culture. The Princeton Faculty Minutes, for example, illustrate this. The Minutes list students who were disciplined between 1787 and 1793. Among the transgressions itemized were tardiness, playing cards on the Sabbath, insolence, contempt, whoremongering, and violence of all kinds, including discharging a gun in college. For this list of approximately 100 different student transgressions, fewer than four individuals were expelled. One, whose crime was listed as "eating to excess in a cafe," was expelled when he pled "not guilty." Found to be guilty by the board of examiners, he was told to leave, no doubt for an unwillingness to demonstrate sufficient penitence and to admit to his own shame. Later, when he professed sorrow, he was reinstated.[9] Other examples exist where a student initially refused to admit guilt and sorrow, but was reinstated when he owned responsibility and pronounced the ritualistic apology.[10]

With this pattern in mind, I began to question the implications for eighteenth-century education and society of a collegiate system based on shame. This is not to suggest that the students were "shame-ridden" or that early America was a "shame-culture."[11] Rather, it is an exploration of how shame was used as a vehicle to maintain social order. In an age riddled with social disruption, the means through which individuals were taught how to form their social personalities to promote stability becomes important to our understanding of the transmission of culture. Therefore, I turned to two fields which have a body of literature that addresses shame: anthropology and psychology.

According to anthropologists, shame is one of the mechanisms which maintains social conformity. It can be used to correct asocial behavior, and it also produces a sense of individual accountability within the public domain.[12] In some societies, such as the pueblo in rural Spain, one of the techniques for maintaining social control consists of dunking neighboring boys in a public fountain before allowing them to court village girls. In other societies, such as that of the St. Lawrence Eskimos, a wrestling match or singing contest may be used to resolve conflict through the ridicule of one of the contestants.[13] There is general agreement, however, that societies concerned with a public social personality employ one or more parts of the shaming process to maintain social control and enforce codes of behavior. These parts of the process include humiliation, degradation, and ostracism—mechanisms which place the focus of attention on the individual who has erred and whom the society seeks to reintegrate.

The emotion of shame is also effective, according to psychologists, in maintaining social conformity. They associate shame with an anxiety which erupts from fear of social expulsion. The person who feels shame (or is made to feel it) fears withdrawal of approval and isolation from the social group of which he is a part and on which he depends. This feeling of loss of approval, potential abandonment, produces vulnerability to rejection because it is based on a situation in which one individual cares what another thinks or feels about him. The author of a recent study on shame, Helen Block Lewis, describes it this way: "In this affective tie the self does not feel autonomous or independent, but dependent and vulnerable to rejection. Shame is a vicarious experience of the other's scorn."[14] A recurring theme throughout all of the literature on shame is that it produces fears of exposure, nakedness in the eyes of others and oneself. For this reason shame is often described as a defense against exhibitionism. The person who feels shame experiences a sense of degradation, a wounded self-esteem, and a sense of not having lived up to standards of excellence.

The significance of a code of discipline based on shame must be understood in terms of the experience of adolescence—that stage of the life cycle when eighteenth-century youth entered college. During adolescence, the time when instinctual conflicts which had remained latent during childhood begin to percolate, one of the ego's mechanisms of defense is an intellectualization of libidinal drives. Anna Freud's pioneer work in this area notes that young people attempt to lay hold of the instinctual processes by connecting them with ideas.[15] Further, we have seen a number of "youth movements" in history which correspond to the tendency for adolescents to become committed to ideas and ideals. This time of the life cycle is described by Erik Erikson as a stage when youth seek "men and ideas to have *faith* in, which also means men and ideas in whose service it would seem worthwhile to prove oneself trustworthy." Erikson remarks that it is the "ideological potential of a society which speaks most clearly to the adolescent who is so eager to be affirmed by peers, to be confirmed by teachers, and to be inspired by worthwhile 'ways of life.' "[16] Adolescence is also a time in life when youth are particularly concerned with what others think of them. The peer pressure assumes a significance it did not have earlier, and young people measure themselves by what others think. Some stress that the relationship between the peer group and feelings of shame is one of utmost significance, more so than the more common parental images which have been introjected to affect super-ego development.[17]

Statements which recognized the significance of the peer group as important for producing shame were written by educators in the eighteenth century as well as psychoanalysts in the twentieth century. Princeton's John Witherspoon, for example, noted that shame "subjects us to the opinion of others." In this way it can be "an assistant or guard to virtue by making us apprehend reproach from others."[18] Pleasing others, or having them approve of one's behavior, was the theme of Charles Nisbet's address to students when they returned from vacation in 1788. Nisbet told the Dickinson College gathering that if parents and friends were not convinced of their progress, then they should apply a constant attention to their behavior "to merit on another occasion, a more favorable opinion of your characters from those whose favor is of so much consequence to you." His address continues as he compares the value of possessing knowledge, as such, to that of proper behavior. "Wisdom affords no infallible receipt for attaining the approbation of the public . . . and attention to propriety of behavior will certainly gain you the favor of all those whose judgment is worth regarding." Nisbet reminds the students to retain a modest attitude toward their learning in order to retain the opinion and esteem of others. In order to do this, to be well regarded, he notes that "all well educated youth will avoid and be ashamed of . . . [being] the occasion of noise, wrath or offense."[19]

The Enlightenment concept of discipline was predicated on assumptions that youth were malleable and that reformation of character was possible. At one time the principal method for punishing students and maintaining order within the institution was corporal punishment.[20] Corporal punishment had been largely abandoned on the American continent by the middle of the eighteenth century, for reasons which Benjamin Rush addresses in his essay on proper punishments in school. Corporal punishments, he noted, "inflicted at school, have a tendency to destroy the sense of shame, and thereby destroy all moral sensibility."[21] Opening the Philadelphia Academy in 1751, Reverend Richard Peters noted that a sense of shame was viewed as one of the "useful passions," a carrier of virtue.[22] President William Smith explained why. Unless rewards and punishments were public, one could not expect students to "submit to the rules of civil society itself when grown up."[23] At Dickinson College, discipline was to appeal as "much as possible to the sense of shame."[24] Nisbet asserted that when "you have lost shame, you have lost everything that can restrain you from the extreme of vice." Quoting an anonymous sage, he added " 'the man, that blushes, is not quite a brute.' "[25] Shame guaranteed that individuals would not behave in a conspicuous fashion, but rather would take their cues for behavior from others in the social vicinity. Through it they would learn when others thought their behavior worthy of reproach or, as Erikson said, how to compare their own senses of self with the opinions of others.

It is within the framework of a concept of shame that the pedagogical technique of emulation must be considered. Educators heralded emulation as the process of identifying with those whose merit had been established. This operated in an academic as well as a social capacity. Academically, the curriculum fostered rote learning: declension of verbs, memorization, oratory. Interpretation or originality were not stressed within the didactic presentation of material. The pedagogical armament of the eighteenth-century college, based on classical authors, promoted identification with figures who had tangible advice to offer aspiring republicans. The author of a recent study of higher education shows how Dickinson's Professor Robert Davidson used grammar to accomplish this:

> When he taught adverbs, he extolled the virtues of the ancients: "Cicero was eloquent, Pliny was *moderately eloquent*, Virgil wrote *admirably*. When conjunctions were the subject of the day, Davidson demonstrated the connection between ambition and slavery: "Rome was enslaved. Caesar was ambitious. Connect them by the conjunction *because* and then it will be Rome was enslaved *because* Caesar was ambitious."[26]

Theories of emulation contributed also to justifications for sending boys to schools rather than relying on private tutors. As John Blair Smith told the audience at the opening of Union College (1796), within the institution's confines "students, who are going to have to live among men and meet the duties of citizenship, are accustomed from early years to dealing, as it were, with the public . . . The mind, by this practice of conversation and matching itself against peers, gathers strength . . . That puffed up pride which inflates itself in exclusive privacy is usually deflated."[27] Basically this was the same theme that Richard Peters sounded in 1751 when he said that, in order "to make every boy discern right and wrong," teachers would have to "raise an inextinguishable emulation."[28]

Emulation, as understood in the eighteenth century, encouraged people to view others with an eye toward comparing one's own deficiencies to their excellence. Thus it produced a form of behavior which was bound also by identifying with one's social unit. In a hierarchically graded, deferential society, emulation helped the eighteenth-century gentleman because it made him want to excel. But emulation, a useful passion, could turn to envy, a dangerous passion, if shame did not intercede. As John Henry Hobart, a student and tutor at Princeton, noted: "Emulation of the excellencies of any one sometimes leads to envying the person in whom they are found."[29] Envy was dangerous because it allowed for individual competition without regard to the good of the social order. It was antithetical, therefore, to promoting organic unity, one of the archstones of republicanism. Just as with shame, emulation taught students to become dependent on outside stimuli.[30]

Advocating shame as a desirable character trait underlay educators' paradigm of the socializing process. They noted its value for producing dependency on, and conformity to a group. Describing philosophical values, pedagogical ideals, and social imperatives is one of the easier tasks confronting educational historians. It is important, however, to compare in the phrase that Gordon Wood has made part of our working vocabulary "the rhetoric and the reality." Exactly how did educators attempt to inculcate shame? What institutional mechanisms tapped or reinforced it? And for what social purpose was it designed? Some of these questions can be answered through an examination of the episodes which most readily illustrate shaming through the process of discipline.

One of the mechanisms which promoted social conformity through activating shame was degradation. Degradation required that students participate in school activities as members of a subordinate class, most often during meals and for chapel attendance. Prior to the end of placement by social status at Yale and Harvard (1767 and 1772 respectively), degradation dropped an errant student one or more places in his own class. In all schools it had the consequence of ostracizing the individual from his class-graded peer group and making his infraction visible to the entire community.[31] This procedure was written into the laws regulating student behavior at the various colleges. At King's College, for example, degradation was used when students disobeyed orders of confinement to the college while they made up deficient work. Myles Cooper's "Book of Misdemeanours in King's College, Alias Black Book" contains a number of entries for students who were confined for a week or more until the missing work was completed. In the case of the four students who "broke thro' the Confinement, which was ordered them . . . " the threat of degradation was held out. Other students were simply degraded for unspecified crimes, but generally for behavior which did not carry respect for honor and station. Contumaciousness and insolence were within this category, and often described as "neglect of speaking proper." This probably explains the cases of the three students who were charged with "different heinous offences." They were degraded until "by their dutiful Behaviour they shall merit Restoration." Three months later Cooper noted that the three guilty students, "in consideration of their regular & dutiful Behaviour, had their Degradation removed."[32] They were then restored to their class and allowed all of the privileges and honors of their classmates.

The most serious offenses, however, were corrected through a process of public humiliation and ritualistic apology in front of the entire college community. It is through these procedures that one sees the shaming technique used to its fullest capacity. Before a student reached this stage in the process he had probably been degraded and admonished by one of the school authorities. Also, a personal apology in verbal and written form had been rendered. The process we witness through the case of a King's student, James Douglass, was designed to correct behavior so incorrigible that failure to comply suggested that he would never learn to be bound by the pressure of the group.

According to Cooper's Black Book, Douglass had stolen eight sheets of paper and a pen knife. For this he

> was reprimanded in the College Hall before all the Students. & after having his Gown stripped off by the Porter, he was ordered to kneel down & read a Paper containing an Acknowledgement of his Crime, expressing much Sorrow for it, & promising Amendment for the future—He was then forbidden to wear his Gown or Cap for one Week.[33]

This episode manifests several aspects of the shaming technique. As with degradation or admonishment before one's class, they made Douglass submit to this in the presence of other students. By the necessity of its attendance, the student body became a part of the shaming procedure. It was with them that a sanctioning power resided. The mechanism was designed so that in the eyes of the group Douglass was to feel his error, and it was the collective organization that was dishonored by his behavior. As Michael Zuckerman notes about the procedure for punishment in New England towns, "more than mere punishment was involved." Because the person was only temporarily outside the group which did the punishing, "the solidarity of the society was not upset. Only the offender who failed to confess stood outside the social order."[34] Since Douglass had the option of leaving beforehand, he must have identified with the social order as he underwent this experience. Otherwise he would not have endured it.

The community defined experience was essential in the shaming process for several reasons. The most obvious is that offered by Rosabeth Moss Kanter, whose work on mechanisms of commitment in nineteenth century utopian societies notes that punishment should occur within the group rather than expel the culprit. This guarantees that "the sanctioning process and product are visible." Since this part of the collegiate experience was part of the larger process of the transition to a new status, one to which membership was based on the approbation of the other members, public shaming permitted all to see the punished individual "as an example to the rest of the community."[35] It showed them that retaining their privileged status as members was always problematic. Myles Cooper would have recognized Kanter's abstractions, for Cooper said something similar about a student who challenged the values of the group when he ignored the conditions of his suspension. In a rage, Cooper asked "for a *formal Expulsion*; in order that *others* may not hope to escape due punishment shou'd *they* act in the same *disorderly* and *undutiful manner*."[36] Membership was indeed problematic for those who refused to accept punishment which was designed to emphasize social cohesion and modulate individual will. The exercise of autonomy—the antithesis of feelings of shame—was simply not acceptable.

Douglass' experience of being stripped of his gown by the person with the lowest status in the community (the porter) was perhaps most powerful. Removing the garb students wore as a visible badge of their social status left him naked and exposed. Ceremonial clothes promoted a closed community and served as a bonding agent for students undergoing the process of incorporation; the removal of the cap and gown isolated Douglass from the group, and it is likely that educators intended him to undergo the process that Helen Merrell Lynd notes is at the root meaning of the word shame: "to uncover, to expose, to wound."[37] Stated another way, "Shame supposes that one is completely exposed and conscious of being looked at—in a word self-conscious," according to Erikson. As they made him kneel, diminished in stature, the intent was to make him feel small in the eyes of others. This corresponds with shame, which "exploits the increased sense of being small."[38]

Apparently the experience proved too strenuous for the young Douglass. Instead of creating the desired self-mortification necessary to produce dependence on and identification with the group, it encouraged him to leave permanently. Clearly he did not feel the shame that educators tried to cultivate. Or perhaps he felt it too greatly, and the episode was too harsh to maintain the appropriate balance. The situation of another student, George Rapalje, had the opposite result, and we can examine this through his own words.

Rapalje had been expelled for having insulted George Harpur "with the most indecent language, repeatedly!"[39] At the same time Harpur was a private tutor, previously having been a Professor of Mathematics at King's College. By the time he was expelled, Rapalje had already apologized to Harpur and to President Myles Cooper and had written a lengthy statement in which he identified himself as an "imploring supplicant" who acknowledged he was "truly culpable" and that the "punishment is but adequate to the crime." He noted a most "distracting anxiety" and a "consumate woe" (sic). Rapalje identified feeling "the shame and disgrace attending my sentence" and recognized that there was a way to become a part of the corporate group again. He requested that the Governors of the college allow him to make a public confession in front of what he called "that tribunal where others have found mercy." He begged to be "once more reinstated in your favor and to have my name inserted amongst the numbers of my fellow students." Promising "submissiveness," he stated that he was "in sincerity penitent for my crime." Finally, Rapalje asked the pardon of the students for "the disgrace I have brought upon the seminary, of which they are members, by my unguarded and ungenteel behavior."[40]

Standard among student apologies was a denial of intent to err. This is important in preserving honor, for it attributes the misdeed to something other than willful or deliberate premeditation. The intentions of the individual speak to his sentiment and to the character from which his conduct derives.[44] Thus we see in Rapalje's statement a denial of any intent to offend, by which, implicitly, he reduced the gravity of the affront. Even Robert Harpur, the injured party, agreed. In a statement on Rapalje's behalf, Harpur believed that there was "no settled design, no malicious intention."[42] Wilfullness in a transgression of such an order would suggest that the individual was outside the boundaries of potential reformation and was insensitive to social pressure. In addition, unintentional transgressions could be attributed to the natural indiscretions of youth, and that, after all, was what educators were expected to correct. With anything less than a denial of intentions to harm, or anything short of presenting himself to the entire community, Rapalje knew he would not be reinstated. Without reinstatement, he feared his character would be "inevitably lost" by being so severely (sic) stigmatized" which would be "an almost insuperable obstacle to my being received into any employment for to what occasion can I with honor apply myself."[43] Though Rapalje did not receive a King's degree, it is unclear whether it had anything to do with the above incident, which occurred the year before the American Revolution forced the closing of this New York institution.

Commenting on the use of shame to supervise behavior in rural Spain,

Julian Pitt-Rivers notes that "it is the social personality, not the person of
the victim which is attained by accepting humiliation in order to be allowed
to return to the normal social relationship."[44] The social personality which
the college hoped to promote was that of a man of honor to himself, to the
institution, and to the larger society, as Benjamin Franklin stated in his
proposals for education.[45] Honor is a corollary to shame, as both are based on the evaluations of others. Just as shame has an infectious quality, so
does honor. Moreover, staying beyond ridicule endowed one with honor,
as John Witherspoon noted in *Lectures on Moral Philosophy* when he said
a sense of ridicule and a sense of honor and shame were allies. In the eighteenth-century college, therefore, as in other societies which employ shame
and shaming techniques to produce honor within and for the group, the
apology before public witnesses constituted a "tribunal before which
claims of honor are brought."[47] When he asked to have his honor reinstated, Rapalje referred to the tribunal as a potentially merciful body.

If Rapalje actually did not feel the shame, he certainly did a good job of
pretending. His statement identified almost all of the aspects important to
the process; he even claimed to feel shame. By noting that he had dishonored the entire community by his personal transgression, he recognized the
implications of an individual's behavior for the entire group. Too, he
recognized the power of the group, which alone could return him to
membership. Implicit in such a remark was that he would be bound by
their values, sensitive to their reproach. It was their good opinion that he
wanted to maintain, and neither personally nor socially could he bear the
ostracism implied in being rejected.

Another of the concerns of eighteenth-century educators that addresses
shame and honor is that of preserving reputation or being held in good re-
pute. Commencement addresses and various faculty lectures abound with
instructions about preserving reputation by preserving character. In addition to the obvious injunctions about avoiding vice, an important way to
preserve character was through the choice of friends and business acquain-
tances. Public opinion measured men as much by their company as by
their behavior, and one could fall from station should he associate with
those whose character did not warrant honor. As Samuel Davies advised
the graduates of Princeton in 1760, "I solemnly warn you against forming
pernicious Connections with bad company. This is the greatest Mischief
into which you can fall . . . "[48]

Davies was probably referring to business and political associations, as
did many who spoke of the importance of maintaining proper honor
through appropriate connections. Anthropologists note that in some cultures an important criterion of male honor is the virginity of their future
brides.[49] Because honor is transferable, the women's honor defines the
status of the males to whom she is related. Guarding a woman's virtue was
a family responsibility, since her dishonor affected its economic and social

profile. That we begin to see shame and honor associated with an acquired male quality forces us to inquire about the role played by the daughters of the same parents who sent their sons to college.

Recent studies hint that what we may have assumed was a dominant nineteenth-century phenomenon, the cult of true womanhood, probably had its origins in colonial culture, especially after the American Revolution, when personal asceticism became a political as well as a social imperative.[50] As early as the 1720s, etiquette books from England began instructing women how to turn charm and delicacy into socially marketable skills which could be used to supplement male achievement. As colleges began to facilitate entry into the occupational networks which did not require the vocational assistance of wives, the adornments of elegant conversation and music slowly became institutionalized for this class. Though the culture needed its women to have honor and virtue, few recognized an autonomous role for women as desirable or virtuous. And, among those who did, the argument was posed in terms of freeing them from the very adornments which fit them for little else than "the precarious chance of establishing themselves by marriage,"[51] as an essayist noted in the 1790s.

In supporting institutions which promoted the associations of their sons and helped them acquire honor, parents provided a network for association for their daughters as well. Though he was not explicit, Charles Nisbet may have been hinting at this when at the second commencement of Dickinson College he noted: "The ancients had a high sense of honor, and a great regard to character and reputation." He then cautioned them to "avoid the infectious Company of sinners."[52]

The infectious company of sinners is exactly what Samuel Barclay did not avoid. A graduate of Columbia College, Barclay applied for the Master of Arts degree in 1800. Within the prerogative of the institution, when an applicant's conduct was in doubt, a committee investigated him to decide whether he warranted receiving the additional degree. In Barclay's case the committee discovered that he had been "addicting himself to criminal intercourse with rude women" and contracted a "loathsome disease which he communicated to his said wife."[53] To have granted the degree to Barclay would have diminished the value of the Master of Arts for the others who held it. As Julian Pitt-Rivers observes, "social groups possess a collective honor in which their members participate; the dishonourable conduct of one reflects upon the honour of all."[54]

Attention to maintaining collective honor was a central concern for members of mutually supporting corporate bodies which sought to produce interdependence. Benjamin Franklin's Junto for Philadelphia is one example. Intended to promote mutual protection, on a list of twenty-four queries asked at the regular meetings was one question which asked, "Hath anybody attacked your reputation lately? And what can the Junto do towards securing it?"[55] Ready to act in a collective way to guard the reputation of a single member, the Junto characterizes an explicit awareness that corporate identity and personal honor are public matters of grave concern.

Honor and shame generally concern people who live in societies which rely on face-to-face, personal relations. In contrast to cultures which rely on anonymous, institutional relations, shame and honor are important "where the social personality of the actor is as significant as his office."[56] A similar emphasis on social personality characterized the eighteenth century debate over leadership in the ideal society, both before and after the American Revolution. After the Revolution, however, when the applicability of republicanism to the new nation was the topic of endless consideration, the characteristics of leadership were inseparable from that of social personality. Republics, noted social and political philosophers, were based on the virtue and character of their participants.[57] When discussing "virtue" a long list of attributes was unveiled, but it was easier to discuss what virtue was not than what it was. Vice, villany, selfishness, and baseness were not the characteristics of which virtue was made. Orderliness, selflessness, and a just performance of duty were among the attributes designated as virtuous. But many found it difficult to define, and even the prize-winning essay proposing a national system of education based on virtue found the author, Samuel Harrison Smith, wriggling: "the terms virtuous and wise do not seem susceptible of absolute definition."[58] Even without absolute definition, it was clear that virtue was synonymous with a fierce dedication to public good.

Smith's proposal, as others which argued for extending the network of educational institutions, addressed the ways in which education could train students to lead with republican virtue. This sprang from the popular idea that the stage of youth "affords a proper season for acquiring wisdom and virtue."[59] At that time in life educators could teach students to use their reason to govern their passions. The control of passions was a precursor to virtue, for it adumbrated a propensity to order and duty, without which republics could not survive. John Witherspoon clearly stated the cause and effect when he said, "Allied to the above virtue is the government of your passions . . . Everyone must be sensible how important it is, both for the success of your worldly callings, and your usefulness in public life, to have your passions in due subjection."[60] The task for students was to control their passions and transform virtue into action to promote public welfare. Students, therefore, were reminded to live "not for yourself but for the public," as Samuel Davies told the Princeton graduating class in 1760.[61] Davies was speaking to the social personality they would be expected to wear as well as to the ideal to which they should aspire. This ideal was just one step away from the ultimate expression of republican virtue. Benjamin Rush expressed it when he said, "Let our pupil be taught that he does not belong to himself, but that he is public property."[62]

A society's concept of honor, according to Julian Pitt-Rivers, "provides a nexus between the ideals of a society and their reproduction in the individual through his social aspirations to personify them . . . it implies not merely one habitual preference for a given mode of conduct, but the entitlement to certain treatment in return."[63] The treatment which graduates of eighteenth-century colleges could expect, as has been noted already, was leadership through public office. Even Ralph Izard, who was one of South Carolina's wealthiest and most powerful elites, noted the unconditional relationship between honor and success. In a letter to William Samuel Johnson, Columbia's new president, Izard announced that he was sending his sons there "so as to afford me the prospect of their being men of abilities, and honor, and of their being useful, valuable citizens of their country."[64] This remark illustrates that even the children of an Izard-Delancey union had to undergo the mechanisms of the rite of passage which would allow them to be endowed with honor. They had to learn a social personality which was useful to the culture, in an institution which was recognized as legitimate. Privilege alone would not suffice.

Because the social personality could not be considered apart from the office, public servants were under constant scrutiny. Behavior had to be a source for emulation and a lesson to those in the lower social orders. As a model for virtue the public leader also had the responsibility to maintain social cohesion through evoking shame in others. As Charles Nisbet noted, the individual would be required to "cover the vicious with deserved reproach and indignation."[65] In the organic society envisioned by social theorists, unharnessed individualism was anathema to the moral code which shame encompassed, and it was up to the leadership to teach subordinates to define their own good in terms of the larger group. This was one important lesson of a college education.

The last time students would be instructed as to how to behave was when they were incorporated into adult status—as a group of bachelors—through the annual rite of passage at commencement. Throughout the eighteenth century this ceremony became increasingly necessary, where earlier it had been more sporadic. It came to codify a set of values to which students should aspire and society should respect. Being graduated implied that the "commencer" was worthy of the college's honor and that his behavior had not brought shame upon the institution. The public ceremony permitted the community to bestow an honor upon the institution, and thus increased the validity of the degree. Similar to the collective activities Rhys Isaac describes for colonial Virginia, the college commencement also "played an important part in the formation and maintenance of personal relationships and assessments of 'worth' in the face-to-face communities . . . "[66] When it left the college halls, William Smith told the first graduating class at the College of Philadelphia, "You are now about to step into life."[67]

When these young men stepped into life they did so after a concerted effort had been made to socialize them to think as well as behave like republicans. The adolescent male was taught the need to know the "will of the people," at least within his immediate social vicinity. He was taught that honor was not heredijary, and given a mechanism for acquiring it. He was taught to disavow luxury and ostentation and made to feel scorn when he engaged in exhibitionist display. He was taught that his relationship to leadership was problematic and that it depended upon his peer's evaluation of him. He was taught to identify with the group.

The rules and regulations officials drafted no doubt anticipated challenges to the parameter of culture. Because these tests serve to integrate "deviants" into the culture, it is appropriate to examine college discipline to view the process through which they occurred. They constituted and symbolized a way of maintaining social cohesion and of transmitting society's definitions of "statuses, rights and obligations, both for the disputants themselves and for the other people."[68] They helped direct youth toward the ideals which constituted the prototypes of the day.

Eighteenth-century prototypes were predicated on being part of a corporate body through which one's social worth could be identified and guarded. The pattern of discipline and ritual in the college of the eighteenth century which gave meaning to republicanism, however, was becoming ill-fitted by the nineteenth century. Fagging, the student practice which allowed upper classmen to initiate the lower classmen into the collegiate culture of hierarchy and discipline, was becoming obsolete. Dartmouth modified fagging for freshmen in 1794, Harvard abolished it entirely in 1798, and so did Yale in 1804.[69] The isolated efforts to have students wear academic garb had been abandoned by various schools.

By the first few decades of the nineteenth century, many aspects of American higher education had changed. In addition to the new schools and increasing student enrollments, patterns of discipline had altered. "Reporting regularly to parents were reforms introduced as disciplinary procedures," notes David F. Allmendinger, Jr., in a study of ante-bellum student life.[70] Perhaps this was part of the general inability to control organized student rebellions which had replaced the individual cases of contumacy. The realtively pacific generation of students had turned into unruly mobs in some institutions. Later in the century secret fraternities would appear across the nation and overtly challenge administrators. The hierarchical differences which republicans had been taught to respect within a corporate context were becoming the basis for comparative factions. Educators could no longer use students as a sanctioning body because they no longer could control the parameters of adolescent culture. Instead they had to rely on individual students to acquire self-control. "The task of achieving a standard of performance each day would demand self-control, and would exact a routine of its own to replace the institutional procedures of the lost collegiate community," Allmendinger observes.[71]

Nineteenth-century changes in discipline removed the culprit from the public stage and corporate body, returning him to his family. Allowing the student to reform in private meant that the concepts of self could become private. Virtue became rooted in personal morality and individual accomplishment and a social personality was to be defined by the situation rather than the transcendent character of the actor. Egalitarian rhetoric, which embraced individuality as a means of measuring worth, dissolved the coalition of public and private morality and placed in its stead the pursuit of romantic self.

FOOTNOTES

This paper was presented at the Columbia University Seminar in Early American Culture, September, 1977. I would like to thank the members of the seminar, as well as friends and colleagues who provided support and criticism: Otis Cavrell, Barbara Finkelstein, Alice Kessler-Harris, Sherry Ortner, Joyce Reigelhaupt, Jinx Roosevelt, Bradd Shore, Amy Swerdlow and Marilyn Young.

1. Thomas Jefferson to George Ticknor, July 16, 1823, quoted in Steven J. Novak, *The Rights of Youth: American Colleges and Student Revolt, 1798-1815* (Cambridge, 1977), 164 and *passim*.

2. The idea that alternatives to the family, which was losing its ability to guarantee a place for its children, could be found in the college is explored in Phyllis Vine, "The Social Function of Eighteenth-Century Higher Education," *History of Education Quarterly*, 16 (Winter, 1976), 409-424. Peter Dobkin Hall explores a parallel theme in "Marital Selection and Business in Massachusetts Merchant Families, 1700-1900," in Rose L. Coser, ed., *The Family: Its Structure and Functions* (New York, 1974 ed.).

3. For a concept of sponsored mobility, consult Ralph Turner, "Modes of Social Ascent Through Education: Sponsored and Contest Mobility," in A.H. Halsey, J. Floud, C.A. Anderson, eds., *Education, Economy and Society* (London, 1967), 121-139.

4. Charles Nisbet, "Address to the Graduates, 1787," Dickinson College Library.

5. Discussions of rites of passage may be found in Meyer Fortes, "Ritual and Office," and Max Gluckman, "Les Rites de Passage," both in Gluckman, ed., *Essays on the Ritual of Social Relations* (Manchester, England, 1962); Arnold Van Gennep, *Rites of Passage* (Chicago, 1975); Bruno Bettelheim, *Symbolic Wounds* (New York, 1962).

6. From the journal of William Wheeler (Yale, 1785), discussed in Cornelia P. Lathrop, *Black Book, Seaport of Old Fairfield* (New Haven, 1930), quoted in Edmund S. Morgan, *The Gentle Puritan: A Life of Ezra Stiles 1727-1795* (New Haven, 1962), 368. This is also discussed in James Axtell, *The School Upon a Hill* (New Haven, 1974), Chapter 6. A more theoretical discussion may be found in an article by sociologist Erving Goffman, "Deference and Demeanor," *American Anthropologist*, 58 (June, 1956), 473-502.

7. Fortes, "Ritual and Office," 55, 87.

8. Walter J. Ong, S.J., "Latin Language Study as a Renaissance Puberty Rite," *Studies in Philology*, LVI (1959), 103-124.

9. This case of July 2, 1790, as well as others, may be found in Faculty Minutes of Princeton University, Princeton University Archives.

10. Edmund Morgan's biography of Stiles notes: "If a body did have to be expelled, he might be readmitted (like a member excommunicated from a church) after proper repentence." See *The Gentle Puritan*, 369. Also see Ann Dexter Gordon, "The College of Philadelphia, 1740-1779," unpublished Ph.D. Thesis, University of Wisconsin, 114, for an account of Robert Strettel Jones, who failed to receive a degree after refusing to apologize to Francis Alison. For a discussion of the four parts of a confession used at Yale, see Axtell, *The School Upon a Hill*, 226.

11. Two works which use the concept of shame culture are Ruth Benedict, *Chrysanthamum and the Sword* (New York, 1946) and E.R. Dodds, *The Greeks and the Irrational* (California, 1951). Recently anthropologists have been challenging the concept of shame and guilt cultures, which have been presented as a dichotomy between external and internal sanctions. The standard challenge is found in Gerhart Piers and Milton B. Singer, *Shame and Guilt: A Psychoanalytic and Cultural Study* (New York, 1971 ed.); Robert I. Levy builds on Piers and Singer in his article "Thati, Sin, and the Question of Integration Between Personality and Sociocultural Systems," in Robert A. LeVine, ed., *Culture and Personality* (Chicago, 1974), 287-306.

12. Three anthologies discuss mechanisms for social conformity and ritual. In Marc J. Swartz, Victor W. Turner and Arthur Tuden, eds., *Political Anthropology* (Chicago, 1966), see: Marc J. Swartz, "Bases for Political Compliance in Bena Villages," 89-109; Paul Friedrich, "Revolutionary Politics and Communal Rituals," 191-220; and Victor W. Turner, "Ritual Aspects of Conflict Control in African Micropolitics," 239-247. For Laura Nader, ed., *Law in Culture and Society* (Chicago, 1972 ed.) consult: P.H. Gulliver, "Case Studies of Law in Non-Western Societies," 11-23; and E. Adamson Hoebel, "Kersan Pueblo Law," 92-116. Perhaps the most useful work on this is J.G. Peristiany, ed., *Honor and Shame: The Values of the Mediterranean* (Chicago, 1966), particularly the Introduction, written by Peristiany; and, Julian Pitt-Rivers, "Honor and Social Status," 19-79.

13. The example of rural Spain comes from Julian Pitt-Rivers, *People of the Sierra* (New York, 1954), chapter 9. A discussion of the St. Lawrence Island Eskimos may be found in Charles Campbell Hughes, "From Contest to Council: Social Control Among the St. Lawrence Island Eskimos," in Swartz, *et al.*, eds., *Political Anthropology*, 55.

14. Helen Block Lewis, *Shame and Guilt in Neurosis* (New York, 1971), 42. Also see Helen Merrell Lynd, *Shame and the Search for Identity* (New York, 1958).

15. Anna Freud, *The Ego and the Mechanisms of Defense* (New York, 1970 ed.), 162.

16. Erik Erikson, *Identity, Youth and Crisis* (New York, 1968), 128-129, 130. Also see Erikson's own chapter in his edited volume, *The Challenge of Youth* (Garden City, 1965 ed.), 1-29. A provocative statement about adolescents becoming alienated due to socio-historical cynicism may be found in Kenneth Keniston, "Alienation and the Decline of Utopia," *The American Scholar*, 29 (1960), 161-200.

17. Piers and Singer, *Guilt and Shame*, 27.

18. John Witherspoon, *Lectures on Moral Philosophy* (Philadelphia, 1822), 25-26.

19. Charles Nisbet, "To the Graduates of the 2nd Commencement, May 7, 1788," Dickinson College Library.

20. Kathryn McDaniel Moore, "The Dilemma of Corporal Punishment at Harvard College," *History of Education Quarterly*, XIV (1974), 335-346; Phillipe Aries, *Centuries of Childhood*, trans. Robert Baldick (New York, 1962), 241-268. A new work on Princeton discusses the Scottish common sense philosophy's science of discipline. See Howard Miller, *The Revolutionary College: American Presbyterian Higher Education, 1707-1837* (New York, 1976), 174-179, 260-268.

21. Benjamin Rush, "Amusements and Punishments Which Are Proper for Schools (1790)," in Dagobert Runes, ed., *The Selected Writing of Benjamin Rush* (New York, 1947), 111-112. Also see William Smith, "An Account of the College, Academy and

Charitable School . . . " in *Discourses on Public Occasions* (London, 1762), 124-125, where he alludes to an age-graded difference in discipline. Smith says some "of the youth are too big for corporal punishment" at the weekly meeting where they assemble so the faculty could "examine the weekly roll, and call delinquents to account."

22. Richard Peters, *A Sermon on Education* . . . (Philadelphia, 1751), 27.
23. Smith, *"An Account,"* 124.
24. Benjamin Rush, "Plans for Dickinson College," Dickinson College Library.
25. Charles Nisbet, "Address to the Graduates, 1787," Dickinson College Library.
26. Miller, *The Revolutionary College*, 180.
27. John Blair Smith, "Inaugural Address, 1796," Union College Library.
28. Peters, *A Sermon*, 26.
29. John Henry Hobart to John How, Feb. 9, 1794, Hobart Letterbook, Princeton University Library.
30. For a discussion of the nineteenth-century debate over emulation as a pedagogical technique, see Michael B. Katz, *The Irony of Early School Reform* (Boston, 1968), part II.
31. Axtell, *The School Upon a Hill*, 219; Myles Cooper, "Book of Misdemeanours in King's College, Alias Black Book, 1771-1775," annotated by Milton Halsey Thomas and reprinted in *Columbia University Quarterly*, XXIII (1931), 3.
32. A discussion of degradation may be found in Harold Garfinkel, "Successful Degradation Ceremonies," *American Journal of Sociology*, LXI (Jan., 1956), 420-424.
33. Cooper, "Black Book," 3-4.
34. Michael Zuckerman, *Peaceable Kingdoms* (New York, 1970), 62.
35. Rosabeth Moss Kanter, *Commitment and Community, Communes and Utopias in Sociological Perspective* (Mass., 1972), 107.
36. Cooper, "Black Book," 14-15.
37. Lynd, *On Shame*, 27.
38. Erikson, *Identity*, 10.
39. George Harpur to the Governors of King's College, July 21, 1774, College Papers, Columbia University Library.
40. George Rapalje to the Governors of King's College, July 21, 1774, *ibid.*
41. Pitt-Rivers, "Honor and Social Status," 26.
42. Harpur to the Governors, July 21, 1774.
43. Rapalje to the Governors, July 21, 1774.
44. Pitt-Rivers, "Honor and Social Status," 42.
45. Benjamin Franklin, "Proposals for the Education of Youth, 1749," in L. Jesse Lemisch, ed., *The Autobiography and Other Writings* (New York, 1961), 172.
46. Witherspoon, *Lectures*, 25.
47. Pitt-Rivers, "Honor and Social Status," 27.
48. Samuel Davies, *Religion and Public Spirit: A Valedictory Address* (New York, 1761), 18.
49. Jane Schneider, "Of Vigilance of Virgins: Honor, Shame and Access to Resources in Mediterranean Societies," *Ethnology*, 10 (1971) 1-24; Pitt-Rivers, *The People of the Sierra*, chapter 7. A discussion of changing patterns of premarital pregnancy may be found in Daniel Scott Smith and Michael S. Hindus, "Premarital Pregnancy in America, 1640-1970: An Overview and Interpretation," *Journal of Interdisciplinary History*, V (1975), 537-570.
50. Carol Berkin, *Within the Conjurer's Circle: Women in Colonial America* (Morristown, New Jersey, 1974); Nancy Cott, "Divorce and the Changing Status of Women in 18th Century Mass.," *William and Mary Quarterly*, 3rd Series, 33 (1976), 586-614; Catherine Scholten, "On the Importance of the Obstetrick Art," *ibid.*, 34 (1977), 426-445. Regina Morantz, "Making Women Modern: Middle Class Women and Health Reform in 19th Century America," *Journal of Social History*, 10 (1977), 490-508.

51. Quoted in Linda K. Kerber, "Daughters of Columbia: Educating Women for the Republic, 1787-1805," in *The Hofstadter Aegis: A Memorial*, eds., Stanley Elkins and Eric McKitrick (New York, 1974), 39.

52. Nisbet, "Address, May 7, 1788," Dickinson College Library.

53. Committee Report, August 5, 1800, College Papers, Columbia University Library.

54. Pitt-Rivers, "Honor and Social Status," 35. Also see Smith, "An Account," 123, where he says that even an honorary degree must receive the mandate of two-thirds of the trustees as "a means of preventing a prostitution of those degrees and honours to the illiterate and the undeserving, which should be the reward of real learning and worth."

55. Franklin, "Standing Queries for the Junto," in Lemisch, ed., *The Autobiography*, 198.

56. Peristiany, *Honor and Shame*, 11.

57. A review of the recent work on republicanism may be found in Robert E. Shalhope, "Toward a Republican Synthesis: The Emergence of an Understanding of Republicanism in American Historiography," *William and Mary Quarterly*, 3rd Series, 29 (1972), 49-80.

58. Samuel Harrison Smith, "Remarks on Education: Illustrating the Close Connection Between Virtue and Wisdom . . . 1797," in Frederick Rudolph, ed., *Essays on Education in the Early Republic* (Mass., 1965), 170.

59. Nisbet, "Address after Vacation, 1787," Dickinson College Library.

60. John Witherspoon, "Address to the Senior Class Preceding Commencement, September 23, 1775," in *Lectures on Moral Philosophy*, 192. In that same volume of interest also is Lecture VI and Lecture X, and "Address to the Inhabitants of Jamaica."

61. Davies, *Religion and Public Spirit*, 6.

62. Benjamin Rush, "Thoughts upon the mode of Education Proper in a Republic," in Rudolph, ed., *Essays*, 14.

63. Pitt-Rivers, in Peristiany, ed., *Honor and Shame*, 22.

64. Ralph Izard to William Samuel Johnson, December 20, 1787, in Herbert and Carol Schneider, eds., *Samuel Johnson, President of King's College: His Career and Writings* (New York, 1929), Vol. III: 196.

65. Nisbet, "Address at the 2nd Commencement."

66. Rhys Isaac, "Preachers and Patriots: Popular Culture and the Revolution in Virginia," in Alfred F. Young, ed., *The American Revolution* (Illinois, 1976), 137. I have explored the significance of commencement in "The Social Function."

67. Smith, "To the Graduates," in *Discourses*, 130-131.

68. P.H. Gulliver, "Case Studies of Law in Non-Western Societies," in Nader, ed., *Law in Culture and Society*, 16; Kai T. Erikson, *The Wayward Puritans: A Study in the Sociology of Deviance* (New York, 1966), especially chapter 1.

69. Novak, *The Rights of Youth*, 12.

70. David F. Allmendinger, Jr., "The Dangers of Ante-Bellum Student Life," *Journal of Social History*, 7 (1973), 82.

71. *Ibid.*

IV

The Perpetual Messiah: Romanticism, Childhood, and the Paradoxes of Human Development

— JUDITH PLOTZ

Infancy is the perpetual Messiah which comes into the arms
of fallen men and pleads with them to return to paradise.
Emerson, "Nature" (1836)

The Romantic movement has a strong claim on the attention of all students of the modern mind. During the Romantic period, those years from
the French Revolution to the Revolutions of 1848, writers, artists, and
philosophers created a body of work that so persuasively re-imagined the
nature of the individual and of society that we latter-day 20th-century
Romantics have not yet exhausted the possibilities of these vivid 19th-
century images. This transformation of many modes of thought—the political, the social, the psychological, the imaginative—is the living legacy of
Romanticism. In fact, transformation itself, conceived in terms of ideal
growth or the utopian fulfillment of potentialities, may be said to be *the*
central Romantic theme. Not since ancient Greece has there been a literature so single-mindedly devoted to what Werner Jaeger called *paideia*, the
fullest possible development of the individual in accordance with his
potentialities.[1]

Major Romantic works, from Schiller's *On the Aesthetic Education of
Man* (1795) through Goethe's *Faust* (1831) to Wordsworth's *Prelude*
(1850), take human growth and development as their central theme.[2]
Shelley calls poets "the unacknowledged legislators of the world" for their

subtle power of making possible "a great and free development of the national will": poetry for Shelley, as for Blake, is the agency of the perfecting of both individual and world.[3]The theme of coming to full consciousness so pervades the work of Keats—presented mythologically in *Endymion* and the two Hyperion fragments, presented with psychological realism in the great odes of 1819—that his educational concerns are manifest even in a casual epistolary comment on the inadequacy of Christianity. Rather than regard this world as a vale of tears, we should regard it as an educational enterprise, as "a vale of soul-making":

> This is to be effected by three grand materials acting the one upon the other for a series of years. These three Materials are the *Intelligence—the human heart* (as distinguished from intelligence or Mind) and the *World* or *Elemental space* suited for the proper action of *Mind and Heart* on each other for the purpose of forming the *Soul* or *Intelligence destined to possess the sense of Identity*. I can scarcely express what I but dimly perceive—and yet I think I perceive it—that you may judge the more clearly I will put it in the most homely form possible—I will call the *world* a School instituted for the purpose of teaching little children to read—I will call the *human heart* the *horn Book* used in that School—and I will call the *Child able to read the Soul* made from that school of its *hornbook*.[4]

Such educational and developmental metaphors are a crucial part of the Romantic idiom, since humanity had come to be defined as a capacity for intellectual, moral, and imaginative growth. "Providence, which distinguished man from the lower orders of Being by the progressiveness of his nature," Coleridge writes, "forbids him to be contented."[5] To conceive man primarily as "progressive" means to see him not within particular achieved social roles but as moving through a continuing process of greater and greater enlightenment.

To embody this emerging Romantic ideal of ever-developing consciousness, an ideal of perpetual growth and improvement, new heroes were needed. The Renaissance man of action, the Restoration wit, the Augustan rational aristocrat were fixed types of excellence, admirable in themselves but set into one particular pattern of achievement. What the new age sought was a hero who could go beyond pattern into limitless potentiality. "I must create a system," cried William Blake's Los, the symbolic embodiment of the human imagination, "or be enslaved in another man's." In their search for normative figures who could elude fixity in the interests of totalization of potentiality, the Romantics frequently turned to two sorts of beings: to artists and to children.

The primacy of these two figures in Romantic literature, particularly the poetry, is striking. Poets, Shelley's "unacknowledged legislators of the world," receive in Romantic poetry full acknowledgment. Wordsworth's greatest poem, *The Prelude*, bears the explicit subtitle: "the growth of a poet's mind"; while most of his other poems more or less explicitly also deal with the poetic process. Blake's *persona*, the poet-prophet Los, plays the role of redeemer of fallen man in Blake's great mythic cycle: "A Poet a painter a Musician an Architect: the Man or Woman who is not one of these is not a Christian."[6] Keats both in mythological and personal poetry makes all his heroes of evolving consciousness poets or dreamers (figures analogous to poets). Coleridge and Shelley take as their habitual theme the imaginative transformation of experience by the divinizing poetic mind. All this is familiar to the most superficial student of Romanticism and also congruent with the traditional veneration for the wisdom of the poetic seer. Less familiar and much more novel in literary tradition, however, is the simultaneous Romantic adulation of the child as central symbol. Nothing in the history of literature compares to the sudden outpouring in the late 18th and early 19th centuries of major imaginative literature and philosophical speculation about children. As Peter Coveney has observed:

> With Blake's *The Chimney Sweeper* and Wordsworth's *Ode on Intimations of Immortality from Recollections of Early Childhood*, we are confronted with something essentially new, the phenomenon of major poets expressing something they considered of great significance through the image of the child . . . [W]ithin the course of a few decades the child emerges from comparative unimportance to become the focus of an increasingly significant proportion of our literature.[7]

Before this time children entered literature only fleetingly—perhaps to exact pathos by their early deaths as in the plays of Shakespeare and many Renaissance elegies, or to be lectured into rapid maturity, as in the popular didactic poetry of Watts. But from the time of publication of Rousseau's *Emile* in 1762 until Dickens' and Twain's great novels of childhood approximately one hundred years later, there is an outpouring of major and serious literature on the theme of childhood. Wordsworth's *The Prelude*, Blake's *Songs of Innocence and Experience*, Coleridge's scattered but brilliant writings on education, DeQuincey's autobiographical explorations of the formative effect of early grief, represent an unparalleled store of richly intelligent and intuitive meditations on childhood.

No language is too lofty for Romantic writers to use in their description of childhood. Far from deserving a benevolent whimsy or indulgent "little language," childhood calls forth the deepest expressions of reverence. Thus Wordsworth:

> Oh! mystery of man, from what a depth

> Proceed thy honours. I am lost, but see
> In simple childhood something of the base
> On which thy greatness stands . . . . [8]

In the great essay *On Naive and Sentimental Poetry* (1795), a psychological explanation of the development of poetry, Schiller begins by examining the human soul in its ideal form:

> The child is . . . a lively representation to us of the ideal, not indeed as it is fulfilled, but as it is enjoined; hence we are in no sense moved by the notion of its poverty and limitation, but rather by the opposite: the notion of its pure and free strength, its integrity, its eternality. To a moral and sensitive person a child will be a *sacred* object on this account . . . . [9]

This earnest exaltation of tone is characteristic of most Romantic writing on childhood. To speak of childhood for the Romantic is to speak of the most profound region of our being, the sole field in which a sublimely human self can grow up. Romantic speculation on childhood is not the quaint extension of literary primitivism with which it has so frequently been linked. Rather such writing is central to the whole philosophic mission of Romanticism—the development of the perfected, totalized individual.

Like the artist, the child represents the high excellence of human nature. For Schiller the excellence of children lies in their "tacitly creative life, the serene spontaneity of their activity, existence in accordance with their own laws, the inner necessity, the eternal unity with themselves."[10] Such a vision of the child's unconscious psychic harmony—a harmony disrupted with the onset of adulthood and regained, if at all, only by a strenuously willed exercise in imaginative self-knowledge—stands behind the elaborate psychological pilgrimage charted by Blake from childhood Innocence through Experience to the higher "Organized Innocence" of fully integrated humanity. Such a vision also animates Wordsworth's elegiac address in his "Immortality Ode" to the visionary six-year-old:

> Thou, whose exterior semblance doth belie
>   Thy Soul's immensity;
> Thou best Philosopher, who yet dost keep
> Thy heritage, thou Eye among the blind,
> That, deaf and silent, read'st the eternal deep,
> Haunted forever by the eternal mind,—
>   Mighty Prophet!Seer blest!
>   On whom these truths do rest,
> Which we are toiling all our lives to find,

In darkness lost, the darkness of the grave . . . .

This adulation of the child as embodying wholeness and self-completion is
an ironic reversal of the prevailing wisdom of the preceding centuries
which had regarded childhood—or, revealingly, "non-age"—as an essentially privative state necessitating an education of imitation and cram. At
their most extravagant, Romantic writers identify the inner harmony
perceived in young children—"the seeming Identity of Body and Mind in
Infants," Coleridge calls it—with the self-creating harmony of Deity.[11]
Bronson Alcott, for example, Transcendentalist poet and educator, baldly
identifies the Divine Image of God with "the form of the child. Herein
have we a Type of the Divinity. Herein is our Nature yet despoiled of none
of its glory." Furthermore, Alcott argues that when all men truly "apprehend the significance of the Divine Type," when "childhood . . . a problem that we have scarce studied, is rightly understood," then the human
race will become "regenerate" in the total "renovation of Nature."[12]
Children in some unspecified fashion are not only godlike, but are our
redeemers. Emerson too endorses this evangel of infancy:

> A man is a god in ruins. When men are innocent, life shall be longer,
> and shall pass into the immortal, as gently as we awake from dreams.
> Now, the world would be insane and rabid if these disorganizations
> should last for hundreds of years. It is kept in check by death and in-
> fancy. Infancy is the perpetual Messiah which comes into the arms of
> fallen men, and pleads with them to return to paradise.[13]

For DeQuincey, too, the adult, if not precisely "a god in ruins," is all too
often a delapidated child despoiled of his heritage. Children, in fact,
possess more amply and richly than adults the attributes of humanity:

> "*The child*," says Wordsworth, "*is father to the man*"; thus calling
> into conscious notice the fact, also faintly or not all perceived, that
> whatsoever is seen in the maturest adult, blossoming and bearing
> fruit, must have pre-existed by way of germ in the infant. Yes; all
> that is now broadly emblazoned in the man, once was latent—seen or
> not seen—as a vernal bud in the child. But not, therefore, is it true
> inversely—that all which pre-exists in the child finds its development
> in the man. Rudiments and tendencies which *might* have found
> sometimes by accident, *do* not find, sometimes under the killing frost
> of counter forces *cannot* find, their natural evolution. Infancy,
> therefore, is to be viewed, not only as part of a larger world that
> waits for its final complement in old age, but also as a separate world
> itself; part of a continent, but also a distinct peninsula. Most of what
> he has the grown-up man inherits from his infant self; but it does not

follow that he always enters upon the whole of his natural inheritance.[14]

These passages present a curious paradox endemic in Romantic thought:
a belief in the absolutism, the perfect completion of the child, is united to a
belief in the desirability of development into a more spacious and fulfilled
adulthood. If the child is regarded with Emerson as "the perpetual
Messiah," with Wordsworth as "father to the Man," how can the process
of growing up be anything other than a descent into a lesser form of being?
To the venerator of childhood sanctity, the educational process must seem
ironic, a forced exchange of a lower for a higher form of wisdom. For all
the concern with growth, maturation, development, cultivated self-
consciousness, there is in Romantic thought a profoundly anti-educational
strain. Wordsworth's six-year-old "Mighty Prophet" of the "Immortality
Ode" delights in his expanding knowledge and mastery of the world, a
knowledge which the poet frankly laments:

> Thou little Child, yet glorious in the might
> Of heaven-born freedom on thy being's height,
> Why with such earnest pains dost thou provoke
> The years to bring the inevitable yoke,
> Thus blindly with thy blessedness at strife.

Yet one can argue that it is precisely the anti-educational strain, coexist-
ing, as it does, with a ceaseless concern with development, that guarantees
both the sincerity and value of Romantic educational thinking. It evinces a
tender respect for the child as the source of every subsequent human excellence; it demands the maximum preservation rather than the maximum
obliteration of childhood experience. The Romantics hold human perfection to abide in that adult who remains most in touch with his childhood
self, who enters, in DeQuincey's fine phrase, "upon the whole of his
natural inheritance." Such continuity of consciousness and capacity is
crucial to adult fullness of being. To be able to grow up without destroying
or maiming the child in oneself is to become the best sort of adult.

Though such a goal is an appropriate end for every human being, since
it is potentially within the grasp of all of us who have ever been children,
the achievement of the goal has been pathetically rare in human history.
The achievement of the goal makes one, in fact, an extraordinary kind of
person: it makes one a creative soul, an artist. What is commonplace in
children is rare in adults; to retain the capacities of childhood into adulthood is, in fact, to be an artist. If only we could hang on to the power that
is ours in childhood we could all be creators of extraordinary vitality, and
the world would be transformed. Consistently in Romantic thought the artist is regarded as the appropriately achieved form of the child: "To carry

on the feelings of childhood into the powers of manhood . . . this is the character and privilege of genius."[15] The person able to retain his childhood powers of perception while acquiring the adult's intellect and moral awareness is the artist—and the best kind of mature adult.

It is this symbiosis between the qualities deemed native to the child and the artist that makes both figures normative for the Romantics. They both possess qualities deemed most humanly valuable—the artist in consciously controlled and developed form, the child potentially and spontaneously.

Both the child and the artist are indigenous to the new Romantic universe. For "nature" as understood by the early nineteenth century was animated by a new set of principles. Romanticism involves a new vision of the nature of the universe. As Wellek, Peckham, and other scholars have pointed out, the philosophy underlying Romanticism is organic and developmental.[16] The universe is no perfected machine set in order once and for all by a clock-maker God. Rather it is a dynamic organism whose leading principles are growth, variation, and energy:

'Nature in late centuries . . . was universally supposed to be dead; an old eight-day clock made many thousand years ago, and still ticking, but dead as brass—which the Maker, at most, sat looking at, in a distant, singular, and indeed incredible manner; but now I am happy to observe, she is everywhere asserting herself to be not dead and brass at all, but alive and miraculous, celestial-infernal, and with an emphasis that will again penetrate the thickest head of this Planet by and by!'[17]

Nature itself is conceived as process, "natura naturans" (in the formulation habitual with Coleridge) or "that which is active through form and figures and discourses to us by symbols."[18] Again and again Romantic writers emphasize the progressive, unfinished, evolutionary, searching, infinite quality of art and of the universe itself, for both use symbolic means of expression: "the Universe is but one vast symbol of God; nay, if thou wilt have it, what is man himself but a Symbol of God . . . ."[19] Carlyle's great *Sartor Resartus* (1833-34) stresses that this universe of change is ever evolving and producing new forms of truth; thus the artist, similarly a producer of new symbolic expressions of truth, is the midwife of universal meaning. Goethe's Earth-Spirit, representing Nature, sings to Faust a terrible song of relentless, endless, active process, a song proleptically representing Faust's own life of perpetual striving:

> In the floods of life and creative storm
> To and fro I wave.
> Weave eternally,
> And birth and grave,

An eternal sea,
A changeful strife,
A glowing life;
At the roaring loom of the ages I plod
And fashion the life-giving garment of God.[20]

To this universe of process and change only the child and the artist are native—the artist by his chosen task of embodying meaning in symbols, the child by his inborn necessity for growth. What better emblem of forward-looking growth than children who are crucial, Coleridge observes, "to keeping up the stock of *Hope* in the human Species/they seem as immediately the secreting-organ of hope in the great organized Body of the whole Human Race, in all men considered as the component Atoms of MAN, as young Leaves are the organs of supplying vital air to the atmosphere."[22] A universe of growth and development is best represented by those human beings in whom growth and development are most manifest. Thus the child stands with the artist as the natural symbol of humanity.

The child and the artist resemble each other too in their mental processes. Both child and artist possess the power of affective thinking, of seeing feelingly with what Coleridge calls "Secondary Imagination" and Blake's "3-fold vision." Wordsworth's is the clearest exposition of this power, first manifested in infancy. The baby growing up in an atmosphere of mother love learns to see the world as "beautified" by that love, suffused with that love:

Blest the Babe,
Nursed in his Mother's arms, who sinks to sleep,
Rocked on his Mother's breast; who with his soul
Drinks in the feelings of his Mother's eye!
For him, in one dear Presence, there exists
A virtue which irradiates and exalts
Objects through widest intercourse of sense.
No outcast he, bewildered and depressed:
Along his infant veins are interfused
The gravitation and the filial bond
Of nature that connect him with the world.
Is there a flower, to which he points with hand
Too weak to gather it, already love
Drawn from love's purest earthly fount for him
Hath beautified that flower (*The Prelude*, II, 11. 233-248).

In a favorite Wordsworthian formulation, "feeling has to him imparted power," so that the "power," the intellectual faculty of perception, is intimately bound up with the feeling of love. In fact, it is the feeling which releases and fuels the power. The child's mind is not a passive register of facts, but an active instrument of creative perception. The use of feelings as the underpinning of intellectual activity is the very thing that constitutes creative power, and is the source of the link between child and artist:

> For feeling has to him imparted power
> That through the growing faculties of sense
> Doth like the agent of the one great Mind
> Create, creator and receiver both,
> Working but in alliance with the works
> Which it beholds. — Such, verily, is the first
> Poetic spirit of our human life,
> By uniform control of after years,
> In most abated or suppressed; in some,
> Through every change or growth and of decay
> Pre-eminent till death (*The Prelude*, II, 11. (255-565).

In like spirit Coleridge observed how much feeling was infused by his young son into everything he learned:

> Having learnt everything almost from the mouths of People,
> Whom he loves, he has connected with his Words and notions a
> Passion & a feeling which would appear strange to those who have
> seen no Children but such as had been taught almost every thing
> in Books.[23]

Such power of infusing objects and facts with a dominant feeling is for Coleridge the very thing in which creative imagination consists.

Further, children are, in Blake's phrase, "on the side of Imagination or Spiritual Sensation" because "in the child's mind there is nothing fragmentary." Children perceive holistically, learning analysis only as they mature. "I saw in early youth," Coleridge writes, "as in a dream, the birth of the planets, and my eyes beheld as *one* what the understanding afterwards divided into [many]."[24]

The "gusto" and "intensity" which Hazlitt and Keats in particular attribute to the artist is the exuberant delight which also enables the child to find a blessing in the world. Coleridge perceives this quality in his three-year-old son:

> I look at my doted-on Hartley—he moves, he lives, he finds impulses
> from within & from without—he is the darling of the Sun and of the
> breeze! Nature seems to bless him as a thing of her own! He looks at
> the clouds, at the mountains, the living Beings of the Earth, and

vaults & jubilates.[25]

The capacious and all-welcoming responsiveness, this non-judgmental joy, is deemed the property of child and artist alike. Oscar Wilde, indeed, depicts a fully redeemed human nature as both aesthetic and childlike:

> It will be a marvellous thing—the true personality of man—when we see it. It will grow naturally and simply, flowerlike, or as a tree grows. It will not be at discord. It will never argue or dispute, it will not prove things, it will know everything. And yet it will not busy itself about knowledge. It will have wisdom . . . . It will not be always meddling with others, or asking them to be like itself. It will love them because they will be different. And yet while it will not meddle with others, it will help all, as a beautiful thing helps us, by being what it is. The personality of man will be very wonderful. It will be as wonderful as the personality of a child.[26]

Allied to the welcoming responsiveness, the susceptibility, of both artists and children is their supra-social independence, their freedom from any fixed social role. Writers who delight in a vision of an actively emergent universe assume the necessity of a similarly changeful human being to inhabit it worthily. "Wie ich beharre, bin ich Knecht" ("As I grow stagnant, I shall be a slave"), Faust boasted. Romantic irony, that characteristically Byronic device of taking antithetical attitudes towards the same experience, treating young love one moment with tenderness, the next with derision, has been traditionally regarded as a way of extending the possibilities of the self. Certainly Friedrich Schlegel holds it to be a way of accommodating an otherwise limited ego to the infinitely varied universe: "Irony is a clear consciousness of an eternal agility, of the infinitely abundant chaos."[27] Romantic irony resembles nothing so closely as child's play —the role-playing at once fully serious and energetically committed, but entirely free and reversible. Further, Schiller's defining of beauty as the work of the Play-urge (*Spieltrieb*) that marries necessity with freedom demonstrates the importance assigned to flexibility and spontaneity in "the aesthetic education of man."[28] Schiller, in fact, considers the road to political liberation to lie through the Play-urge, with its power to liberate men from the fixity of their conditions. Such playfulness, such rapid shifting of roles, is the natural condition of childhood and the acquired genius of mature artistry. Freedom from a fixed social role—Blake calls it the "spectre," Jung the "persona," Wordsworth simply the "earthly freight" of custom—enables the child to try out imaginatively many other possible selves without irrevocably fixing himself into one single identity. Delighting in this capacity of "little children from 3 to 6 years old" to play a multitude of roles, Coleridge notes:

The first lesson, that innocent Childhood affords me, is—that it is an instinct of my Nature to pass out of myself, and to exist in the form of others. The second is—not to suffer any one form to pass into *me* and to become a usurping *Self* in the disguise of what the German Pathologists call a *fixed idea* . . . the representative of our Self.[29]

The child, in other words, can play at many roles—doctor, lawyer, cook, hunter—without ever allowing one of these "representative Selves" to usurp the true, playful, various self. Children, like artists, are playful, able to take on the parts of others without mistaking those parts for their entire selves, without being locked irrevocably into a permanent "representative" self. Thus, in Blake's touching poem "The Chimney Sweeper," the innocent speaker tells of comforting another sweep:

> There's little Tom Dacre who cried when his head,
> That curl'd like a lamb's back, was shav'd; so I said
> 'Hush, Tom! never mind it, for when your head's bare
> You know that the soot cannot spoil your white hair.'

For these exploited little chimney sweepers some freedom still exists. Tom does and does not have blond curls; he both *is* a chimney sweeper and, simultaneously, *is not*, for he is also the cherished lamb of God. The delusion of the child is not at issue here; what is important is to recognize the child's capacity to be simultaneously in and out of his determined, conditioned role. For the child of innocence, the non-existent curls are every bit as real as his blackened shaved head. The innocent is not mentally bounded, as is the spectrous adult, by his condition. In the child whose imagination has not been crushed, possibility is as vast as conception:

> From my early reading of Faery Tales & Genii &c &c—my mind had been habituated *to the Vast*—& I never regarded *my senses* in any way as the criteria of my belief. I regulated all my creeds by my conceptions and not by my *sight* . . . . [30]

This Blakean example suggests the reason for so much Romantic concentration on the *innocence* of childhood, an innocence, curiously, that leagues the child with the imaginative artist. The word *innocent* has multiple meanings, but it never refers simply to a privative state of ignorance and inexperience. Childhood innocence almost always involves—for Lamb, for DeQuincey, for Schiller, and for Coleridge, among others—a refusal to admit the force of circumstances. Whatever the moral will determines to do, must be done. This is what Schiller means by contrasting adult *determination (Bestimmung*, i.e., the actualizing of potentialities) to "the unlimited *determinacy*" (*Bestimmbarkeit*, i.e., possible potentialities) of the innocent child. Childhood innocence, the "naive of temperament," ignores all practical constraints on good action:

> If a father tells his child that some man or other is expiring from poverty, and the child goes and gives the poor man his father's purse, such an action is naive; for healthy nature is acting through the child, and in a world in which healthy nature were predominant he would be entirely right to act so. He sees only the distress and the means nearest at hand to alleviate it; such a development of property rights as permits a portion of humanity to perish has no basis in simple nature. The child's act, therefore, puts the world to shame, and this our hearts also confess by the satisfaction they derive from such an act.[31]

It is not so much that childlike innocence implies natural goodness (though that usually is included in the term), as that it implies an utter translucency of behavior—a totally *lived* application of all concepts that are mastered. Looking back with embarrassment at this superior childhood self, Lamb feels his present decline:

> I know how it shrank from any the least colour of
> falsehood—God help thee, Elia, how art thou changed!
> Thou art sophisticated.—I know how honest, how
> courageous (for a weakling) it was—how religious , how
> imaginative, how hopeful! From what have I not fallen, if
> the child I remember was indeed myself . . . . [32]

Most often admirers of childhood innocence impute to it, as does Hartley Coleridge, a moral excellence: "All possess/Once in their life fair Eden's sinlessness."[33] But Blake and, intermittently, Wordsworth associate innocence with a pre-moral freedom and spontaneity in which the psyche is fully at one with itself. Precisely because infancy is pre-moral, Blake argues, it has the wisdom which is shut out by mature moralizing and repression (Satan, for Blake, is a figure not of sinfulness but of righteousness and the accusation of sin):

> Infancy, fearless, lustful, happy, nestling for delight
> In laps of pleasures: Innocence! honest, open, seeking
> The vigorous joys of morning light.[34]

For Blake, uninhibited, unselfconscious power of act, i.e., infantile innocence, is a source of exemplary joy. The child who is happy, innocent of the knowledge of good and evil, is for Blake the symbolic forerunner of the adult who must imaginatively transcend his impulses towards self-mutilation and tyranny. Innocence is thus a wide and complex idea suggesting both unconditioned goodness of a very traditional kind and and also transcendence of good and evil. Childhood is frequently associated with both kinds of innocence and is therefore regarded as symbolic of human excellence.

Romanticism thus finds childhood obsessively fascinating for its inner harmony, for its powers of affective and unitary thought, for its congruence with an emergent organic universe, for its freedom from social conditioning, for its innocent rejection of adult limitation—or, in a word, for its manifestation of the qualities appropriate to the highest type of adult, the creative artist. It is hardly surprising, therefore, to find the figure of the child as a leading symbol in Romantic poetry.

Recognizing the symbolic function of the child in Romanticism, M.H. Abrams, among others, has identified the Romantic treatment with the traditional Biblical emphasis on the particularly *chosen* role of children:

> Modern preoccupation with the experiences of childhood has usually and with some justification been traced to Rousseau . . . . Reference to the child as norm, however, reminds us, it was not a Romantic primitivist, but Christ who posited the return to the state of a child as the condition for entering the apocalyptic kingdom: "Except ye be converted, and become as children, ye shall not enter the kingdom of heaven." [35]

Yet one must be skeptical of any insistence on the traditional nature of the child symbol in Romanticism. Children have become centrally important in a new way. It is not only the tremendous and sudden amount of major work on childhood that is new, but—more important—the point of view towards childhood. The children depicted in Romantic literature are not simply allegorical representations of the human spirit, but are very real, empathically realized boys and girls.

The Romantic attitude towards childhood manifests itself in a newly empathic language of stunning immediacy. Most accounts of children prior to that time, in English and American literature at any rate, treat children as projections of adult sins and desires, or as symbolic emblems of moral frailty, or else as incomplete and volatile beings in need of correction. The child is most frequently seen as a *temporary* being—temporary either in his probably brief life, or in his ultimate transition to the real life that is adulthood—whose childishness is best put aside as soon as possible. Against this tradition there emerges in the late eighteenth century a new point of view that cherishes children not for what they may become, but for the reality of what they are. Rousseau in *Emile* best enunciates this new philosophy respecting the special childishness of children. Speaking of Emile's happy and uncomplicated early years, Rousseau says:

He has reached the perfection of childhood; he has lived the life of a child; his progress has not been bought at the price of his happiness, he has gained both. While he has acquired all the wisdom of a child, he has been as free and happy as his health permits. If the Reaper Death should cut him off and rob us of our hopes, we need not bewail alike his life and death, we shall not have the added grief of knowing that we caused him pain; we will say, "His childhood, at least, was happy; we have robbed him of nothing that nature gave him."[36]

Alluding to the melting tenderness of such passages, Peter Coveney has commented: "No one of Rousseau's stature and influence has written in this way of children before [with such] lyrical enthusiasm . . . humanist rhetoric . . . sentimental appeal to nostalgic regret."[37] What is novel, however, is not the gentleness towards a child all too likely to die—there are many precedents for that—but the recognition that the child has a life *here and now* to be delighted in for its own sake. There is as much value in childhood experience as in adult experience. The reality of life is every bit as present to the infant as to the sage: "My Baby has not lived in vain," Coleridge writes of his son Berkeley who died in his first year, "this life has been to him what it is to all of us, education and development."[38] Wordsworth, too, in a central passage of *The Prelude* asserts the vital creative humanity of even the baby too young to crawl or speak:

> Emphatically such a Being lives,
> Frail creature as he is, helpless as frail,
> An inmate of this active universe (II, 11. 252-254).

The writings of the English Romantics exhibit a dazzling participatory skill at conveying the lived experiences of childhood. Coleridge's notebooks and letters testify to this alertness to his children's energies:

Hartley . . . a fairy elf—all life, all motion—indefatigable in joy—a spirit of Joy dancing on an Aspen Leaf. From morning to night he whirls about and about, whisks, whirls, and eddies, like a blossom in a May-breeze.

It is in very truth a sunny, misty, cloudy, dazzling, howling, omniform, Day! I have been looking at as pretty a sight as a Father's eyes could well see—Hartley & little Derwent running in the Green, where the Gusts blow most madly,—both with their hair floating & tossing, a miniature of the agitated Trees below which they were playing inebriate both with pleasure—Hartley whirling around for joy—Derwent eddying half willingly, half by the force of the Gust—driven backward, struggling forward, & shouting his little hymn of joy.[39]

Coleridge depicts this childhood exuberance, this whirling and darting, as resonant wth meaning, for he repeatedly identifies such motion as "eddying," his favorite image of spontaneous, self-generated, quasi-divine activity. The child's joy, for Coleridge, represents Life Unconditioned. Wordsworth analogously depicts the sensations of childhood sports not as frivolously time-wasting but as dense with meaning. The description of ice-skating in *The Prelude* is justly famous:

> and oftentimes,
> When we had given our bodies to the wind,
> And all the shadowy banks on either side
> Came sweeping through the darkness, spinning still
> The rapid line of motion, then at once
> Have I, reclining back upon my heels,
> Stopped short; yet still the solitary cliffs
> Wheeled by me—even as if the earth had rolled
> With visible motion her diurnal round!
> Behind me they did stretch in solemn train,
> Feebler and feebler, and I stood and watched
> Till all was tranquil as a dreamless sleep (I, 11. 452-463).

Wordsworth here conveys both the physical and psychological density of the childhood experience with sufficient richness to explain its memorable effect, to explain why, to cite DeQuincey, "the *primary* convulsions of nature," experienced in seemingly trivial form in youth, "come round again and again by reverberating shocks."[40]

It is not simply the *idea* of childhood, then, but the very experience of real children, vividly recounted as dense with meaning, that appears so crucial and significant and resonant of hope to the Romantics.

This heightened value placed upon childhood necessarily suggests a new educational emphasis. To prize childhood qualities as crucial to full humanity rather than dismissing them as impediments to maturation requires a new educational mode, one in which "the feelings of childhood" may be merged with the "powers of manhood." While the Romantic writers most heavily concerned with the quality of childhood sensibility are not, except for Coleridge,[41] concerned with specific institutional reform, they are obsessively interested in an issue intimately bound up with education, i.e., the methods by which childhood qualities can be developed into perfected adulthood. Although Wordsworth, Coleridge, and Blake made very little practical contribution to the history of institutional educational change, their pervasive and passionately held ideas about the fundamental nature of education are to this day immensely suggestive.

The primary educational axiom of the Romantics is that all true education is a natural process implied by the very constitution of human nature. All genuine education recognizes, in Coleridge's phrase, that human nature is "in every sense a *progress*, both body and mind." Education, then, is simply "the *method* of self-development" deriving its procedures from a wise scrutiny of the natural processes by which the mind unfolds itself.[42] Wise education is the process of growth, rationalized and understood.

The Romantic vocabulary of education, as Gill Cook has pointed out, is consequently organic.[43] A process dictated by our very evolving natures is, as Wordsworth says, "everything that *draws out* the human being."[44] Education, Coleridge insists, means "to educe, to call forth, as the blossom is educed from the bud. The vital excellences are within; the flower is but educed or brought forth from the bud."[45]

The assumption that education must proceed from within explains the Romantic disdain for mere instruction, an overlay on the true properties of the mind. "Thank God," Blake writes, "I never was sent to school/To be Flog'd into following the Style of a Fool."[46] Thus Coleridge asserts, "It is not merely a degradation of the word education, but an affront to human nature to include within its meaning the bare attainment of reading and writing, or of Latin and Greek."[47] Education is not acquirements any more than the mind is a storage bin. Though instruction may all too often degenerate to be "merely mechanical and like a Carpenter's Ruler, having its whole value in the immediate outward use to which it is applied, without implying any portion of the science in the use itself," true education involves the introduction of knowledge that *re-acts* on the mind. The object of education for Coleridge is the same as that which he attributes to Plato:

> We see, that to open anew a well of spring water, not to cleanse the stagnant tank, or fill, bucket by bucket, the leaden cistern; that the EDUCATION of the intellect, by awakening the principle and *method* of self-development, was his proposed object, not any specific information that can be *conveyed into it* from without: not to assist in storing the passive mind with the various sorts of knowledge most in request, as if the human soul were a mere repository or banqueting room, but to place it in such relations of circumstance as should gradually excite the germinal power that craves no knowledge but what it can take up into itself, what it can appropriate, and reproduce in fruits of its own.[48]

In fact, Coleridge reserves the term education for what he deems the naturally cultivated development of the mind:

Alas! how many examples are now present to our memory, of young men, the most anxiously and expensively be-schoolmastered, be-tutored, be-lectured, anything but *educated*: who have received arms, and ammunition, instead of skill, strength, and courage; varnished rather than polished; perilously over-civilized, and most pitiably uncultivated! And all from inattention to the method dictated by nature herself, to the simple truth, that as the forms in all organized existence, so must all true and living knowledge proceed from within; that it may be trained, supported, fed, excited, but can never be infused or impressed.[49]

It is such a faith in the natural faculties of the mind, demanding a slow ripening, that lies behind Wordsworth's condemnation of the knowledge-stuffed child in the 1805 version of *The Prelude*:

> 'tis a child, no child,
> But a dwarf man; in knowledge, virtue, skill . . . .
> Briefly, the moral part
> Is perfect, and in learning and in books
> He is a prodigy. His discourse moves slow,
> Massy and ponderous as a prison door,
> Tremendously embossed with terms of art;
> Rank growth of propositions overruns
> The stripling's brain; the path in which he treads
> Is choked with grammars; cushion of divine
> Was never such a type of thought profound
> As is the pillow where he rests his head.
> The ensigns of the empire which he holds,
> The globe and sceptre of his royalties,
> Are telescopes, and crucibles, and maps.
> Ships he can guide across the pathless sea,
> And tell you all their cunning; he can read
> The inside of the earth, and spell the stars;
> He knows the policies of foreign lands;
> Can string you names of districts, cities, towns,
> The whole world over, tight as beads of dew
> Upon a gossamer thread; he sifts, he weighs;
> Takes nothing upon trust; his teachers stare;
> The country people pray for God's good grace,
> And tremble at at his deep experiments.
> All things are put to question; he must live
> Knowing that he grows wiser every day
> Or else not live at all, and seeing too
> Each little drop of wisdom as it falls

Into the dimpling cistern of his heart
(V, 11. 294-295, 318-345).

This child, this homunculus, as Wordsworth describes him is hedged in
and maimed by the very training that seems to give him power. A "noon-
tide shadow" of a real man, but not a real man, this boy has been made
the prisoner of his education; his language moves "massy and ponderous
as a prison door"; the formal terminology of logic "overruns" his brain;
the movement of his mind "is choked" with learning. Self-conscious and
skeptical, this child knows only those things he has been explicitly taught.
His heart is a "cistern," an enclosed tank filled from outside; the inner
sources of living water have been suppressed since his infancy. "The cistern
contains; the fountain overflows": Blake's fine aphorism suggests the central place of a model of mind that is active and productive. Without so
trusting a metaphor of mind to rely upon, the educator is liable to fall into
the error of training such shadow-men, stuffed men, as this poor child
whose inner life (if there is any left) has no way of informing and shaping
the unwieldy bulk of data.

Over against an education which stresses cognitive acquisition of information, the Romantics favor one which stresses the development of the
naturally existent faculties of the mind. For this reason the Romantics
speak constantly of the need for continuity of consciousness from
childhood to adulthood. In order to be most fully alive, "the whole
faculties of man must be exerted"; yet such wholeness is the property of
those only who are able to remain alive to their past lives in their present:

> Every parent possesses the opportunity of observing how deeply
> children resent the injury of a delusion; and if men laugh at the
> falsehoods that were imposed on themselves during their childhood,
> it is because they are not good and wise enough to contemplate the
> past in the present, and so to produce by a virtuous and thoughtful
> sensibility that continuity of self-consciousness, which Nature has
> made the law of their animal life. Ingratitude, sensuality, and hard-
> ness of heart all flow from this source. Men are ungrateful to others
> only when they have ceased to look back on their former selves with
> joy and tenderness. They exist in fragments.[50]

We are most ourselves and most admirable when we have the freest access
to our early life and experience. With tremendous optimism about the ordinary possibilities of the normal self, Coleridge and Wordsworth regard
creative power, true distinction of mind, as potentially within the reach of
all men and women—all boys and girls rather. Genius is not so much the
possession of rare and transcendent powers as it is the ability to integrate
parts of one's life into a whole; to make fullest use of experiences common

to us all. It is, in fact, "the character and privilege of genius, and one of the marks which distinguish genius from talents" to be able to remain so fully alive as "to carry on the feelings of childhood into the powers of manhood." Thus nothing can be more important than to ensure the natural and harmonious development of the child into the adult.

Continuity and development are the dominant themes of Wordsworth's poetry.[51] It is because "the child is father to the man" that the task of childhood must be to store up emotional wealth and sensuous riches to supply the adult years. As Barbara Garlitz has pointed out,[52] Wordsworth's "Intimations Ode" was an extraordinarily influential utterance that permeated the sermons and childhood literature of the 19th century. For all its ambiguity of tone and feeling, the poem clearly invokes childhood as a source of strength, and suggests that maturity is only tolerable or even possible to that person who has tasted the possible joys and unique perceptions of childhood to the full Speaking in *The Prelude,* itself a monumental examination of "the growth of the poet's mind," of such moments of perception, Worsdworth claims central and permanent importance for them:

> Oh! mystery of man, from what a depth
> Proceed thy honours. I am lost, but see
> In simple childhood something of the base
> On which thy greatness stands; but this I feel,
> That from thyself it is that thou must give,
> Else never canst receive. The days gone by
> Come back upon me from the dawn almost
> Of life: the hiding-places of my power
> Seem open; I approach, and then they close;
> I see by glimpses now; when age comes on,
> May scarcely see at all, and I would give
> While yet we may, as far as words can give,
> Substance and life to what I feel, enshrining,
> Such is my hope, the spirit of the Past
> For future restoration (XII, 11. 272-286).

To retain childhood capacities in adulthood, to integrate childhood attributes into the mature psyche, that must be the task of education. In a very real sense, therefore, the poetry of Wordsworth and Blake is expressly educational. The former charts the development of the childhood self; the latter explicitly attempts in "The Songs of Innocence" to make such modes of perception once more available to adults.

The Romantic stress on the retention, the development, the continuity from the childhood to the adult self is tied up with a much more capacious notion of what constitutes the adult self than had been traditional. With a

wider sense of the permissible limits of being than had existed earlier,
Romantic writers take an unprecedentedly genial view of even traditionally
unhallowed aspects of childhood. What had hitherto been regarded as
childhood amorality is not only tolerated but extolled. It is striking that
Wordsworth, Coleridge, and Blake all regard as profoundly benign and
formative certain childhood traits which had traditionally been regarded as
signs of sinfulness.

All three writers delight in infant sensuousness. John Wesley had regarded the baby's headstrong propensity to seek sensuous gratification as a
sign of original depravity;[53] but the Romantics treat the same phenomenon
as a necessary means of growth. Coleridge is the most comprehensive of
the three writers in perceiving the self-absorbed, appetitive character of infancy not as a moral fault but as a formative stage of life not to be inhibited or frustrated. Sunk blamelessly in their senses—"fearless, lustful,
happy! nestling for delight/In laps of pleasure"—the infants are all the
same moving through the great progressive task of infancy: the task of
moving out of the totally subjective sensuous cocoon into a delighted
awareness of the objective world without. In Coleridge's formulation, the
infant begins his experience of the world with the experience of taste. The
primal experience and first "education" of infancy is nursing. Observing
his infant son Derwent, Coleridge notes:

> Exceeding Expressiveness of the motion of the Tongue of
> Toothless Infants.

From taste the babies move to touch:

> Babies touch *by taste* at first—then about 5 months they go from the
> Palate to the hand—& are fond of feeling what they have tasted—/
> Association of the Hand with the Taste—then the latter by itself
> recalls the former.

From these tactile sensations infants work outwards:

> The first education which we receive, that from our mothers, is given
> us by touch; the whole of its process is nothing more than, to express
> myself boldly, an extended touch by promise. The sense itself, the
> sense of vision itself, is only acquired by a continual recollection of
> touch.[54]

What is most real, therefore, to the infant is not his own separate identity,
but his initial experience of taste, which gradually extends itself to a sensuous mastery of the world. What is crucial, in Coleridge's view, to the
child's development is a secure sensuous beginning. First the child sucks

and tastes milk from the breast. Then the child touches the breast, experiencing both the immediate sensation of touch on his fingers and the remembered—therefore mediated—pleasurable sensation of sucking milk. The pleasure in touch is reinforced by the memory of taste. To impute to that finger touch the joy of the mouth's tasting is an imaginative, mentally unifying act by the baby that unites touch, taste, and pleasure into a single apprehension. Further it is an educationally progressive act for the baby in that the gratifications of taste have impelled him to use them as a way of perceiving and mastering a larger sphere. Thus the child looks out at the world and sees, not knowing he sees, a flower or a stuffed toy; he reaches to touch it. Thus *sight*, tending towards and stemming from *touch*, is "an extended touch by promise" in that the seen world is perceived as something to be touched, just as the tangible world is ultimately perceived as something to be tasted. The earlier stages of perception both impel and reinforce the later stages. Observing that his son Hartley "seemed to learn to talk by touching his mother,"[55] Coleridge infers that mental progress is a matter of incorporating primary processes into more advanced ones. Thus the growing sensory and intellectual skills of a child involve no sacrifice of primal gratifications, but are rather an extension of satisfactions. The progressive openings out of the senses enable a child imaginatively to attach the same intensely pleasurable emotions involved with nursing, involved with his earliest tender nurturing, to all the experiences of his senses, even that "touch by promise" in the world of sight. During infancy the self is centered in the world of the senses. The original infantile narcissism that would ingest the world into itself, that cannot distinguish the world from the self, gives way to a joyous apprehension of the experience of the senses. The task of infancy is fully to exercise the senses at that time of life in which the distinction between self and the external world is least keenly felt, so as to store up for the future the power of a perception which is at once objective and touched with joy. The earliest education, and the most crucial, takes place during the first year of life, and is dictated by the child's natural propensities.

A similar trust in the child's nature stands behind the licensed idleness Wordsworth and Coleridge endorse for older children. Mere child's play—treated in earlier literature either as a metaphor for transience or as evidence of insignificance—takes on a lofty educational purpose. Every functioning mind requires images, concrete objects grasped in all their sensuous fullness. In childhood, the response to natural objects is at its height. Thus, Romantic writers from Rousseau on down agree on the desirability of childhood absorption into the world of sights, sounds, and concrete objects. "I think," Coleridge writes,

> the memory of children cannot, in reason, be too much stored with
> the objects and facts of natural history. God opens the images of

nature, like the leaves of a book, before the eyes of his creature, Man—and teaches him all that is grand and beautiful in the foaming cataracts, the glassy lake, and the floating mist.[56]

Important as it is, nature's education of the senses must be spontaneous. There is a deep wisdom in childhood spontaneity, in the seeming idleness of the child at play. In Wordsworth's great poem of self-development, *The Prelude*, a work concerned throughout with the preservation and development of a fully imaginative human mind, one book is expressly devoted to formal education. Yet Book V, titled "Books," is emphatic in its praise of the ordinary untrained playfulness and undirected passion of commonplace children:

> A race of real children; not too wise,
> Too learned, or too good, but wanton, fresh,
> And bandied up and down by love and hate;
> Fierce, moody, patient, venturous, modest, shy;
> Mad at their sports like withered leaves in winds. . .
>   (V, 11. 411-415).

Skeptically condemning manipulative educators who trust nothing to the child's own nature (who in that differ from the wisdom of Wordsworth's mother, who had "virtual faith that He/Who fills the mother's breasts with innocent milk,/Doth also for our nobler part provide,/Under his great correction and control,/As innocent instincts, and as innocent food"), Wordsworth urges a very loose-reined education:

> Sages who in their prescience would control
> All accidents, and to the very road
> Which they have fashioned would confine us down,
> Like engines; when will their presumption learn,
> That in the unreasoning progress of the world
> A wiser spirit is at work for us,
> A better eye than theirs, most prodigal
> Of blessings, and most studious of our good,
> Even in what seem our most unfruitful hours?
>   (V, 11. 355-363).

"Even in what seem our most unfruitful hours"—especially in hours of childhood idleness—we are becoming most ourselves. As a clear counterimage in Book V to the deathly prodigy, Wordsworth sets out the curious and beautiful portrait of the Boy of Winander. The prodigy, a young John Stuart Mill or Macaulay, knows many things from his intensive training, but the child who has received nature's education is portrayed as knowing one rather odd thing, as being involved (as Francis Jeffrey was quick to point out) in time-wasting foolishness: "all [Wordsworth] is pleased to communicate of *his* rustic child is that he used to amuse himself with shouting to the owls, and hearing them answer."[57] For such a dubious accomplishment, Jeffrey goes on, "the author frequently stood mute, and gazed on his grave for half an hour together." There is no doubt that Wordsworth is demanding admiration for this child as a counter-example to the prodigy. Yet the child's most obvious accomplishment is simply hooting like an owl. Clearly something more must be at work:

> There was a Boy; ye knew him well, ye cliffs
> And islands of Winander!—many a time
> At evening when the stars had just begun
> To move along the edges of the hills,
> Rising and setting, would he stand alone
> Beneath the trees or by the glimmering lake,
> And there, with fingers interwoven, both hands
> Pressed closely palm to palm, and to his mouth
> Uplifted, he, as through an instrument,
> Blew mimic hootings to the silent owls,
> That they might answer him; and they would shout
> Across the watery vale, and shout again,
> Responsive to his call, with quivering peals,
> And long halloos and screams, and echoes loud,
> Redoubled and redoubled, concord wild
> Of mirth and jocund din; and when it chanced
> That pauses of deep silence mocked his skill,
> Then sometimes, in that silence while he hung
> Listening, a gentle shock of mild surprise
> Has carried far into his heart the voice
> Of mountain torrents; and the visible scene
> Would enter unawares into his mind,
> With all its solemn imagery, its rocks,
> Its woods, and that uncertain heaven received
> Into the bosom of the steady lake (V. 11. 364-388).

The child's unselfconscious intense absorption into nature, his heightened concentration, his simultaneous receptiveness to the vastness of nature—all are creating in him a power of feeling that will make growth possible. "Never . . . imagine," Coleridge enjoins in a similar vein, "that a child is idle who is gazing on the stream or lying upon the earth. The basis of all moral character may then be forming; all the healthy processes of nature may then be ripening."[58]

Crucial to Romantic thinking about education and development is what

Rousseau in *Émile* had called "negative education" and what Wordsworth subsequently called "wise passiveness": the keeping of the child's mind free of cant, free of cumbersome preconceptions, free to grow according to what Coleridge calls "the method of nature":

> In the infancy and childhood of individuals (and something analo-
> gous may be traced in the history of the communities) the first know-
> ledges are acquired promiscuously.—Say rather that the plan is not
> formed by the selection of objects presented to the notice of the
> pupils; but by the impulses and dispositions suited to their age, by
> the limits of their comprehension, and the volatile and desultory ac-
> tivity of their attention, and by the relative predominance or the
> earlier development of one or more faculties over the rest. This is the
> happy delirium, the healthful fever of the physical, moral, and intel-
> lectual being,—nature's kind and providential gift to childhood. In
> the best sense of the words, it is the light-headedness and light-
> heartedness of human life! There is indeed, "method in't" but it is
> the method of nature which thus stores the mind with all the material
> for after use, promiscuously indeed and as it might seem without
> purpose, while she supplies a gay and motley chaos of facts, and
> forms, and thousand-fold experiences, the origin of which lies
> beyond the memory, traceless as life itself, and finally passing into a
> part of our life more rapidly than would have been compatible with
> distinct consciousness and with a security beyond the power of
> choice![59]

The tremendous Romantic trust in the unfolding processes of mind in the child's early years means a casual attitude towards subject matter (what Coleridge called "the selection of objects presented to the notice of the pupils") and a scrupulous attention to the pre-existent faculties, the "im-pulses and dispositions suited to their age." This accounts for the easy contempt with which Wordsworth is able to dismiss a prodigy and flagrantly to idealize a seemingly idle child. The way lies clear for Huckleberry Finn.

The primary impulses, the primary appetites, which must be fed in childhood are two—a passive faculty and an active faculty:

> We should address ourselves to those faculties in a child's mind
> which are first awakened by nature, and consequently first admit of
> cultivation, that is to say, the memory and the imagination. The
> comparing power, the judgment, is not at that age active, and ought
> not to be forcibly excited.[60]

This is as striking for what it rejects as for what it endorses. Wordsworth and Coleridge consider that educational cramming is morally damaging to children, creating in them nothing but a habit of invidiousness and conceit. The child taught to weigh, balance, set himself in judgment on moral issues is so given to vanity that he exists "within the pinfold of his own conceit" (*The Prelude*, V, 1. 333):

> It was a great error to cram the young mind with so much knowledge as made the child talk much and fluently. What was more ridiculous than to hear a child questioned what it thought of the last poem of Walter Scott? A child should be child-like, and possess no other idea than what was loving and admiring.[61]

To be truly childlike means to be imaginative. The association of childhood with imagination had long been part of the rationalist tradition. As Thomas Babington Macaulay remarked darkly, "Of all people children are the most imaginative. They abandon themselves without reserve to every illusion . . . . Such is the despotism of the imagination over uncultivated minds."[62] From such a viewpoint, however, imagination was an impediment to learning, a quality to be repressed or deracinated as soon as possible. But for Wordsworth and Coleridge imagination was not only the quality most important to the mature adult, but the faculty by which maturity could come to pass. "The imagination is the distinguishing characteristic of man as a progressive being."[63] Imagination is thus crucial to the entire educational development of the child.

Imagination for Wordsworth and Coleridge is not simply a gift possessed by a few artists. (If it were simply that, then art itself would be of considerably less value to us.) It is a psychological process common to us all in greater or lesser degrees, a process by which we unify our experience. It is, as Thomas McFarland has pointed out with respect to Coleridge,[64] a dual power, at once testifying to the mind's dependence on nature for images and to the mind's creative independence of nature. It is a faculty which manifests itself in three main ways. First, imagination is that power which attests our susceptibility to images. As what Coleridge calls "Primary Imagination," Wordsworth the "dramatic" imagination, and Keats the "Shakespearean" imagination, it is the power by which we perceive the fullness of being of things and relate them to ourselves.[65] It is thus an agent for the assimilation of the otherness of the world into ourselves. Second, imagination is the faculty that uses images to body forth totalities, visions of organic wholes. It is the great faculty of unification of multiplicity under a leading idea or emotion. It is a power, in Coleridge's formulation,

> by which one image or feeling is made to modify many others, and by a sort of fusion to force many into one . . . and which, combining many circumstances into one moment of consciousness, tends to produce that ultimate end of all human thought and feeling, unity,

and thereby the reduction of the spirit to its principle and fountain who is alone truly one.[66]

Third, and most important, imagination is the faculty which makes manifest to us the power of our own minds. As we become conscious that the patterns and meanings we perceive in the world are as much created by us as given to us, we recognize our power of mental autonomy as does Wordsworth in his famous tribute to "Imagination . . . the power so called/Through sad incompetence of human speech":

> That awful Power rose from the mind's abyss . . . .
> Under such banners militant, the soul
> Seeks for no trophies, struggles for no spoils
> That may attest her prowess, blest in thoughts
> That are their own perfection and reward,
> Strong in herself and in beatitude
> That hides her, like the mighty flood of Nile
> Poured from her fount of Abyssinian clouds
> To fertilise the whole Egyptian plain
>   (*The Prelude*, VI, 11. 592-594, 609-616).

Wordsworth metaphorically likens the imaginative mind to the Nile, the river whose source was then unknown, and which flowed thousands of miles without tributaries "to fertilise the whole Egyptian plain." So the stream of imagination flowing from within has power to enrich the world. By acts of imaginative unification we come to realize, in Dewey's formulation, that the world is not only given to us, but taken.

Since children's thinking is by nature imaginative in each of these three ways, wisdom dictates that the educator should help children use this faculty of imagination for the "progressive" ends of furthering their self-development. Imagination is the best means for the active assimilation and integration of knowledge into the self.

Children are naturally imaginative in all three modes. Through his astonishingly adhesive grasp of words and images—"the memory of words and images which the . . . young child manifestly possesses in an unusual degree—even to sealing wax accuracy of rétention & representation"—the child is unselfconsciously able to absorb the images of nature and suspend them in his mind as does Wordsworth's Boy of Winander:

> the visible scene
> Would enter unawares into his mind,
> With all its solemn imagery, its rocks,

> Its woods, and that uncertain heaven,
> Received into the bosom of the steady lake
>   (V, 11. 384-388).

This non-judgmental exercise of memory, this fixing and storing of images, is a process allied with imagination, and may be thought of as passive imagination at work. To *remember*, to store the mind with natural images of beauty, aids moral development in several ways: first by withdrawing the child's consciousness from himself and directing it healthily outwards; second by creating a habit of seeing clearly and precisely, a habit Wordsworth and Coleridge regard as the intellectual correlative of truthfulness. Even though early childhood is the appropriate time for storing, stocking, loading the memory with natural images and facts, both Wordsworth and Coleridge are unequivocally opposed to all rote memorization of disconnected facts and arbitrary grammatical rules. Insofar as a young child—up to about seven—is given any specific academic training—and Coleridge urges some instruction in the rudiments of Greek grammar as well as in reading, writing, and arithmetic—he should be asked to learn the subject in question with great accuracy, never be allowed even to call a long leaf round or a red ball blue. The effect of such training is to educe veracity as a habit of mind. Coleridge speaks earnestly of "the connection of *intellectual accuracy* with *moral veracity*; for this end boys should not be accustomed to utter words which they did not understand. Having first used words of no meaning, they soon use those of half meaning, then those of vicious meaning."[68] To Wordsworth and to Coleridge, as to Rousseau before them, the mind of a child is naturally concrete, averse to abstract moralizing. The teacher who would follow nature in teaching honesty must educe the habit of clear thought rather than the abstract cant of truth.

The child is also imaginative in his habit of affective thought. As Blake and Wordsworth make emphatically clear in their poetry of infancy, the innocent eye is the one which sees feelingly, harmonizes the world by means of an informing emotional state. Thus the Wordworthian infant who basks in his mother's love, inhabiting an atmosphere of love, is able to reach out to perceive the world in the light of that love:

> For him, in one dear Presence, there exists
> A virtue which irradiates and exalts
> Objects through widest intercourse of sense.
> No outcast he, bewildered and depressed:
> Along his infant veins are interfused
> The gravitation and the filial bond
> Of Nature that connects him with the world.
> Is there a flower, to which he points with hand
> Too weak to gather it, already love

Drawn from love's purest earthly fount for him
Hath beautified that flower; already shades
Of pity cast from inward tenderness
Do fall around him upon aught that bear
Unsightly marks of violence of harm
(*The Prelude*, II, 11. 238-251).

For Coleridge the "joy" of the infant gives it the power of learning: "Hartley seemed to learn to talk by touching his mother." It is the affective underpinning of the mind that enables the mind to function at all in a productive and progressive way. Since the mind is prior to any of its functions, true education must be affective. Childhood learning best begins in the affective life, which is unitary, rather than in the intellectual life, which is analytic:

Have you children, or have you lived among children, and do you not know, that in all things, in food, in medicine, in all their doings and abstainings they must believe in order to acquire a reason for their belief?[69]

Thus love must be prior to instruction; faith to judgment; goals to methods:

In the education of children, love is first to be instilled, and out of love obedience is to be educed. The impulse and power should be given to the intellect and the end of a moral being exhibited.

My experience tells me that little is taught or communicated by contest or dispute, but everything by sympathy and love. Collision elicits truth only from the hardest heads.[70]

This, in fact, is the central Romantic insight: the necessity of a prior mental set, an emotional context, for learning to take place. Though it is clearly possible to regard the human mind as passive and to apply knowledge upon the passive senses, all truly humane and imaginative teaching proceeds from within.

Finally children are naturally imaginative in their unitary mode of perception. They see wholes before parts:

In the child's mind there is nothing fragmentary; its numeration table is truly Pythagorean. The numbers are, each and all, units and integers, and slowly and difficultly does it exchange this its first awakened arithmetic for that of aggregation, apposition, in one word, of result.

I saw in early youth, as in a dream, the birth of the planets; and my eyes beheld as one what the understanding divided into (1) the origin of their masses, (2) the origin of their motions, and (3) the site or position of their circles and ellipses.

. . . & when I came home, he showed me how [the stars and planets] rolled round—/I heard him with a profound delight and admiration; but without the least mixture of wonder or incredulity. For from my earliest reading of Faerie Tales, & genii &c &c—my mind had been habituated *to the Vast*—& I never regarded my senses in any way as the criteria of my belief. I regulated all my creeds by my conceptions, not my *sight*.[71]

Their taste is naturally attuned to images of vastness and wonder—and for very good reasons: such images satisfy the human hunger, most uncritically urgent in youth, for grandeur, sublimity, and pattern:

> A gracious spirit o'er this earth presides,
> And o'er the heart of man: invisibly
> It comes, directing those to works of love
> Who care not, know not, think not what they do.
> The tales that charm away the wakeful night
> In Araby; romances; legends penned
> For solace by dim light of monkish lamps;
> Fictions, for ladies of their love, devised
> By youthful squires; adventures endless, spun
> By the dismantled warrior in old age,
> Out of the bowels of those very schemes
> In which his youth did first extravagate;
> These spread like day, and something in the shape
> Of these will live till man shall be no more.
> Dumb yearnings, hidden appetites, are ours,
> And *they must* have their food. Our childhood sits,
> Our simple childhood, sits upon a throne
> That hath more power than all the elements
> (*The Prelude*, V, 11. 491-509).

Against all the utilitarian defenders of practical morality, against all the humanitarian opponents of emotional extravagance, like Rousseau and the Edgeworths, who would have prohibited to the 19th-century child, as they would to our own children, the reading of works of fantasy, Coleridge declares his faith in the value of wonder:

Should children be permitted to read Romances, Relations of Giants

and Magicians, and Genii?—I know all that has been said against it;
but I have formed my faith in the affirmative—I know no other way
of giving the mind a love of 'the Great' & 'the Whole.'[72]

Such moments of exaltation as children feel in response to stories of
romance and grandeur are tremendously valuable in two respects. Such a
grandiose exaltation gives the child what Wordsworth calls "an obscure
sense/Of possible sublimity" (*The Prelude*, II, 11. 317-318). Reaching out
to grasp vast and beautifully patterned images, scarcely understood,
awakens the mind to the possibility of a total order. A richly imaginative
early mental life is the necessary preliminary for an adult who is able to put
the scattered pieces of life together into a meaningful pattern. Furthermore, such childhood absorption into romance has the healthful effect of
promoting self-forgetfulness:

> Oh! give us once again the wishing cap
> Of Fortunatus, and the invisible coat
> Of Jack the Giant-killer, Robin Hood
> And Sabra in the forest with St. George!
> The child, whose love is here, at least doth reap
> One precious gain, that he forgets himself
> (V, 11. 341-346).

"Nothing should be more impressed on parents and tutors than to make
children forget themselves; and books which only told how Master Billy
and Miss Ann spoke and acted were not only ridiculous but extremely
hurtful. Much better give them 'Jack the Giant-Killer' or the 'Seven
Champions' or anything, which, being beyond their sphere of action,
should not feed self self-pride."[73]

Imagination in both positive and negative ways is thus the primary agency of earliest education. Negatively it draws off the child's attention from
self-conscious judgment, analysis, egotism, so that the processes of growth
can take place spontaneously, uninhibited by self-consciousness. Positively
it is the holistic faculty which enables the child to integrate his knowledge
into a meaningful intellectual and emotional synthesis: "The *Heart* should
have *fed* upon the *truth*," Coleridge writes, "as Insects on a Leaf, till it be
tinged with the colour, and shew its food in every the minutest fibre."[74] To
speak properly of education—"Knowledge not purchased with the loss of
power"—means to speak not of instruction alone but of our total humanity: "By deep feeling we make our *ideas dim*, and this is what we mean by
our life, ourselves."[75] True education then must proceed from and return
to the affective life. "To carry the feelings of childhood into the powers of
manhood" may be an arduous and extravagantly optimistic program, but
the Romantics offer it as the best hope for childhood happiness and adult
self-realization.

REFERENCES

1. Werner Jaeger, *Paideia: The Ideals of Greek Culture*, trans. Gilbert Highet, 3 vols. (Oxford: Basil Blackwell, 1954).

2. Both Goethe and Wordsworth labored over their masterpieces for much of their lives. *Faust*, begun around 1770, was not completed until 1831. Wordsworth began *The Prelude* in 1799, completed a full draft by 1805, but worked and reworked the poem until his death in 1850. Both poets seem to have regarded their poems of growth and development as co-extensive with their very lives, tacitly identifying growth with life itself.

3. "A Defence of Poetry" (1821), *English Romantic Writers*, ed. David Perkins (New York: Harcourt, Brace & World, 1967), pp. 1086-1087.

4. *The Letters of John Keats*, ed. Maurice Buxton Forman, 4th ed. (New York: Oxford University Press, 1952), p. 335.

5. *The Watchman*, ed. Lewis Patton, *The Collected Works of Samuel Taylor Coleridge: 2*, ed. Kathleen Coburn & Bart Winer, Bollingen Series LXXV (Princeton, N.J.: Princeton University Press, 1970), p. 131.

6. "The Laocoon," *The Poetry and Prose of William Blake*, ed. David Erdman and Harold Bloom (Garden City: Doubleday, 1965), p. 272. All subsequent references to Blake are this text.

7. *The Image of Childhood: The Individual and Society: A Study of the Theme in English Literature* (1957; rev. ed. Harmondsworth, Middlesex: Penguin Books, 1967), p. 29.

8. William Wordsworth, *Poetical Works*, ed. Thomas Hutchinson, rev. Ernest de Selincourt (London: Oxford University Press, 1969), *The Prelude*, XII, 11. 272-275. Except where noted, all further citations from Wordsworth's poetry are from this edition.

9. Friedrich von Schiller, *Naive and Sentimental Poetry and On the Sublime: Two Essays*, trans. Julius A. Elias (New York: Frederick Ungar, 1966), pp. 86-87.

10. p. 85.

11. *The Notebooks of Samuel Taylor Coleridge*, ed. Kathleen Coburn, 3 vols. (New York: Pantheon Books, 1956-   ), #4398. This edition will hereafter be cited as *CN*.

12. "The Doctrine and Discipline of Human Culture" (1836), *Essays upon Educatoin by Amos Bronson Alcott* (Gainesville, Florida: Scholars' Facsimiles & Reprints, 1960), p. 52; p. 54.

13. "Nature," *Selections from Ralph Waldo Emerson*, ed. Stephen E. Whicher (Boston: Houghton Mifflin, 1960), p. 54.

14. *Autobiography, The Collected Writings of Thomas DeQuincey*, ed. David Masson (1889; rpt. New York, AMS Press, 1968), I, p. 121.

15. *The Friend*, ed. Barbara Rooke, 2 vols., *Collected Works: 4* (Princeton, N.J.: Princeton University Press, 1969), I, pp. 109-110.

16. René Wellek, "The Concept of 'Romanticism' in Literary History," *Comp. Lit.*, I (1960); Morse Peckham, "Toward a Theory of Romanticism," *PMLA*, 66 (1951).

17. Thomas Carlyle, *Past and Present* (1843), ed. Richard D. Altick (Boston: Houghton Mifflin, 1965), p. 33.

18. "On Poesy or Art," *Criticism: The Major Texts*, ed. Walter Jackson Bate (New York: Harcourt, Brace Jovanovich, 1970), p. 393.

19. *Sartor Resartus* (New York & London: Dent and Dutton, 1908), p. 139.

20. *Goethe's Faust*, trans. Walter Kaufmann (Garden City: Doubleday, 1963), p. 103.

21. *The Letters of John Keats*, p. 335.

22. *CN*, #2549.

23. *Collected Letters of Samuel Taylor Coleridge*, ed. Earl Leslie Griggs, 6 vols. (Oxford: Clarendon Press, 1956-1971), #529. This edition will be hereafter cited as *CL*.

24. Erdman & Bloom, p. 677; *Anima Poetae* (London: William Heinemann, 1895), p. 77.

25. *CL*, #352.

26. "The Soul of Man under Socialism" (1891), *The Artist as Critic: Critical Writings of Oscar Wilde* (New York: Random House, 1969), p. 263.

27. Friedrich Schlegel, *Dialogue on Poetry and Literary Aphorisms*, trans. Ernst Behler and Roman Struc (University Park & London: Pennsylvania State University Press, 1968), p. 155.

28. *On the Aesthetic Education of Man*, trans. Reginald Snell (New York: Frederick Ungar, 1965), pp. 73-75.

29. *Inquiring Spirit*, ed. Kathleen Coburn (New York: Pantheon Books, 1951), pp. 68-69.

30. *CL*, #210.

31. *Naive and Sentimental Poetry*, p. 87; p. 216n; p. 93.

32. "New Year's Eve," *The Essays of Elia*, ed. Geoffrey Tillotson (New York & London: Dent and Dutton, 1962), p. 33.

33. "Childhood," *The Complete Poetical Works of Hartley Coleridge*, ed. Ramsay Colles (London: Routledge, 1906), p. 177. Samuel Taylor Coleridge's "doted on" precocious son Hartley grew up to be a self-styled "small poet" who wrote obsessively of infancy and childhood.

34. *Visions of the Daughters of Albion*, p. 48.

35. *Natural Supernaturalism: Tradition and Revolution in Romantic Literature* (New York: W.W. Norton, 1971), pp. 381-382.

36. *Emile*, trans. Barbara Foxley (New York & London: Dent & Dutton, 1974), pp. 126-127.

37. *The Image of Childhood*, p. 46.

38. *CL*, #274.

39. *CL*, #376, #462.

40. *Suspira de Profundis* (Boston: Tichnor, Reed & Fields, 1852), p. 210.

41. Coleridge, who was interested in almost everything, was a well-informed propagandist for Andrew Bell's Madras System of monitorial tuition, an early exponent of a system of universal national education, and a frequent public lecturer on educational issues. K. Gill Cook's forthcoming George Washington University dissertation on Coleridge's educational thought, "Unity with Progression," promises to be the definitive work on this subject. I am especially indebted to Ms. Cook for her suggestive observations on Coleridge's linking of imagination, progression, and education.

42. *Shakespearean Criticism*, ed. Thomas Middleton Raysor, 2 vols (Cambridge, Mass.: Harvard University Press, 1930), II, p. 296; *The Friend*, I, p. 473.

43. Unpublished Prospectus to "Unity with Progression," a dissertation in progress.

44. *Letters of the Wordsworth Family*, ed. William Knight (Boston: Ginn & Co., 1907), II, p. 341.

45. *Shakespearean Criticism*, II, p. 290.

46. Erdman and Bloom, p. 502.

47. *Shakespearean Criticism*, II, pp. 290-291.

48. *CL*, #1558; *The Friend*, I, pp. 472-473.

49. *The Friend*, I, p. 500.
50. *The Friend*, I, p. 40.
51. The theme has structural concomitants too. The concern with continuity fundamentally determines the structure of Wordsworth's blank verse, an elaborate sequence of interrelated clauses in apposition, each growing out of a preceding clause, each linking to a successor. Much of the real difficulty in reading Wordsworth's poetry stems from his reluctance to cut off the complexity of perceived relationships; such reluctance takes the syntactical form of exceedingly long, suspended sentences.
52. "The Immortality Ode: Its Cultural Progeny," *SEL*, VI (1966), pp. 639-649.
53. John Wesley, "Sermon on the Education of Children" (c. 1783), *Child-Rearing Concepts, 1628-1861*, ed. Philip J. Greven Jr. (Ithaca, Ill.: Peacock Publishers, 1973).
54. *CN, #960; #924; Philosophical Lectures*, ed. Kathleen Coburn (New York: Philosophical Library, 1949), p. 115.
55. *CN, #838*.
56. *The Complete Works of Samuel Taylor Coleridge*, ed. W.G.T. Shedd (New York: Harper Brothers, 1858), p. 318.
57. "Review of *Poems* by George Crabbe," *English Romantic Writers*, p. 365.
58. *Shakespearean Criticism*, II, p. 292.
59. *Coleridge on Logic and Learning*, ed. Alice D. Snyder (1929; rpt. Folcroft, Pa.: Folcroft Library Editions, 1973), p. 105.
60. Shedd, IV, p. 317.
61. *Shakespearean Criticism*, II, p. 291.
62. "Milton" (1825), *Critical, Historical, and Miscellaneous Essays* (New York: A.C. Armstrong, 1860), I, p. 209.
63. *Miscellaneous Criticism*, ed. Thomas Middleton Raysor (Cambridge, Mass.: Harvard University Press, 1936), p. 195.
64. *Coleridge and the Pantheist Tradition* (Oxford: Clarendon Press, 1969), pp. 306-310.
65. *Biographia Literaria* (New York & London: Dent & Dutton, 1960), p. 167; Wordsworth, "Preface to *Poems*" (1815), *Literary Criticism of William Wordsworth, ed.* Paul M. Zall (Lincoln: University of Nebraska Press, 1966), p. 150; Keats, *Letters*, pp. 226-227.
66. "Shakespeare as a Poet Generally," Bate, pp. 388-389.
67. *CN, #1828*.
68. *Shakespearean Criticism*, II, p. 296.
69. *Aids to Reflection*, ed. Henry Nelson Coleridge, 2 vols. (London: William Pickering, 1843), I, p. 144.
70. *Miscellaneous Criticism*, p. 194; *Shakespearean Criticism*, II, p. 57.
71. *Coleridge on Logic and Learning*, p. 127; *Anima Poetae*, p. 77; *CL, #210*.
72. *CL, #210*.
73. *Shakespearean Criticism*, II, p. 293.
74. *CL, #65*.
75. *CN, #921*.

V

The Double-Vision of Education in the Nineteenth-Century: The Romantic and the Grotesque

— STERLING FISHMAN

During the last years of the 18th century, artists and writers began to surround education with a rosy hue. In word and picture teachers and students, after centuries of controlled warfare, laid down their cudgels and began to live in blissful harmony. In verbal and visual portrayal, education was depicted as a gentle and affectionate activity rather than a violent or potentially violent one. Teachers no longer appeared with their omnipresent instruments of violence. Students were no longer universally sullen. Artists and writers began to idealize and romanticize this important area of human activity. A new cultural theme emerged, a new set of symbols: the loving and caring teacher; the eager and happy child.

The purpose of this essay is to explore this change in the *visual realm,* to show how Romanticism provided a new educational theme thereby creating an alternative educational ideal which barely had existed earlier. Obviously, Romanticism did not totally obliterate the "old view" of education in art or life. In classrooms and nurseries teachers and tutors persisted in punitive pedagogy and learners everywhere continued to cringe. Nor did the portrayal of education as an adversarial and hostile activity disappear entirely from the sketch pad and canvas. The "old way" found a new means of visual representation in the development of the grotesque, the caricature.

Romanticism, however, has proven durable; it still inspires us. It has survived the hard edge of Realism and Naturalism in the late 19th century. It still provides us with dreams and ideals; and in the world of dreams we are all artists.

Did Romanticism affect only art and literature or did it affect life as well? Was it only a sentimental ideal which flourished in the world of pen and palette, or did it alter the lives of people? With respect to education, did the new set of ideals actually transform tormentors into mentors and suffering victims into happy learners? These are the questions which have inspired this essay.

How does one show that a significant historical change occurred in the manner in which education was portrayed by artists? Should one begin by collecting and dating all of the available visual representations of education? Should one then analyze and classify these under such headings as "Benign," "Hostile," "Violent," etc., after observing attitudes, facial expressions, etc.? Should one then add up the various columns to determine if some chronological pattern occurs? There is, of course, good precedent for employing this method of content analysis and worthwhile results may ensue.[1] In a project such as I have described, however, this would be impractical. What percentage of the total number of visual representations of education will I have observed? Would this represent a satisfactory sample? How could I honestly determine that a significant change had occurred?

Unfortunately, "iconology," or the analysis of the visual past for historical research, does not possess a satisfactory methodology. Historians have normally employed visual materials for anecdotal or illustrative purposes. The study of history has followed the lead of its patron saint, Leopold von Ranke, and concentrated on verbal documentation largely ignoring the visual remnants of the past. In writing diplomatic or political history, historians were on sound ground in following this lead. But as the fields of cultural and social history emerged, one might have expected this new breed of historian to observe the walls of museums as often as they studied the written archives. Like old horses whose blinders are finally removed, however, they continued to stare in one direction. At the end of the last century, the newly founded field of art history fell heir to this vast treasure of visual remains. But to no avail. Art historians became infatuated with the study of changes in artistic style and technique. The daily lives of the thousands of people who inhabited the canvases and drawing paper of the past remained virtually unscrutinized. An occasional historian interested in the history of clothing or toys might make the effort, but otherwise historians perpetuated their visual torpor.[2]

Several recent initiatives have begun to alter this pattern. First, historians began to write the history of peoples without a written record of their past. This frequently meant appropriating the methods of the cultural anthropologist and archeologist, examining artifacts and visual remnants as well as carefully recording oral history. It represented a striking achievement that could not go unnoticed. Writing history without archives became possible and even respectable. Equally striking was the use made of visual sources by that pioneer in family history, Philippe Aries. In writing his *Centuries of Childhood,* he peppered the text of his work with references to visual sources, not merely to illustrate the results of archival research, but as primary documentary evidence. The original text included copies of many of these sources.[3] Unfortunately, the seedling which Aries planted has been something of a disappointment in this respect. While not totally barren, it has not borne the luscious and ripe fruit one might have expected.

In any case, what kind of methodology other than quantitative content analysis can one employ using visual sources to document historical change? First, let me suggest a rather simple one and provide a few examples. You must begin with a gentle assumption: that the historian is an honest and honorable person who has spent a significant portion of a recent research leave looking at many hundreds of pictures in which the subjects are engaged in "education." As will soon be apparent, this does not necessarily mean schooling. Education is defined here as any *deliberate* effort to transmit skills or knowledge from an older generation to a younger one, whether in the home, shop, field, or school. The historian, having observed as many examples as possible, then selects several specific representations of what he regards as typical of the portrayal of education in a particular period.

Let us assume that the historian takes his typical examples from Germany and England in the mid-19th century. The first might be a portrait of Pestalozzi engaged in teaching a class of orphans painted by Konrad Grob in 1879 (Figure 1). The entire scene is permeated with affection between the teacher and his students. Pestalozzi looks lovingly at one little waif while another climbs on his back. Light falls on another child seated beside Pestalozzi with his primer in hand. A woman stands at the door staring in adulation at the "great teacher." Even the perspective of the artist makes it appear that he has painted this work at floor level. His subject is elevated to semiroyal or semidivine status. Incidentally, one reason for selecting this painting is the low social status of the pupils, which provides additional breadth for comparison.

As a second example, let us observe a Victorian music lesson painted by James Collinson (Figure 2). The artist depicts the teacher and child in a moment of great affection. They are staring lovingly into each other's eyes. Various objects in the room intensify the feeling of warmth, e.g., a geranium standing on a lace covered table. The face of the young piano teacher expresses essentially the same loving feeling as does Pestalozzi's

Figure 1

Figure 2

in the previous example.

Whereas artists rendered educational scenes in this rosy manner as a matter of course in the mid-19th century, virtually none had done so a century earlier. This particular genre of idealizing and romanticizing education began in the late 18th century and gained momentum throughout the following century. Even the most gentle scenes depicted prior to 1750 usually contain some symbol of implied hostility or violence (see Figure 3), and are never loving and affectionate in the manner of these two examples. Clearly, a significant change has occurred in the visual depiction of "education."

Figure 3

Visual depictions of tender teachers, devoted pupils, and commodious surroundings not only represent a new set of artistic images, but also signify the creation of a totally new set of popular myths and beliefs concerning one of the most important areas of human activity, education. Art and life are closely linked. The artist not only renders a vision of perceived reality, but is also engaged in mirroring and forming popular ideals.

As human beings, we possess a rich visual sense and vivid imaginations. This permits us to indulge in flights of visual fancy and fantasy—to imagine places we have never visited, to undress people who are fully clothed, and to concoct daydreams and nightdreams about a world we shall never have. Of course, we may also create visual frenzies as well, and frighten ourselves with monsters and maelstroms.

Yet, no matter how absurd and far-fetched our visual fantasies may seem, they are linked to the realities of perception..The visual symbols of our fantasy world are derived from actual visual experiences. Even our wildest creations bear a resemblance to what we know. One could argue that "to imagine" literally means to exceed our actual experience. In the visual realm, as well as the verbal, "to imagine" means to rearrange experience. A creative writer rearranges words in a novel in an aesthetically pleasing way. A creative painter does likewise with visual symbols. Whether it is the pleasure garden of Kubla Khan or the hellfires of Hades that we seek to imagine and describe, we are limited by our horizons.

Our visual fantasies are therefore confined to a given spectrum. "What," one might ask, in order to define the breadth of that spectrum, "is the most far-fetched vision you can imagine?" Perhaps some scene from Hieronymous Bosch would come to mind. Most of us operate on a daily basis, however, by remaining within a narrow range of remembered perceptions. We are not deliberately trying to test the limits of our visual imagination. If anything, we are more concerned with recalling various images as accurately as possible, than with trying to embellish them. We try in vain to recall the features of a long-lost friend or lover, rather than intentionally distort them. Frequently we are struck by our inability to recall such people without the assistance of an old photograph or painting.

Now, let us asssume that we are trying to recall visually a moment in our lives remembered as lovely—for example, a walk down a country road or a family gathering on a holiday. If our ability to recall precisely is less than perfect in any case, do not other emotional factors begin to shape our visual recollections as well? Is there, for example, not a "nostalgia effect," i.e., a tendency to romanticize the "good old days"? Are we not prone to deceive ourselves about the past in order to make sense of the present? We live our lives in terms of various myths and ideals and undoubtedly use the past, visually and verbally, to support these. Why not?

Although the artist may be superior to the rest of us at rendering or remembering visual images, he is still limited by his skills, his manual dexterity, and the artistic style in which he is trained. Let us for a moment assume that the aim of the artist is to reproduce a bucolic scene as precisely as possible. What factors will enhance his achievement? His eyes, his skill, and his *mental set*. We should not forget that we see with the brain and not the eyes. The eyes merely transmit impressions. As with the rest of us, factors such as "nostalgia" and "wish fulfillment" influence the artist's vision. He may either intentionally or unintentionally ignore the telephone wires which mar an otherwise perfect pastoral scene and omit them from his canvas.

The point of this is to show that popular as well as professional imagery is based on a particular mental set. We usually see what we expect to see. We organize our visual world to support the myths in which we believe. Nor is this a solitary endeavor; frequently we share a collective vision. Most of our beliefs and fantasies are mass beliefs rather than ours alone. In fact, we are engaged at all times in a grand conspiracy to deceive ourselves. We conspire with our eyes, our friends, and our professional artists to organize the world in which we live.

The iconology of education, therefore, reveals that the myths surrounding "education" underwent a radical transformation in the last third of the 18th century. The study of visual evidence also shows that this "new" depiction of education in a rosy and romantic manner would gain momentum throughout the 19th century, and reach mass proportions in the middle-class family magazine which became popular in the last half of the century.

Given what we already know, this should not prove surprising. It is only that the study of visual sources has been so neglected that makes it so. In the first place, we already know that artists began to idealize and romanticize "childhood" at approximately the same time, i.e., the late 18th century. Instead of merely painting portraits of individual children, as artists had done since the Renaissance, many artists began to seek to capture the "essence" of childhood. The effort alone represents a significant step in the history of childhood. Artists customarily began to depict "childhood," one of the principal elements in any portrayal of education, in a benign manner. Anticipating the Romantics, for example, Joshua Reynolds and his *protégé*, Thomas Lawrence, devoted immense energies to portraying the innocent and lovable nature of "childhood." On the continent, a similar tendency emerges in the works of artists such as Jean Baptiste Greuze in France and Johann Georg Meyer in Germany.[4] The new theme encompassed all social classes, poor children as well as wealthy ones. A new metaphor of childhood appeared, and a new mythology as well.

This new view of childhood led necessarily to a new view of pedagogy and education. Rousseau, Pestalozzi, and their contemporaries began to

Figure 4

popularize this new methodology in their writings, a pedagogy based on respect, understanding, and love. The methods of Rousseau's tutor and Pestalozzi's Gertrude quickly found their way into the popular educational literature of Europe. It is equally instructive and historically illuminating to trace the new methodology in the visual realm. Interestingly, the frontispiece to the first edition of *Emile* published in Amsterdam in 1762 did not yet capture the new spirit (see Figure 4). The artist found the "hardening process" advocated by Rousseau as the theme worth portraying. He shows the infant Achilles being thrust into the River Styx by his mother to make him invulnerable to his enemies. The viewer could also interpret the scene as infanticide. In subsequent editions of *Emile*, however, a loving tutor appears (see Figure 5) as the counterpart to the new child (as well as a mother nursing her own child).

The new imagery appeared everywhere in Western Europe. A new set of beliefs about education found visual expression. Children became amiable and sympathetic and teachers became their tutors rather than

Figure 5

their tormentors. This new portrayal became an intrinsic part of Romantic lore. Romantic artists and writers removed the wings from angelic Baroque putti and gently lowered them to fields and forest glens. Here they were instructed by nature assisted by loving tutors. Even when these secular cherubs moved indoors, they began their lessons in a *Kindergarten*, a "children's garden." Friedrich Frobel, the founder of the *Kindergarten,* now joined Rousseau and Pestalozzi in the visual hagiolatry of 19th-century Europe. (See Figure 6.)

Children and teachers were not the only members of the educational circle to receive a new imagery, however. Concerned and loving parents completed the new picture. As the family home and the peasant cottage provided the locales for a considerable portion of 19th-century education, the changing image of parents is also educationally significant. In middle-class homes, private tutors and doting parents constitute a new genre for artists. Observe for example C. R. Leslie's "Dancing Lesson" of 1832 (see figure 7). The entire family gathers to watch the children demonstrate their new dancing skills. A distinguished-looking male not only tenderly holds the hand of a very young child, but he is also staring with earnest intensity at the performance of the dancing students. This is a scene without precedent from a century earlier.

Figure 6

Similarly, the peasant cottage received new visual treatment as well. Of course the skills being taught were not those of the dancing master or piano teacher, but of the weaver or woodworker. Nevertheless, a new set of relationships received visual expression. In this setting, romantic ideology clearly prevailed over the harsh realities of rural life. For the cultural historian, however, the mythology is important. Even the industrial slums did not totally defy sentimental treatment. Artists frequently depicted industrial schools (see Figure 8) and monitorial schools in a benevolent manner. With the large numbers of children portrayed, however, any feeling of pedagogical warmth became depersonalized.

Figure 7

Figure 8

The new visual image, of course, corroborates what we find in literary accounts of education in this period—fictional, pedagogical, and official. In all of these representations, we observe the growing emotional and material investment in children and education. "Childhood" assumes an almost exaggerated importance in 19th-century expression, as does education. The triumph of middle-class society means the triumph of education. It becomes the middle-class means, par excellence, of perpetuating its position in society. Schools provide access to the professions for the sons of the middle class, while at the same time providing social control of the masses. Education and the values associated with it become the social panacea of the 19th-century. Is it any wonder that the new mythology finds such widespread verbal and visual support; or that it is even romanticized?

Nor is it surprising, given the growth of middle-class ideology, that childhood and education should have become popular themes for 19th-century artists. Pedagogical portraiture found its adherents among artists of every style and movement, and it remained an enduring theme throughout the 19th-century. Many of the Romantics who normally painted epic and historical scenes have also given us educational portraiture. James Collinson, one of whose works we have already seen, belonged to the Pre-Raphaelite Brotherhood. Nor is there any lovelier depiction of education than the Impressionistic painting by Renoir of "Gabrielle and Coco Reading" (see Figure 9).

Figure 9

Of course, the educational genre doesn't exist in isolation, but as a corollary to the increased interest in domesticity as subject matter. The growth of family portraiture meant that artists became interested in every aspect of family life, including that activity of ever-increasing importance, education. The Louvre owns literally hundreds of canvases by 19th-century French artists devoted to domestic and educational subjects. Similarly, the catalogues of Professor Robert Alt of East Berlin, the world's leading iconologist of education, are filled with photographic copies and descriptions of 19th-century pedagogical scenes.[5]

With the growth of illustrated middle-class family magazines in every Western country after 1850, the theme of idealized education gained mass distribution. Although a complete analysis of these journals and their audience goes beyond the scope of this essay, a few examples should support the point. The *Gartenlaube,* for example, which dominated the family-periodical field in Germany, portrayed a pedagogical scene in its monthly masthead. Presumably the father is reading the *Gartenlaube* with his flock, but the pedagogical nature of the theme is clearly evident, as is the feeling of warmth that exists between adult and child. With the founding of illustrated American family magazines at the end of the century, the theme becomes too common to document. Even the advertising industry in its infancy grasped the possibility of using popular mythology as a visual marketing device. The theme has become a persistent one as well. The greatest 20th century visual mythologizer of American life, Norman Rockwell, has frequently employed this theme. His *Saturday Evening Post* cover of March 27, 1956, "Teacher's Birthday," provides the apotheosis of the educational genre. (see Figure 10).

What then happened to the older vision of education as an adversarial activity? Did it disappear entirely in face of the new blissful imagery? Did the cruel pedant and the tormented student become visually extinct? Where did they go? Of course, all of these educational images continued in the visual as well as the ideological realm, but they clearly became a secondary theme in serious depictions of education. The adversarial theme became largely archaic. The theme did not fall into disuse, however, but moved into a popular visual realm where it found new "vitality": that of caricature.

All good histories of caricature tell us that caricature, like satire, has a long and noteworthy history. Yet caricature, unlike satire, has rarely received the serious treatment it deserves. Standard histories of art seldom make more than passing references to it, although many of the great painters practiced caricature. Usually treated as a lesser accomplishment, it receives scant attention. Perhaps, from the perspective of the art historian, caricature does not have any greater significance. The art of visual mimicry and comic exaggeration strikes the scholar as frivolous and superficial, as a lesser achievement in purpose and execution. Only such undeniable masters of the genre as Goya and Daumier receive serious treatment. Generally, caricature is neglected by art historians.[6]

Figure 10

My purpose, however, is not to correct this omission, but to indicate the significance of this visual source to the cultural and social historian. First, the caricaturist usually intends to reach a large viewing public. In doing so, he sheds the elitist role assumed by most artists. This was true in the 16th century when Luther attacked the Pope through caricature for a largely illiterate following. It has remained true in the 19th and 20th centuries, with the growth of mass circulation periodicals and a large reading public. In distorting the features of prominent public figures, the political cartoonist intends his daily caricature to reach a far larger audience than the serious portrait painter. New methods of lithography introduced in the early 19th century especially enhanced this possibility.

Second, as a popular art, caricature must devote itself to popular themes and subjects. A grotesque rendering of an obscure subject or situation has no comic value, no matter how well it is accomplished. To have drawn a superb caricature of Jimmy Carter for a national publication before his presidential candidacy would have been a futile and fruitless exercise. Following Carter's initial primary electoral successes, caricaturists avidly competed with each other to capture the toothsome smile which became the hallmark of the Carter caricature. Employing only a few well-wrought lines and unable to use lengthy explanations, the caricaturist must find a widely known subject or theme.

Furthermore, the visual nature of caricature almost assures that the entire clientele of a publication will encounter it. One cannot make this assumption about articles, essays, and books, where circulation figures can be misleading. One can more readily assume that more of the highly literate subscribers of *The New Yorker* look at the cartoons (not all of which are caricatures, of course) than read all or any of the articles. For the historian, the popular nature of this art and its visibility become especially significant.

Returning to our original theme, we can see that the transfer of the adversarial teacher and students into the realm of caricature does not indicate a loss of popularity as a visual subject. This theme probably reached an even larger public. How the caricaturist treats the theme becomes the significant factor, i.e., with affection or hostility, benignly or with ill will. Caricature can convey either friendly or unfriendly feelings; it is seldom neutral, and it is usually not difficult to interpret the intention of the artist. With respect to portraying the teacher as the tormentor of his students and the students as sufferers, it is clear that almost all of the caricaturists of the 19th century picked up their pens in anger. They depicted a genre of teacher and a situation which their public knew as well and probably despised as strongly as they did. Several examples should illustrate the point.

Let us first consider the educational caricatures of Honore Daumier, an artist who occupies a prominent position in the history of French art in the 19th century. Daumier possessed an uncanny ability to capture facial expressions. He turned this skill on the continuing warfare between teachers and students in the mid 1840's. His published his savage lithographs in *Le Charivari,* a newly founded satirical journal. Each issue of the paper contained a full-page lithograph, which formed its chief attraction. Why, one might ask, would its chief contributor, Honore Daumier, choose education as the subject for so many of these drawings? Clearly the subject had broad appeal for the readers; it represented an area of intense public scrutiny.

His lithographs devoted to education, thirty-two in all, portray the teachers and overseers as pedants and social misfits. Frequently they bear pedagogical armaments, e.g., whips, hand slappers, etc. They have repugnant facial features and personal habits. In Figure 11, for example, we see a teacher about to use a hand slapper on a sullen student. Interestingly, the title of this drawing is "The Old Method." What a far cry

Figure 11

from the loving tutors being portrayed affectionately in other popular
journals. The oppressed students, of course, are waging constant warfare
against these repulsive teachers. In the lithographs of Daumier, the
students are usually triumphant.[7]

As noted, Daumier represents a rare instance of a caricaturist whose
fame has endured. Others, whose names are forgotten or lost, attacked
the "old methods" with equal vigor. In every country of Western Europe,
their satirical portrayals found a popular audience. Sometimes appearing
in the pages of the newly-emerging middle-class family magazines or
published in satirical collections, the classroom as a battleground became
an object of infamy. Even in the case of Joseph Lancaster's monitorial
schools, which gained great popularity in Europe and America in the
first decades of the 19th century, the harsh punishments prescribed by
Lancaster became the subject of vicious caricature. In a collection
published in Nuremberg in 1826, ironically titled *Teaching Methods and
Teachers (Die Padogogick und die Padogogen),* we find an especially
biting attack. In conjunction with rewards, Lancaster had described
several forms of punishment which could even be portrayed as cruel and
sadistic in his day. In Figure 12 we witness a visual assault on such Lancasterian innovations as the wooden shackle (lower left and right) and

the "hanging basket," which Lancaster prescribed and described as
"one of the most terrible that can be inflicted on boys of sense and
abilities."[8] Clearly, the artist was opposed to such methods even if Lancaster was not.

Figure 12

To summarize: popular imagery had changed by the beginning of the
nineteenth century. Dreamers and dream merchants conspired to create
scenes of loving tenderness where none had existed before. Of course, the
few examples presented above cannot conclusively prove my point; the
reader and viewer must accept the existence of hundreds of similar visual
representations. Nor should this thesis be misinterpreted: educational
brutality and warfare continued unabated in home and classroom.
Teachers flogged students, and students cringed in fear or rebelled in
anger, phenomena that now entered the world of frightful caricature and
fitful nightmares. The tensions produced by the gulf between the dream
and the nightmare must have caused considerable anguish. My aim,
however, has not been to describe the problems of a schizopedagogical
society. I have described the growth of a new educational mythology,
however fractured, its visual enshrinement, and the banishment of its
predecessor to a tabloid underworld where it continued to thrive.

FOOTNOTES

1. For an excellent recent example of the use of this methodology, see Stephen Brobeck, "Images of the Family: Portrait Paintings as Indices of American Family Culture, Structure, and Behavior, 1730-1860" in *The Journal of Psychohistory,* Vol. 5, No. 1 (Summer, 1977), pp. 80-106.

2. For a brief but excellent discussion of the history of art history see E. H. Gombrich, *Art and Illusion: A Study in the Psychology of Pictorial Representation* (Princeton, 1972), pp. 9-30. See also Erwin Panofsky, *Meaning in the Visual Arts* (Garden City, New York, 1955), for a discussion of iconology.

3. Philippe Aries, *Centuries of Childhood: A Social History of Family Life* (New York, 1962).

4. Estelle M. Hurll, *Child Life in Art* (Boston, 1906), Chapter I and pp. 65-84. See also Madge Garland, *The Changing Face of Childhood* (London, 1963), and Ursula Kellelhut, *Das Kind in der Kunst* (Leipzig, 1977).

5. Robert Alt, *Bilderatlas zur Schul- und Erziehungs Geschichte* in 2 volumes (Berlin, 1966 and 1971). Professor Alt's collection in East Berlin contains contact prints of more than 10,000 visual sources. Lloyd deMause, editor of *The Journal of Psychohistory,* owns a large personal collection of visual materials.

6. See Gombrich, *Art and Illusion,* Chapter X. Also C. R. Ashbee, *Caricature* (London, 1928), and Bohum Lynch, *A History of Caricature* (Boston, 1927).

7. Raymond Ricard, ed., *Teachers and Students* (Boston,1974). This work contains an excellent introduction and notes as well as 32 prints by Daumier on this theme.

8. Joseph Lancaster, "Improvements in Education as it Respects the Industrious Classes of the Community...," in Carl F. Kaestle, ed., *Joseph Lancaster and the Monitorial School Movement* (New York, 1973), p. 81.

VI

Reading, Writing, and the Acquisition of Identity in the United States: 1790-1860

— BARBARA FINKELSTEIN

*"We are not lumps of clay; and what
is important is not what people
make of us, but what we ourselves
make of what they have made of us."*
(Jean-Paul Sartre, *Saint Geist*)

This essay is designed to explore educational history as it reveals relationships between what is done to people and what it means to them, between what is externally imposed and what is subjectively experienced, between what is taught and what is learned. It represents an attempt to explore human consciousness as it was being organized, and as it developed as children learned to read and write in nineteenth-century America. Exploring learning environments in which children of rich and poor, slave and free, urbanites and ruralites acquired the rudiments of literacy, the essay is a first attempt to assess the capacity of four different groups of people to learn from educational experiences.

In all cultures and in any era, the acquisition of literacy involves children in what Walter Ong has characterized as a silent world of books and print.[1] As they learn to read and write, children are perforce withdrawn from face-to-face communities and compelled or seduced into environments which require them to process information as it is contained and organized in the visual world of books and print. Projected into a world of orderly structure and sequence, of fixed and contained culture, students experience a different sort of learning reality from that which is defined in personal, face-to-face communities. They can cultivate a capacity to "de-tribalize."[2] As they read and write, they can transcend, withdraw and re-evaluate moral and social imperatives that are nurtured in personal face-to-face communities.[3] Indeed, the acts of reading and writing provide for nothing less than the possibility of gaining autonomy, of defining a self as independent as well as part of social settings and emotional relationships.

The capacity and willingness of individuals to become autonomous, to transcend the moral and intellectual confines of face-to-face communities, to form individual judgments, to imagine new social possibilities, and to find distinct forms of self expression are importantly molded as they learn to read and write.

Children can acquire the rudiments of literacy in atmospheres where thrusts toward autonomy can either be approved or disapproved, organized or obliterated. They can learn to read and write in settings where the silent and fixed world of books is either cherished, ridiculed, or feared. They might be encouraged to engage the written world in psychological and social isolation, or in an atmosphere of communal conviviality.

By exploring the early experiences of children as they learned to connect the written with the spoken word, we can begin to speculate about the relationships between the acquisition of literacy and the cultivation of creativity and independent thinking—in short, about relationships between literacy and autonomy.

The experience of becoming literate was in no way uniform for children in nineteenth-century America. Learning to read and write organized at least four distinct sorts of psycho-educational realities, in which four distinct styles of self-expression were being cultivated. Indeed, at least four distinct emotional processes were underway as children learned to connect the world of the written word with the oral world of face-to-face communities.[4]

The first, which I will be describing as a *process of communal exposure,* involved children, such as those of modestly endowed farmers, in formal pedagogical settings both within households and in school settings outside the domestic orbit. Learning to read and write enclosed these children within environments that required communal exposure. For them, schooling and public exhibition proceeded simultaneously, and the written word was instantly incorporated into the face-to-face community of oral discourse.[5] The second route to reading and writing, which I am going to be calling a *process of obliterated selfhood,* involved children who attended large urban schools in a wrenching and abrupt removal from family and street into a school setting of relentless regulation and of intrusive control.[6] The third, a *process of domestic enclosure,* commonly initiated children of high-born Americans into a personal network of household relationships with parents, brothers, sisters, and other relatives.[7] The last, a *process of stolen selfhood,* defines the emotional reality that slaves appear to have experienced as they learned to read and write.[8]

PROCESS OF COMMUNAL EXPOSURE

Becoming literate in rural America did not typically involve children in a sustained or unrelenting withdrawal from adult company, nor from informal associations with friends and relatives. Whether they learned to read and write in intensely involved families where parents actually taught children to read and write themselves, in families where parents caused children to go to school, or where tutors were brought into households, the world of books was a sometime world. Learning to read and write were occasional activities for the young, proceeding during evenings or slack seasons—usually winters or summers.[9]

For rural children, learning to read and write constituted a process which embedded the written word in the oral-aural world of face-to-face communities. Within households, churches, and schools—wherever children acquired the rudiments of literacy—learning limited, if it could not suppress, individual expression; reflected, if it did not always advance, the rhetorical character of community life.

It was not unusual for children to begin to read as they were learning the catechism. By definition a verbal exchange, intended to structure dialogue between adult and child, catechetical teachings reflected a simultaneous commitment to the pedagogical virtues of oral communication and to the restraining possibilities of reading. Indeed children commonly learned to read and speak the Catechism in settings of religious and psychological austerity. Bronson Alcott, for example, born in Wolcutt, Connecticut in 1799, was dispatched at the age of four to his grandparents. In their household, efforts to become literate were part of the preparation for conversion. Catechisms were memorized and recited; prayers were constantly spoken. Descriptions of religious rituals, too, required the public expression of literary accomplishment. Autobiographies are suffused with descriptions of ritual readings. The experience of Frances Wayland, though he was city-bred, is nevertheless typical: "On the Lord's day, the rule of the family was for all the children to learn a hymn before dinner, and a portion of the Catechism ....The former was repeated to my mother; the latter to my father....After tea, at candle-lighting we were all assembled in the parlor; my father, or one of the older children read some suitable passage of scriptures."[10]

In less austere households, the tendency to communalize literacy was no less visible. In the household of Alice Kingsbury in Waterbury, Vermont, in the '30s, family prayer and Bible reading could be stopped for questions. In still other households, where learning to read the Bible and to chant the Catechism was systematically pursued, other social activities also reinforced the tendency to communalize the written word. As recorded in her diary, Caroline Cowle Richards read newspapers as well as recited the Catechism for her grandparents. In the household of Mary Austen, a prize of five dollars was awarded to the grandchild who could first complete the oral reading of the Bible. A teacher who had been hired by a Vermont family to teach their children in a nearby schoolhouse alternated the 107 long answers to the Catechism with a few poems, which she allowed the children to recite aloud.[11]

For the thousands of rural children who learned to read and write in schools rather than within households, the acquisition of literacy also involved them in a series of highly structured face-to-face encounters with teachers, parents, and classmates. Like their counterparts who learned to read and write primarily at home, children who acquired literacy in school became involved in a series of social events which were designed, however unconsciously, to socialize learning—to endow intellectual accomplishment with community meaning and to divert individuals from mere self-expression.

The buildings in which students acquired the rudiments were themselves typically reflections of the primarily oral, rather than visual, transmission of culture which proceeded within them. Before the 1860s, country schoolhouses resembled amphitheaters, with benches surrounding a central space housing either a teacher or a stove.[12]

Learning in country schools before 1860 consisted typically of a series of oral exercises. Students were asked to study a portion of a text, and were then called to the teacher to "say their lessons." The catechetical exercise—consisting of dialogues between students and teachers—also reinforced the communal orientation of pedagogy:

8. Q. How is the Art of Writing acquired?
    A. By learning to draw and combine six principal strokes.

9. Q. Is it needful to know what strokes these are?
    A. Yes, for unless we get a perfect idea of each separately, we can never write handsomely.[13]

Where students learned in classes or groups, they proceeded in choral form, the teacher acting as choirmaster. Speaking schools and spelling schools were universally described by observers and participants. They required students to display a capacity to read by "declaiming" a piece, by reciting selections from readers, by engaging in spelling contests—all reflected the oral orientation of the pedagogy. Writing, like reading, involved students in social presentations of their work. Instructed to copy phrases, words, sentences, they were rarely asked to compose. Writing was scarcely an occasion for individual self-expression. Rather, it became an opportunity to be social—to engage in the formation of letters that everyone could read together. Exercises in chanting or singing geography, like exercises in reading and spelling, were ultimately social. Students literally sang the capitals, populations, and main products of the states and nations—to the tune of the hickory stick, wielded, of course, by the teacher.[14]

The persistence and popularity of spelling and speaking exhibitions for which the entire community turned out also symbolize the importance of the community as a focus of intellectual expression. Student anxieties were commonly focused on Friday afternoon spelling and speaking matches—times of potential public humiliation or triumph.[15] End-of-term exhibitions also absorbed intellectual accomplishment into community rituals and provided occasion for communal get-togethers.

Whether children in the countryside learned to read and write at home or in school, they were constantly required to display two capacities—the capacity to memorize and the capacity to speak. They were not expected to question or criticize, to create or re-create meaning through the written word. Indeed, they were frequently punished for trying to do so. They were, instead, being provided with the twin intellectual props without which the oral transmission of culture is doomed. They were taught to remember and to talk, to become speakers of the word. Learning to read became, for rural children, a training in oral communication.

Although the process of learning to read and write involved country children in educational settings that discouraged self-expression and the use of the imagination, it did not, it seems, suppress them effectively. The autobiographical literature suggests that the children commonly used books to withdraw into imaginative worlds of their own creation. The pictures in primers not infrequently caught the fancies of imaginative children, even as they sat in class. Nor was it uncommon for children to retreat into fields to read novels—especially those that parents and teachers disapproved.[16] Though punishment frequently accompanied their efforts to use books to withdraw from communal involvements and responsibilities, students were not effectively repressed. The process of learning to read and write did not apparently require or nurture the obliteration of selfhood.

PROCESS OF OBLITERATED SELFHOOD

Different indeed were the experiences of children who learned to read and write in low-cost popular primary schools in the cities. Going to school projected these children into a pedagogical culture that effectively suppressed both the informality and the spontaneous character of oral communities. It was a culture in which the written word was used to detach children from the communities in which they had been reared.[17]

Whether they came to school occasionally, or systematically over the entire school year; whether they were sent by families who valued literacy or who were indifferent to it; whether they were boys or girls, six or sixteen years of age, city children who attended low-cost schools learned to read and write in an atmosphere of relentless regulation. It was an atmosphere designed to stamp out differences among individual students, to secure a rigid conformity to rules and regulations as dictated by teachers, to substitute the rule of law for the rule of personal persuasion, to disconnect children from networks of personal communication and engage them, instead, in a highly controlled world of books and print. For these children, learning to read and write constituted a process which detached the written world from the public world of face-to-face communication. As they entered school, they entered an isolating world in which teachers used the printed word to effect a psychological transformation in their students. The schoolroom was a place in which learning to be a student meant learning to withdraw from informal sociability and to present a prescribed self—to develop, in short, a public personality.

The systematic isolation of students from one another and from their families was expressed and accomplished through a series of regulations that distinguished the process of acquiring literacy in city schools from the process in country schools. Enclosed within a rigid world of regulated time and space, children in large urban schools were required to purge themselves of their individuality by incorporating the goals of the teachers as their own, by identifying themselves in relationships to pedagogical tasks, and by becoming "social personalities."[18]

Throughout the nineteenth century, teachers in low-cost urban schools sought to secure conformity not only by expelling disorderly students, delivering sermons, and physically overpowering recalcitrant students—as did their rural counterparts—but also by applying principles of military discipline to the classroom. Joseph Lancaster provided a model for countless teachers in the half-century before 1850, and exemplified the spirit of the typical urban teacher throughout the century. Lancaster provided for every minute of the day. The plans were symbolized by his declaration: "A place for everything and everything in its place."[19]

Lancaster arranged the instructional system so that students would at all times be responsible to a designated authority. There were monitors to take attendance, to keep order, to oversee recess, and to oversee each other. "The beauty of the system," remarked an English traveler, "is that nothing is trusted to the boy himself; he does not only repeat the lesson before a superior, but learns it before a superior...under the eye and command of a master."[20]

Not only did the monitorial system provide for a hierarchy of offices to which every student was bound by threat of physical or mental punishment, but Lancasterian masters enforced rules which proscribed every conceivable physical movement of the students as well. In effect, teachers forced students to suspend impulse and habit and made them derive standards of conduct from the will of the master. The elaborate and carefully enforced rituals were designed to substitute the mechanical and systematic for the spontaneous and unpredictable. Not only did students have to hang up their coats on signal, but they had to perform intellectuals tasks in proper physical form.

Opening exercises, for example, were conducted in this manner: "He [monitor] opens the door, rings the bell, and the scholars without, leave off their sports and pour into the school. They array themselves against the wall around the room as military companies, each class under its own monitor as captain..."[21]

Physical regulations were no less stringent during recitations:

> While reading, as the eye rises to the top of the right hand page, the right hand is brought to the position, with the forefinger under the leaf, the hand is slid down to the lower corner, and retained there during the reading of the page....This also is the position in which the book is to be held when about to be closed; in doing which the left hand, being carried up to the side, supports the book firmly and unmoved, while the right hand turns the part it supports over the left thumb... The thumb will then be drawn out between the leaves and placed on the cover; when the right hand will fall by the side.[22]

A student who attended a Lancasterian school in New York recalled that every boy had to have his "left palm enclosed in his right behind his back, in a sort of self-handcuffed state, and woe be to him who is not paying attention when the order is given, or is tardy in obeying it..." "Hadn't hands behind" was a significant offense in this school.[23]

The isolation of students continued unabated in non-Lancasterian urban schools, legion after 1850. Like their predecessors, teachers, who were now teaching in classes grouped by age, tended to identify the enforcement of physical ritual with the conformity to rules of whatever nature. Some observers from Baltimore admired this procedure in a New York school:

The regularity of their movements, their simultaneous enunciation, their young voices mingling in the melody of their childhood's songs....When they sing "Now we all stand up," they spring to their feet, the entire mass with apparently a single motion. When they sing "Now we all set down," they drop into their seats. "Now we fold our arms," all arms are folded. "Now we are nodding, nid, nid, nodding," the sea of little heads move to right and left....[24]

An anonymous critic of other New York City public schools interpreted what he saw in this way:

They sat, the girls on the one side and the boys on the other, each eye fixed upon the wall directly in front. There was no motion.... The rows of children, right and diagonal, were as regular as rows of machine-planted corn. A signal was given at which every face turned instantly, as though on a pivot, toward the face of the directress. She bade them good morning, and, in one breath, the whole school responded. At another signal every face swung back on its pivot to the original position....[25]

The observations, criticisms, and recollections of various writers all suggest that the physical uniformity symbolized in the opening exercises carried over to the classroom recitations. When a mathematics problem was proposed by the teacher, recalled one writer who described New York schools in the 1860s, "down would go all the slates and the work of ciphering would proceed...[A]s the work was completed...the slates would pop up against the breast, one after another; and when a boy was called upon to explain, up he would jump, rattle off his explanation, and then thump down again amongst the perfect stillness of the rest."[26]

The attempt to instill habits of obedience and conformity is most dramatically illustrated, perhaps, in a description written by Joseph Mayer Rice. In the New York City classroom which he described, the teacher had carried the passion for obedience and mechanical submission to regulations so far that she had confused them with the instructional task at hand:

During several daily recitation periods, each of which is from twenty to twenty-five minutes in duration, the children are obliged to stand on the line, perfectly motionless, their bodies erect, their knees and feet together, the tips of their shoes touching the edge of the board in the floor. The slightest movement on the part of the child attracts the attention of the teacher. The recitation is repeatedly interrupted with cries of "Stand straight," "Don't bend the knees," "Don't lean against the wall," and so on. I heard one teacher ask a little boy: "How can you learn anything with your knees and toes out of order?"[27]

In their effort to create a social personality in their students, teachers in cities relied more completely than did their rural counterparts on shame rather than muscle to control the behavior of their students. While humiliation was practiced in country schools—witness the omnipresence of dunce stools, fools' caps, squatting students—it was carried to its ultimate extreme in cities. In monitorial and non-monitorial schools alike, all aspects of student behavior were advertised, opened to public scrutiny. Not only was the relative academic standing of each student displayed in labeled rows, but achievement and failure lists were commonly published. It was not uncommon for urban teachers to involve whole classes in collective rituals of humiliation. A man who received the rudiments of literacy in a large monitorial school run by the Catholic Church in New York City in the '20s shuddered as he recalled this shaming punishment:

> ...two other "implements of culture" were called respectively the "fool's-cap" and the "hangman's-cap." The former was a kind of skull-cap, without a visor, which made a person look, and I presume, feel like a fool indeed. The Hangman's-cap jutted all over with indescribable angles and snaky curves... A boy, having the Fool's or Hangman's cap on, was marched...to the lower end of the hall and made to get up in the recess of one of the windows. The scholars were ordered to turn and face him. The master then gave the order, and the whole assemblage, with fingers pointed, commenced to deride and insult their school-mate in every conceivable manner, and to set up so horrible a hissing at him, that one might have thought this academic place had suddenly been turned into a serpentry of the whole Ophidian race...[28]

The systematic use of public humiliation, like the attempt to regulate every observable public movement, literally forced students to express themselves in a ritually prescribed fashion that was designed to suppress face-to-face, spontaneous communication of any sort.

Vigorous efforts to prevent eye contact among students were also designed to convert them from being sociable into being acceptable. To prevent eye contact among them, in the monitorial schools of the cities, masters literally forced students to look at the monitor and the textbook when they assumed their positions for recitation. Edward Austin Sheldon, a Boston schoolmaster in the '70s, described a school in which students who stood on the floor "had the attitudes of soldiers. They stood in a perfectly straight line, held books equidistant from their noses.'' And Joseph Mayer Rice made the following observations of a New York City teacher, whose principal had presided over the school since the mid '60s:

> All children in the room stare fixedly at a point on the blackboard. When material, of whatever nature, is handed to the children..[it] is then passed along sideways until each child in the row has been supplied. During this procedure the children are compelled to look straight in front of them, and to place their hands sidewise in order to receive the material, without looking whence it comes.[29]

Systematic efforts to isolate students from one another also took place in the form of a series of musical exercises, which emerged in large city schools during the century. Though orally conducted and sung in communal harmony, music exercises were impersonal in the extreme, requiring students to match their voices one to the other so as to be undifferentiated.

Unlike country schools, which were noisy in the extreme, silence characterized many well-run urban schoolrooms throughout the century. Indeed, the literature of school description is burdened with both praise and censure of teachers who successfully commanded silence.

The tendency to draw students away from familiar communities and to impersonalize communication is also reflected in the nature of relationships between families and schools in the cities. Neither hiring nor firing teachers, attending or participating in communal activities focused around literacy, meetings between parents and teachers were formalized. Homework and report cards rather than exhibitions and spelling matches were the connecting links between home and school.[30] Individual rather than communal, impersonal rather than personal, schooling for children of the middling poor did not tie literacy to familiar communal settings.

There is a final thing to be said about the acquisition of literacy as it occurred in large urban schools. It appears to have conferred a sense of powerlessness, required the submergence of individual consciousness, of individuality, and created a social personality called "student." Of all the settings in which literacy was acquired, this one was the most profoundly isolating. Small wonder that there is a paucity of autobiographical recollection, and that particpants have left us few written records describing their efforts to learn to read and write. Learning to read and write literally required these children to withdraw from meaningful social communities.

PROCESS OF DOMESTIC ENCLOSURE

For children of the high-born—a term I am using loosely to describe families of wealthy merchants, even evangelical Protestants, judges, lawyers, doctors, and publishers—becoming literate commonly proceeded within the household. Less likely than country children of modest means or children of the laboring poor to acquire the rudiments of literacy at school or from friends, high-born children were, instead, enclosed within a network of domestic relationships with mothers, fathers, tutors, and family friends.

For these children, the family defined, organized, managed—indeed, constituted—the community within which they were to acquire the rudiments of learning and the adornments of language. There is evidence suggesting that parents systematically withheld children from outside educational agents, preferring, instead, to exercise near-total personal control over the nature and substance of their children's early education. A goodly portion of the *Autobiography* of Charles Francis Adams is given over to lamentations over his father's decision to withhold him from schools and to pick his tutors, his books, and his companions for him. Other autobiographies, too, document a widespread disposition to avoid public, i.e., extra-domestic, schooling in the early years of learning.[31]

Yet another reflection of the tendency to enclose children within a domestic web as they learned to read and write was the systematic censorship of certain books. Fearing the effects of a burgeoning metropolitan vulgarity, high-born parents commonly censored books, protecting their children from what they believed to be dangerous and vulgar social fare. In the household of Andrew Dickson White, for example, novels and romances were regarded as unfit for children and were kept under lock and key. The Griscom family, too, limited their library to religious books. Young John had to plead with his father to get a copy of *Aesop's Fables*. Bronson Alcott's parents celebrated the Sabbath not only by special praying, but by closeting all books except the *Bible, Pilgrim's Progress,* and *Baxters.*[32]

Learning to read and write commonly involved children of affluence in a series of intense emotional relationships with their parents. Often fed, clothed, and otherwise nurtured by servants or young relatives—adults other than parents—educational tasks commonly composed the principal substance of parent-child relationships. This reality may have led the son of Joanna Bethune, the New York philanthropist, to define his inheritance in educational rather than material or social terms.[33]

For high-born children, the acquisition of literacy involved them in daily face-to-face communication with parents. Austerity, isolation, and the anxiety of public trial did not characterize their attempts to master the world of visual symbols. Mary Austen, for example, learned the alphabet in her kitchen. For her, the letter "i" evoked the scene of her mother kneading bread and of her brother doing his alphabet. The mother of Isaac Roberts, Dean of the College of Agriculture at Cornell, taught her children in the 30s and 40s to read and figure while she sat at the big fireplace knitting stockings, socks, or mittens. The kitchen became a schoolroom, with older brothers or sisters helping the younger. James Burrill Angell, later to become president of the University of Michigan, learned the alphabet with his grandfather, as together they read the great letters in his father's old law books. And George Putnam of the publishing house Putnams identified reading with motherhood and with other educational amusements over which she presided.[34]

Learning to read enclosed children in a world of personal and private relationships. The capacity to read and write was rendered immediately sociable through a near-instant incorporation of the printed word into the face-to-face culture of the household. Indeed, family rituals commonly reflected, expressed, and advanced a love of the culture of books, and an affection for the social uses of the mind. "In the little home world, my mother filled the largest place," remembered Henry Cabot Lodge. "She was a great reader, and from earliest years associated in my mind with reading and a love of books."[35] Hapgood Hutchins, too, recalled ritual readings happily:

> The best part of my definite education I received at home. Beyond all civilizing influences was my mother's reading of Shakespeare....I think I could not have been more than five or six years old when she first read *Hamlet*....In the evenings the whole family gathered in the spacious parlor and there my mother read an act or two of one of the great plays....These readings of my mother educated, charmed, and soothed me....He [Shakespeare] was an epoch of experience to me and not a book.[36]

Within the family of Alfred Victor Dupont, French was spoken and journals were read. And Henry Cabot Lodge had these literary recollections of his father: "My father was very fond of Cervantes, and I early became familiar with Don Quixote....[I]n my tenth year I read all the Waverly novels from beginning to end...I also devoured eagerly all the children's books of the time."[37] Even Abigail Alcott, Bronson's unjustly ignored wife, herself a high-born woman, carried on a tradition of ritual family readings: "...one of our number...would read aloud while the mother and the two elder daughters sewed. Thus we read Scott, Dickens, Cooper, Hawthorne, Shakespeare, and the British poets."[38]

Writing, like reading, became a vehicle for domestic communication. Unlike their counterparts in the countryside, children of the high-born

used their handwriting skills as vehicles of self-expression, as well as occasions to display "a fine hand." Children commonly kept journals and
diaries and wrote poetry, essays, and plays. Writing letters to various
members of the family became a form of communication within these
households.[39] Bronson Alcott, an unusually attentive father, constantly
sent letters combining affection and admonition to his daughters. To
Louisa, on her eighth birthday, he wrote: "Be like Jesus and please your
father. Try in all your resolutions to mind what that silent teacher in your
breast says to you...A birthday is a good time to begin to live anew."
Sometimes he was more specific. To Elizabeth, age five, he wrote: "You
make us very happy every time I look at your smiling face, and make us
sorry every time I see your face look unpleasant."[40] Letters between
parents and children who were separated from each other for one reason
or another also reflect a commitment to the written word as a vehicle of
self-expression and of intergenerational communication. Not infrequently a tool of social discourse, girls prepared invitations, menus, notes and
the like.[41]

Conversations, arguments, and discussions also involved the incorporation of the written word into daily face-to-face activity. The
autobiographical literature is suffused with recollections of political
discussions revolving around newspaper articles, with theological discussions of sermons and/or portions of scripture, and with instructive
dialogue organized around readings of novels, poetry, and the like.

This sort of household culture probably accounts for the high esteem
in which hearthside education was held by some foreign travelers,
domestic observers, and childrearing advisors.[42] Even the children's
playmates recognized the literary quality of parent-child relationships.
"You don't know how much I gained educationally from going to lunch
with you and hearing your father talk,"[43] remarked a friend of Eliza
Kingsbury. One son, whose differences with his father led him to leave
home, nonetheless "respected him for his wide range of reading and love
of knowledge. He was, in his demonstrative moments, one of the most
cultivated and delightful companions I have ever known."[44]

Translated almost immediately into a language of oral discourse, the
universe of visual symbols was inextricably introduced into relationships
between parents, children, relatives, and friends. As they re-created, re-
imagined and structured the visual world of books and newspapers in
their efforts to become literate, children in high-born families combined
literacy and sociability, merged the worlds of visual and oral discourse,
and became part of a self-contained, exclusive culture of literacy. The
culture was one in which the formality of visual symbols merged with
and qualified the informality of face-to-face communication, and where
the content of books and other visual media was consistently subject to
individual judgment, creating a unique and exclusive world of verbal

discourse.

It is interesting to note that the culture of literacy as it proceeded within the households of the high-born was not necessarily reflected in the behavior of tutors or of teachers when high-born children had to go to school. Henry Cabot Lodge's first book-connected whipping occurred when, at age 11, he went to Mr. Sullivan's school. The shadow of a fool's cap lingers over Samuel Pennypacker's recollection of a tutor-governess. Hutchins Hapgood recalled that home provided, in his opinion, his only education. "At school, occupations were fighting, whispering and trying to avoid meaningless work." At the little dame school she attended, Alice Kingsbury recalled, girls were hit on the shoulder with whale bones, and boys were hit, harder, with rulers.[45] It is hardly any wonder that boarding schools became important educational vehicles after 1850 for high-born children who had mastered the fundamentals. A major aim of the boarding school, according to James McClachlan, has been to preserve the innocence of childhood in a setting removed from the corrupting temptation of street and city.[46] Boarding schools could extend, advance, and sophisticate the unique verbal world in which children of the high-born acquired the rudiments of literary distinction.

The same characterization that Lawrence W. Levine has made of a black secular song seems equally applicable to the process of becoming literate in high-born society. "It allowed individuals to express themselves communally and individually, to derive great aesthetic pleasure, to perpetuate traditions, to keep values from eroding, and to begin to create new expressive modes." High-born literacy, like black secular songs, revealed a culture which kept large elements of its own autonomous standards alive, and which continued a rich internal life.[47] Unlike black secular songs, however, literary culture of the high-born set standards for others to imitate and pursue.

PROCESS OF STOLEN SELFHOOD

For slaves, learning to read and write engaged them in a kind of emotional and social no-man's-land into which few, understandably, were willing to enter. Unlike most children living in the United States in the first half of the nineteenth century, slave children were typically enclosed within a world where the transmission of culture proceeded almost completely through the spoken word. In the world created by the slaves, the consciousness of children was being formed within a community that maintained integrity, coherence, and solidarity by creating what Lawrence W. Levine has called "a sacred world." It was a world that enabled slaves to transcend the one in which they were forced to live, simultaneously creating a meaningful, richly expressive, psychological and moral reality. The sacred world of black slaves was contained, reflected, and transmitted in song and tale, through prayer and dance, in cabins and in fields, both day and night.[48] Participation in the expressive culture of Afro-American slaves did not require literacy, though there is evidence suggesting that the ability to read and write was both respected and supported within the slave community.

If the acquisition of literacy was not a requirement for participation in the sacred world of slaves, it certainly promised no integration ino the world of power that was inhabited and controlled by slave-holding whites. Indeed, the desire and the ability to read and write were vigorously and forcefully punished, especially after 1835, when the last of the prohibitions on literacy were made into law. Like visiting a relative on another plantation, or running away, learning to read and write was a punishable offense. Wherever slaves attempted to acquire the rudiments of literacy, they courted danger and invited punishment. Narratives commonly contain recollections of beatings that were administered when slaves were caught trying to read or write. "De White folks didn't 'low us even to look ata book. Dey would scol' an' sometimes whup us efen dey caught us and our head in a book!" "I shall never forget my first attempts to learn to spell...," recalled Josiah Henson, alleged role model for Uncle Tom. "I was thirteen years of age when I nearly lost my life because I made an effort to gain this kind of knowledge." Finding Hanson with a spelling book in the apple orchard, his master beat him over the head, saying, "I'll teach you to get apples...for such a vile purpose. Give me that book." Henson says that he failed to open a book again until he was forty-two. "Who taught you how to write...?" asked the master of Octavia Albert. "...An educated Nigger is a dangerous thing, and the best place for him is six feet underground, buried face foremost." The owner of Frederick Douglass, too, became outraged when he found out that Douglass was learning to read. "Learning will spoil the best Nigger in the world." Being sold away for reading and writing apparently was not regarded as an idle gesture, and the narratives are suffused with the fear of literacy detection.[49]

Enclosed in a community which incorporated individuals, transmitted culture, and defined tolerable psychological and moral reality through the powers of speech and hearing, slave children had no need of literacy in order to fully participate in the world that the slaves made. Controlled from the outside by people who limited, if they could not entirely suppress, access to the world of printed and visual symbols, slave children were prohibited from translating literary skills into meaningful economic or political action. It is hardly surprising to find that a relatively small percentage of slaves had learned to read and write before emancipation.[50]

For slaves who decided to try to master the written world, and engage the world of books and print, learning to read and write reorganized their relationships to the communities both of masters and of fellow slaves. The acquisition of literacy commonly required withdrawal, at least for a time, from social relationships. Acquiring the rudiments was, for slaves, an essentially solitary process carried on in secret, in special places and during in-between times—away from the communal noise of quarters, the rigors of work, and the punitive advances of masters.[51]

Only rarely did children acquire the rudiments of literacy from parents, or from schools carried on secretly in cabins, or from masters, mistresses, or ministers willing to risk legal penalties.[52] Narratives suggest that slaves who learned to read were, perforce, skilled in the art of "stealing time." Listening at schoolroom doors, talking friends into helping them, attaching themselves to people able and willing to instruct, helping themselves to books from the masters' library, attending closely to Bible readings, they learned to read and write by stealth, and essentially in isolation. For Peter Randolph, who learned letters from a friend, learning to read involved him in a shuttle from a church door, where he listened to a white preacher read a text, to home, where he labored over a Bible, matching spoken sermons to visual symbols. Nettie Henry, a Mississippi slave, also labored her way to literacy, explaining to her children the proper procedure: "...de same words in dis book what's in de Bible...larn 'em de way de is fixed...dem de firs' thing you know you can read the Bible." Similarly, William Hayden, a Virginia slave, picked up leaves of a spelling book and learned to read the Bible by matching sounds and letters. Storing paper in secret places and cabins, Octavia Albert learned to read and write in social isolation. "I used almost constantly to carry a copy of Webster's spelling book in my pocket, and when sent on errands, when play was allowed me, I would step aside...and take a lesson in spelling." A hat was a popular place in which to hide a book, and the narrative literature contains several accounts of slaves who dropped into orchards, bushes, cabins, forests, and swamps to catch a word or two.[53]

If learning to read and write required slaves to remove themselves from the centers of community activity, their isolation was neither total, nor, as it had been for urban children, necessarily alienating. Rather, there is evidence suggesting that they used literary skills to expand, enhance, dignify, and deepen the sacred world in which slave consciousness dwelled. Indeed, literacy among slaves before the Civil War was a means of verification and reinforcement of the psychological and moral meaning of the sacred world.[54] Rather than diluting the predominance of the oral tradition—a process which was well underway by the twentieth century—literacy actually became an instrument of community enrichment prior to emancipation.

There is evidence suggesting that the drive to acquire literacy reflected a desire to draw close to centers of community and belonging, to incorporate the sacred world into the rigors of daily life ever more completely. Harriet Jacobs identified and described the melding of the sacred and the daily in this recollection:

> I knew an old black man, whose piety and childlike trust in God were beautiful to witness...He had a most earnest desire to learn to read. He thought he should learn how to serve God better if he could only read the Bible. He came to me, begged me to teach him to read...After asking if he knew that slaves were whipped for teaching each other to read he still wanted to. He thought he would come three times a week...I selected a quiet nook...and there I taught his A, B, C....As soon as he could spell in two syllables he wanted to spell out words in the Bible. The happy smile that illuminated his face put joy into my heart. After spelling out a few words, he paused and said, "Honey, it 'pears when I can read dis good book I shall be nearer to God....I only wants to read dis book, dat I may know how to live; den I hab no fear 'bout dyin.''[55]

Other narratives, too, document the identification of literacy with religious expression. Peter Randolph, the only literate slave on a Virginia plantation of eighty-one other slaves, was inspired to read by religious sentiment. For eleven years he labored to master the rudiments:

> I became impressed that I was called to God to preach to other slaves...But then I could not read the Bible...A friend showed me the letters and how to spell words of three letters. Then I continued until I got so as to read the Bible—the source of all knowledge. It was my desire to read easily this book. I thought it was written by the almighty himself. I loved this book, and prayed over it and labored until I could read it.[56]

"Education...," recalled John Thompson, a fugitive slave who was reared on a Maryland plantation, "was one of my greatest blessings. Through this, I have been able to read the word of God, and thereby learn the way of salvation." "My father learned to read, so that he could enjoy the priceless privilege of searching the Scriptures," recalled Samuel Reingold Ward.[57]

The capacity to read the word of God appears to have focused and occasioned close relationships between adults and children. Indeed, the narrative literature suggests that reading, religiosity, and domestic harmony were inextricably related. "It was with great delight," recalled a North Carolina slave in the early part of the century, that her mother heard the Bible read by her son. "It was the highest pleasure she had ever known."[58]

That Bible reading organized a sense of domestic felicity is evident in recollections which tied motherhood, literacy, and religious sentiment inextricably together. Recalling the efforts of his mother to encourage him to read, one slave recalled this explanation: "Look to Jesus and that he who protected the widow and fatherless would also take care of me." In the memoirs of Josiah Henson, Bible reading and maternal concern were linked.[59]

The fact that literate slaves commonly led prayer services held secretly in slave quarters at night also suggests that the capacity to read and write had community focus. As sources of Biblical inspiration, as mediators of Biblical injunctions, literate slaves were incorporated into the center of slave community life.[60]

If learning to read enabled literate slaves to enhance the sacred world of religion, to draw closer to parents, to inform communal activity, and otherwise to submerge themselves in the face-to-face world of the quarters, literacy had other functions as well. Indeed, it enabled slaves to extricate themselves from the enveloping web or oral community and to imagine an earthly future that was profoundly different from the one they were experiencing.

The acquisition of literacy and the capacity to read and write organized a particular sort of political self-consciousness. It was a consciousness that enabled slaves to project an earthly future in which blacks and whites would relate on a more nearly equal political footing. It was not unusual for slaves who learned to read and write to recall periods of time when their relationships with whites were relationships of companionship rather than subordination. Indeed, it was the issue of literacy itself which commonly focused power realities for young slaves. Lunsford Lane, who grew up on a North Carolina plantation, described his surprise at unequal treatment: "When I began to work, I discovered the difference between myself and my master's white children.... They were learning to read, while I was not permitted to have a book in my hand.... They had learned to read, while in me it was an offense." A Virginia slave, James Williams, also associated reading and writing with a conscious recognition of his subordinate status. Of his boyhood friend, he recalled: "I was his playmate and constant associate in childhood. I used to go with him to his school, and carry his books for him, and meet him there when school was dismissed. We were very fond of each other....He taught me the letters of the alphabet, and I should soon have acquired a knowledge of reading, had not George's mother discovered her son in the act of teaching me."[61] The narrative literature suggests the presence of a kind of omnipresent anger that was kindled in the hearts and minds of slaves as they were learning to read and write.

Not unexpectedly, we find that slaves used their abilities to read and write in a series of efforts to subvert and evade the law. They used literacy to effect control over their lives and to extend their freedom in a variety of creative ways. Some used the ability to write to fashion passes for themselves and for fellow slaves, enabling them to become geographically mobile, to visit friends and family on nearby plantations or towns, without harassment from white patrols who were placed in charge of rounding up unaccounted-for slaves.[62] Others, like Louis Hughes, knew that writing was the ultimate key to liberation, and forged their own passes to freedom. Facilitating contact with abolitionist sentiment as it was contained in newspapers and pamphlets, literacy not only inspired, directed, and encouraged slaves to run away, but presented an alternative view of life for blacks on this earth.[63] Indeed, reading and writing enabled slaves to imagine an earthly as well as a sacred world in which black dignity was a reality.

Nurtured in two worlds—one that was hostile to slave literary efforts, the other in which literacy was valued but not necessary—learning to read and write constituted an act of self-assertion, a courageous assertion of independence, a strike for identity that was without precedent in nineteenth-century America. No wonder that so many freed men rushed, as Harriet Beecher Stowe had remarked, "not for the grog shop but for the schoolroom."[64] Literacy enriched the special moral and psychological worlds of slaves, as well as advancing their position in the economic and political centers of the nation. It is hardly surprising that they poured into classrooms after emancipation.

Becoming literate was in no way a uniform experience for children in nineteenth-century America. Carried on in a multiplicity of institutional settings, in a plurality of cultural environments, and in the presence of overwhelming social difference, the process of becoming literate organized various sorts of realities for nineteenth-century children.

For the progeny of the high-born, the acquisition of literacy involved them in an exclusive domestic and social circle, in which was reflected and advanced a distinctive sort of social presence. For this group, the acquisition of literacy and the manipulation of words and ideas proceeded simultaneously. As they learned to read and write, they were required to cultivate the capacity to retrieve the written word, and to place it in the service of social and political persuasion and subjective imagination. Required to practice the arts of criticizing, arguing, persuading, and exhorting, in close proximity to their parents, high-born male children were learning how to acquire influence, and to keep it. High-born female children were learning the delights of escape into literature.

Like the high-born, slave children, too, were acquiring a daily knowledge of political reality as they learned to read and write. Unable to depend on their parents or on schools to sustain and transmit knowledge of the written word, slave children learned to identify literacy and independence. Through the lonely, secret process of "stealin' " an education, they were able to enhance their private psychological worlds, and in some small ways to manipulate the economically and politically oppressive reality into which they were born. As unambiguously voluntary students, learning to read and write focused in them a fierce commitment to self-expression.

For students who learned to read and write in schools, the process of acquiring literacy was not as unequivocally liberating as it was for the very rich and the very lowly. In both the country and the city, students were required to memorize and declaim, to imitate and reproduce texts, to repeat rather than formulate ideas, to recite rather than criticize a piece. As both of these groups of children learned to read and write, they were learning to associate book-learning with the exercise of adult authority. In the cities, however, children entered large schools carrying different sorts of social, religious, ethnic, and psychological baggage. Within classrooms they were confronted by a uniform set of pedagogical circumstances in which they were required to obliterate their individuality. As they learned to read, these urban children were learning to suspend judgment, to obey instantly, to read and write unwittingly, to derive standards of conduct from rules and regulations imposed by teachers. Paradoxically, the opportunity to learn represented an opportunity to engage in a network of restraining regulations and impersonal relationships with adults and friends. For these students, schooling and thoughtlessness were closely identified. If some were able to use the ability to read and write creatively, it was not because their schooling had taught them how. Unlike their urban counterparts, children in country schools did not learn to read and write in an atmosphere of unrelenting impersonal regulation. Although they too were required to memorize and declaim, to imitate and reproduce, they were not asked to look the same, stand the same, sit the same, or recite "in one voice." Required to socialize learning by turning it periodically into group play, country children were learning to equate books with communal conviviality as well as with personal restraint, and, in the process, learning to separate themselves from their communities.

FOOTNOTES

The research for and writing of this essay was facilitated by an Independent Fellowship from the National Endowment for the Humanities.

I would like to thank Dominic Cavallo and Judith Plotz for excellent criticisms and suggestions. A preliminary draft was presented at the International Psychohistorical Association Convention, June 8, 1978.

1. Walter J. Ong, *Interfaces of the Word.* (Ithaca: 1977), *passim.*
2. Marshall McLuhan, *The Gutenberg Galaxy: The Making of Typographic Man*

(Toronto: 1962); Ong. Ibid; *The Presence of the Word* (New Haven: 1967).

3. Ong, *Ibid; Knowledge and the Future of Man* (New York: 1968); *Rhetoric, Romance and Technology* (Ithaca: 1973).

4. These four processes emerged in the course of examining literally hundreds of autobiographies. For a basic list, see: Barbara Finkelstein, "Schooling and School-teachers: Selected Bibliography of Auto-biographies in the Nineteenth Century," *History of Education Quarterly* XIV (Summer, 1974), pp. 292-300; see also Federal Writers Project, W.P.A. *Slave Narratives,* Library of Congress Mss division.

   The effort to explore the educational process as it was experienced by students involves the historian in some interesting methodological problems. Forced to rely on autobiographies, diaries, observations of social critics, or, as in the case of illiterate slaves, on the narratives of agents of the W.P.A., it is necessary to advance generalizations cautiously. There is a kind of particularity in the experience of individuals as they acquire literacy. Recognizing that no two families, no matter how apparently similar, behave in precisely the same way, it is nonetheless possible to tease out patterns of behavior and ranges of attitudes. Relying on about one hundred reminiscences and an assortment of advice literature, and involving slaves in this analysis, I have tried to represent a socioeconomic range of Protestant sentiment and behavior, recognizing, of course, the limitations inherent in using subjective sources.

5. For a comprehensive list, see Finkelstein Bibliography, *Loc. Cit.*

6. *Ibid.*

7. For examples, see footnotes attached to analysis of high-born literacy below. A splendid unpublished paper of Bertram Wyatt-Brown also explores parent-child relationships in evalengical families.

8. Oral histories collected by W.P.A. Federal Writers Project as well as dozens of slave narratives and autobiographies constitute the substance of the documentation for this portion of the essay. See footnotes below.

9. For examples see: Julia Tevis, *Sixty Years in a School-Room; An Autobiography of Mrs. Julia A. Tevis* (Cincinnati: 1978), p. 55; in Kentucky; John Dean Caton, "Memoirs and Observations of John Dean Caton," Library of Congress Mss. Collections, The John Dean Letters, 1870; in New York State; William Dean Howells, *A Boy's Town* (New York: 1904), Flo V. Knisely Menninger, *Days of My Life: Memories of a Kansas Mother and Teacher* (New York: 1939) pp. 21; 119 in Kansas; Fassett Allen Cotton *Education in Indiana: 1793-1934* (Bluffton, Indiana: 1934), p. 28; Eli M. Rapp, "The Eight-Cornered School-Building at Sinking Spring," *Transactions of the Historical Society of Berks County 11* (1905-1909), pp. 213-33; Eli M. Rapp, "The Eight-Cornered School-house at Sinking Spring," *Ibid.,* p. 221.

10. Amos Bronson Alcott as quoted in Clara Gowing, *The Alcotts as I Knew Them* (Boston: 1909), p. 46. See also: Benjamin Rush, "Letter to his Son James," in Valentine, Alan, Ed., *Father to Sons: Advice Without Consent* (Norman, Oklahoma: 1963) p. 91; Lyman Beecher, *The Autobiography of Lyman Beecher* in Two Volumes (Cambridge: 1961) p. 104; Mary Peabody Mann, ed., *Life of Horace Mann.* (Washington, D.C.: 1937), Vol. IV, p. 136; Amos Bronson Alcott, *Memoirs...*(Boston: 1915), pp. 16-23. Francis Wayland and H. L. Wayland, *A Memoir of the Life and Labors of Francis Wayland* (New York: 1972), p. 15. *Conversations on the Memoirs of Pious Children* (Philadelphia: 1837), p. 7.

11. Alice E. Kingsbury, *In Old Waterbury: The Memoirs of Alice E. Kingsbury* (Waterbury: 1942); *Diary of Caroline Cowles Richards, 1852-1872* (New York: 1908) p. 14; Mary Austen, *Earth Horizon* (Boston: 1932), p. 67; Lucia B. Downing, "Teaching the Keeler District School," *Vermont Quarterly, A Magazine of History,* Ns. XIX, 4 (Oct. 1951), pp. 233-40.

12. Henry Barnard, *American Journal of Education,* all *volumes, passim;* See also, Autobiographical source in Finkelstein Bibliography of Autobiographies, *Loc. Cit.*

13. Barbara Finkelstein, "The Moral Dimension of Pedagogy,R' *American Studies* (Fall, 1974), pp. 79-89, "Governing the Young: Teacher Behavior in Popular Primary Schools in the United States: 1820-1880" (Unpublished dissertation, Teachers College, Columbia University, 1970) Chapters 1 and 2.

14. *Ibid.,* Chapters 1 and 2.

15. Barbara Finkelstein, "In Fear of Childhood: Relationships Between Parents and Teachers in Popular Primary Schools in the Nineteenth Century," *The History of Childhood Quarterly,* III, 3 (Winter, 1976) pp. 327-28; For particularly graphic descriptions, see: New England: "Common Schools of Connecticut," *American Annals of Education and Instruction,* II (April 15, 1839), p. 249; John Howard Redfield, *Recollections...* (n.i., 1900) p. 56; for the West: Carpenter, *op. cit.* p. 77; Howells, *op. cit.,* p. 42; Enoch Edwin Byrum, *Life Experiences* (Anderson, Indiana: 1928), p. 35; James Langdon Hill, *My First Years as a Boy* (Andover: 1927) pp. 99-100. Middle States: William Summers "Early Public Schools of Norristown," Historical Society of Montgomery County Pennsylvania *Proceedings,* VI (1929), p. 351; South: John Lewis Herring, *Saturday Night Sketches; Stories of Old Wiretrass Georgia* (Boston: 1918), p. 33; George Clark Rankin, *The Story of My Life, Or More Than a Half-Century As I Lived It* (Nashville: 1912), p. 40; Felton, *op. cit.,* p. 59; Killits, *op cit.,* p. 367; Clinkscales, *op. cit.,* p. 90.

16. The autobiographical literature is suffused with imaginative uses of literacy. For examples, see: *Alcott Memoirs, Posthumously Compiled from Papers, Journals and Memorabilia of the Late Frederick L. H. Willis,* (Boston: 1915), pp. 16-17; For other examples, see Rachael Q. Buttz, *A Hoosier Girlhood* (Boston: 1934), p. 54; See also Calvin Coolidge, *The Autobiography of...* (New York: 1929), p. 30 Clara Harlowe Barton, *The Story of my Childhood* (New York: 1907), pp. 27-28.

17. Sentiment of this sort suffuses in the literature of school reform as well as in school committee reports in the cities. See for example: Boston Association of Masters of the Public Schools, *Remarks in the Seventh Annual Report of the Honorable Horace Mann,* Secy. of the Mass. Board of Education (Boston, n.i., 1844) Baltimore Commissioners of Education Reports of 1835-38 (Baltimore: 1838); see also the sections involving Immigrants, in Sol Cohen, *Education in the United States,* pp. 991-99; Schools for the Poor, pp. 975-90. For secondary works see: Michael B. Katz, *The Irony of Urban School Reform: Educational Innovation in Nineteenth Century Massachusetts* (Cambridge: 1968); Stanley K. Schultz, *The Culture Factory: Boston Public Schools 1789-1860* (New York, 1973); David B. Tyack, *The One Best System: A History of Urban Education* (New York, 1974). We should note that schools from children of wealthier families resembled country schools, engaging students in a process of communal exposure.

18. Barbara Finkelstein, "Pedagogy as Intrusion: Teaching Values in Popular Primary Schools in Nineteenth-Century America," *History of Childhood Quarterly,* 2 (Winter, 1975), 349-78.

19. Joseph Lancaster, *The British System of Education. Being the epitome of the improvements and inventions practiced by Joseph Lancaster: to which is added a Report of the Trustees of the Lancaster School at Georgetown, Columbia* (Washington: Joseph Milligan, 1812); Joseph Lancaster *The Lancasterian System of Education with Improvements by Its Founder* (Baltimore: published for the author, 1821), p. 4. The sources around which this discussion of Lancasterian schools turn portray schools in eastern cities—New York, Philadelphia, Washington, Baltimore, Pittsburgh. But there is guidance to suggest that monitorial schools in cities further west resembled those of the eastern metropolises. Civic leaders from places such as Cincinnati and

136 BARBARA FINKELSTEIN

Lexington dispatched men to study schools in Baltimore, Philadelphia, New York, and Boston. Richard C. Wade, *The Urban Frontier, The Rise of Western Cities, 1790-1830* (Cambridge: Harvard University Press, 1959), pp. 105-125. Articles appear frequently in the *American Annals of Education and Instruction* that describe the progress made by western cities in establishing monitorial schools.

Allusions to Lancasterian schools can also be found in other periodicals. See for examples: *American Journal of Education 1826-1830; Western Academician and Journal of Education and Science;* The Joseph Lancaster Papers, located in the American Antiquarian Society in Worcester, Massachusetts, also contain references to Lancasterian schools in many cities.

Manuals, prepared by Masters of Lancasterian schools in particular locations, too, indicate their omnipresence. See for example: William Dale, *A Manual of the Albany Lancasterian School* (Albany: n.i., 1820); There are also monographs which describe the development of Lancasterian schools. See: Charles Calvert Ellis, *Lancasterian Schools in Philadelphia* (Philadelphia: n.i., 1907); John Franklin Reigart, *The Lancasterian System of Instruction in the Schools of New York City* (New York: Teachers College, Columbia University Press, 1916); Several other historians allude to the prsence of Lancasterian schools in particular states. See for examples: Moses Edward Ligon, *A History of Public Education in Kentucky* (Lexington: University of Kentucky Press, 1942), p. 33; Charles Lee Coon, *North Carolina Schools and Academies: 1790-1840: A Documentary History* (Raleigh: Edwards and Broughton Printing Company, 1915), pp. 722-45; William Arthur Maddox, *The Free School Idea in Virginia Before the Civil War* (New York City: Teachers College, 1915).

20. Joseph Lancaster, *The Lancasterian System of Education with Improvements by Its Founder* (Baltimore: Published for the Author, 1821), *passim.*
    Quoted in Paul Monroe, *Founding of the American Public School System: A History of Education in the United States* (New York: The Macmillan Company, 1940) p. 369.
21. "My School-Boy Days in New York City Forty Years Ago," *New York Teacher and American Educational Monthly,* VI (March, 1869), p. 93.
22. Quoted in Paul Monroe, *Founding of the American Public School System: A History of Education in the United States* (New York: The Macmillan Company, 1940) pp. 367-68.
23. "My School-Boy Days in New York City Forty Years Ago," *Loc. Cit.,* p. 95.
24. *Report of the Committee Appointed to Visit Public Schools of Philadelphia, New York, Brooklyn and Boston of Commissioners of Baltimore* (Baltimore: H. A. Robinson, 1867), pp. 35-36.
25. "Two Representative Schools," *New York Teacher, and American Educational Monthly,* V (July, 1868). pp. 275-78.
26. Joseph Mayer Rice, *The Public School System of the United States* (New York: The Century Company, 1893), *passim;* Paul Henry Hanus, Adventuring in Education (Cambridge: Harvard University Press, 1937), pp. 28-29; Ellwood P. Cubberley, *The Portland Survey: A Textbook on City School Administration Based on a Concrete Study* (Yonkers-on-Hudson: World Book Company, 1916); Andrew J. Rickoff, *Past and Present of Our Common School* (Cleveland: Leader Printing Company, 1877), p. 79; "Two Representative Schools," *Loc. Cit.,* p. 256.
27. Rice, *Loc. Cit.,* p. 95.
28. "My School-Boy Days in New York City Forty Years Ago," *New York Teacher, and American Educational Monthly,* VI (March 1869), 89-100; John Griscom, *Memoir of John Griscom,* LLD (New York, 1859), 200-07; John Howard Redfield, *Recollections of John Howard Redfield* (New York, 1900), 201; Edward Strutt Abdy, *Journal of a Residence and Tour in the United States of North America, From April, 1833, to October, 1834* (London, 1835), I:152; Thomas Hamilton, *Men and Manners in America*

(Philadelphia, 1833), 52-57; Isaac Fidler, *Observations on Professions, Literature, Manners, and Emigration, in the United States and Canada, made during a residence there in 1832* (New York: 1833) 39-40; William Bentley Fowle, "Boston Monitorial Schools," *American Journal of Education* I:1 (March 1826), 160-66.

29. Joseph Mayer Rice, *The Public School System of the United States* (New York: The Century Company, 1893), p. 33; See also: *Report of the Committee Appointed to Visit Public Schools of Philadelphia, New York, Brooklyn and Boston to the Board of Commissioners of Baltimore* (Baltimore: H.A. Robinson, 1867), p.83.

30. See Barbara Finkelstein, "In Fear of Childhood..." *Loc. Cit., for elaboration.*

31. Charles Francis Adams, *An Autobiography,* (Boston, 1916) pp. 13-15; Alice E. Kingsbury, *In Old Waterbury: The Memoirs of Alice E. Kingsbury.* See also: George Haven Putnam, *Memories of My Youth* (N.Y.: London: 1914), p. 235; Samuel Whitaker Pennypacker, *The Autobiography of a Pennsylvanian* (Philadelphia 1910), p. 6; Norman B. Wilkinson, "The Education of Alfred Victor Dupont," *Pennsylvania History* XXVIII, 2 (April, 1961), pp. 110-11.

32. Andrew Dickson White, *The Autobiography of Andrew Dickson White* (New York: 1898), p. 14; John Griscom, *Memoir of John Griscom* (New York: 1859), p. 18; *Alcott Memoirs, Posthumously Compiled from Papers, Journals and Memorabilia of the Late Frederick L. H. Willis,* (Boston: 1915), pp. 16-17.

33. Rev. George W. Bethune, *Memoirs of Mrs. Joanna Bethune, by her son, Containing Extracts From the Writings of Mrs. Bethune* (New York: 1896) p. 38. Three unpublished biographical studies also elaborate this pattern. See: Margo E. Horn, "The Effect of Family Life on Women's Role Choices in Nineteenth-Century America: The Case of the Blackwell Women" (Center for Family Research, Washington, D.C. 1978); see also the work of Barbara Sicherman on the family of Edith Hamilton, and Cathleen Dalton on the family of Theodore Roosevelt.

34. Mary Austin, *Earth Horizon* (Boston: 1932); p. 67; Roberts, *op. cit., p. 59;* James Burrill Angell, *The Reminiscences of James Burrill Angell* (Freeport: 1971), pp. 4-5; Lyman Beecher, *The Autobiography of Lyman Beecher,* ed. Barbara Cross (Cambridge, 1961), p. 104.

35. Henry Cabot Lodge, *Early Memories* (New York: 1913), p. 39.

36. Hapgood Hutchins, *A Victorian in the Modern World* (New York: 1930) pp. 38-39; Sarah (Weld) Blake, *Diaries and Letters of Francis Minot Weld* (Boston: 1925), p. 5.

37. Lodge, p. 30; Dupont, *op. cit.,* pp. 10-11.

38. Alcott. Memoirs, *Loc. Cit...,* p. 25.

39. See Charles A. Strickland, "A Transcendentalist Father," *History of Childhood Quarterly,* I, 1973. Amos Bronson Alcott, *The Journals of Bronson Alcott,* Odell Shepard, ed. (Boston: 1848), *passim; The Letters of Bronson Alcott,* ed. Richard Herrnstadt (Ames), p. 38.
   Ibid., p. 50; *Ibid., passim.* See also: Elizabeth Cady Stanton, *Eighty Years and More: Reminiscences,* (New York: 1897) pp. 4-27; Harriet Beecher Stowe, *Life and Letters* pp. 6-8; Louisa Mae Alcott, *Her Life and Letters,* ed. Edna O. Cheyney (Boston: 1928), p. 19.

40. *The Letters of Bronson Alcott...*p. 38. The Blackwells, The Alcotts, The Hamiltons, The Lodges, The Roosevelts and innumerable high-born families were voracious letter writers.

41. In Barbara Welter, *Dimity Convictions* (Athens: 1977) chapter on Growing Up Female.

42. Francis J. Grund, *Their Moral, Social, and Political Relations* (London: 1837) I, p. 36.

43. Alice E. Kingsbury, *In Old Waterbury...* Ch. 3; Putnam, *op. cit.* Bethune, *Ibid.,* 43.

44. Isaac Jones Wistar, *Autobiography, 1827-1905* (Philadelphia: 1937), p. 25; Wilkin-

son, *op. cit.,* pp. 110-11; Austen, *op. cit.,,* p. 62.

45. Lodge, *op. cit.,* p. 65; Pennypacker, *op. cit.,* p. 34; Henry James, *A Small Boy and Others* (New York: 1913), p. 16; Hutchins, *op. cit.,* p. 36; Kingsbury, *op. cit.,* p.3.
46. James E. McClachlan, *American Boarding Schools* (New York: 1970).
47. Lawrence W. Levine, *Black Culture and Black Consciousness: Afro-American Folk Thought From Slavery and Freedom* (New York, 1977), p. 297.
48. Levine, *passim: 5see also for an analysis of law and custom. Eugene Genovese, Roll, Jordan, Roll: The World The Slaves Made* (New York, 1973); Herbert G. Gutman, *The Black Family in Slavery and Freedom* (New York: 1975); John Blassingame, *The Slave Community* (Baton Rouge: 1972).
49. Anne Maddox, *Alabama Narrative,* p. 273-76; Mary Ellen Granberry, *Alabama Narratives,* p. 10; Rev. Josiah Henson, *An Autobiography,* (London: 1870), p. 19; Mrs. Octavia V. Rogers Albert, *The House of Bondage; or Charlotte Brooks and Other Slaves* (New York: 1890), pp. 3, 14; Frederick Douglass, *Life and Times.*
50. Historians have estimated diversely. Figures range from 5%-27%.
51. Charles Ball, in Jolin F. Baylis, ed. *Black Slave Narratives* (New York: 1970), pp. 99-100; *Narrative of James William An American Slave* (Boston: 1838), p. 48. Linda Jacobs; p. 156; *Aunt Sally,* p. 96; Mrs. Octavia V. Rogers Albert, *The House of Bondage or, Charlotte Brooks and Other Slaves* (New York: Hunt and Eaton, 1890), p. 3, 14; Henry Bibb, *Narrative of the Life and Adventures of Henry Bibb, An American Slave* (Philadelphia; 1969), p. 42; William Green, *Narrative of Events in the Life of William Green...* (Rhistoric Publication 219), p.9; *The Life of John Thompson, A Fugitive Slave* (Worcester, 1856) p. 17; Mrs. Martha Griffith Braun, *Autobiography of a Female Slave* (New York: 1857), p. 23.
52. Almost every account details the need as well as the process of stealin' time and an education. There were of course exceptions.
53. Peter Randolph, *Sketches of Slave Life, or Illustrations of the Peculiar Institution* (Boston: 1835), p. 15; Nettie Henry, *Mississippi Narratives,* p. 62; William Hayden, *Narrative of...written by himself* (Cincinnati: Rhistoric Publications, 1911), p. 31. Octavia Albert...*op. cit.,* pp. 8-9; Some slaves learned from white playmates. See: *Narrative of Life of Moses Grady, Late A Slave* (Boston: 1844), p. 36; John Thompson... *op. cit.,* p. 104. Sometimes parents were taught by children. See: *Virginia Slave Narratives,* Elizabeth Sparks, Vol. 17, p. 53. See also: Douglass, pp. 51-53; p. 114. *Alabama Narrative,* Emma Jones, p. 237; Rev. W. E. Northcross, p. 280; *Aunt Sally; or, The Cross, The Way to Freedom* (Cincinnati: 1858), p. 81; Charles Hays, *Alabama Narratives,* I. p. 175; Alonzo Kowles, *Alabama Narratives,* p. 385.

     Alabama Slave Narrative, Dellie Lewis, I, p. 257; John Thompson, *Life...* p. 103. See also: Peter Randolph, *Sketches...* p. 15; Henson, *An Autobiography...* p. 18; p. 40; Austin Steward, *Twenty-Two Years a Slave, and Forty Years a Free Man* (Rochester, N.Y., 1859), p. 158.
54. The narratives and autobiographies contain dozens of instances in which literate slaves either presided over prayer meetings or helped others to learn to read and write. Lawrence W. Levine suggests that preachers were able to identify and explicate the Book of Moses, hence defining a different scripture from the ones their masters had cited.
55. Harriet Jacobs, *Linda...* p. 111. See also: Mrs. Octavia Rogers Albert, *House of Bondage...* p. 1810; Samuel Ringgold Ward, *Autobiography of a Fugitive Negro,* (London, 1855), pp. 6, 27; Peter Randolph, *Sketches of Slave Life,* or *Illustrations of the Peculiar Institution* (Boston: 1855), p. 15; Jim Guilliard, *Alabama Narrative,* I, 145; Necktie Henry, *Mississippi Narratives,* p. 62.
56. Peter Randolph, pp. 13-15.
57. John Thompson, *The Life of John Thompson: A Fugitive Slave* (Worcester: 1856), p.

106; Samuel Ringgold Ward, *Autobiography of a Fugitive Negro* (London: 1855), p. 6.

58. *Aunt Sally; or The Cross: The Way to Freedom* (Cincinnati: 1858), p. 81.
59. Henson.
60. Elizabeth Sparks, *Virginia Narratives*, Vol. 17, p. 53; Octavia...Albert, pp. 8-9; Charles Hays, *Alabama Narratives*, I, p. 175; Mrs. Harriet Jacobs, p. 119; James Smith, *Autobiography of James Smith* (Norwich: 1881), p. 44; Hayden, p. 32.
61. Nettie Henry, *Mississippi Narrative*, Vol. 9, p. 62; Frederick Douglass, p. 14. Lunsford Lane, *Narrative of ...Formerly of Raleigh, N.C.* (Boston: 1842), p. 7; See also: Mrs. Harriet Jacobs, *op. cit.*, p. 11; James Williams, *Narrative of James Williams, An American Slave* (Boston: 1838).
62. Octavia Albert, *House of Bondage*, p. 108. Peter Randolph, *Sketches...* p. 15.
63. Louis Hughes, *Thirty Years a Slave: From Bondage to Freedom, The Institute of Slavery as Seen on the Plantation and in the Home of the Planter* (Milwaukee, 1897), pp. 100-01; 103; Jacobs, Douglas...

VII

Una and the Lion: The Feminization of District School-Teaching and its Effects on the Roles of Students and Teachers in Nineteenth-Century Massachusetts

— DEBORAH FITTS

"No, sir, a man should never be a schoolmaster. That's a woman's business." Henry Ward Beecher placed these words into the mouth of the sage Uncle Ebenezer in his novel *Norwood, or Village Life in New England,* published in 1887.[1] By that date, teaching was in fact a "woman's business." In the nation as a whole, women teachers outnumbered men by a ratio of more than three to one, and in Massachusetts women made up 90% of the teaching force.[2]

This "feminization" of the nation's teaching force had begun in the Northeast in the 1830s and '40s and spread to the West, and to some extent the South, in the middle decades of the nineteenth century. Educators past and present have speculated about the possible effects of a shift from male to female teachers, particularly in terms of the development of sex-role identities of both students and teachers.[3] This essay seeks to explore the meaning of feminization as it related to the social and psychological functions of schools, and as it was expressed in student/teacher relationships during a specific time and in a specific place. The place is Massachusetts, where feminization of common school teaching first occurred and most rapidly advanced. The time is from 1820 to 1860, the period of transition from a predominantly male to a predominantly female teaching force. By looking at the writings of educators, analyzing local school board reports, and examining the reminiscences of teachers and students, I hope to delineate some concrete differences between male-run and female-run classrooms, and to explore the significance of these differences as they affected teacher and student roles and relationships, and ultimately the social meaning of schooling.

Teaching was not an entirely new role for women in the 1840s. Women had kept schools in America, both public and private, since colonial times. Their roles as teachers, however, were limited: they taught young children (up to about age seven) and occasionally older girls. They generally presided over classrooms only in summer and sometimes in fall or winter in city private schools for "young ladies." Schooling between the time of the Revolution and the 1830s followed the agricultural timetable, and the summer schools in particular performed more than a strictly educational function. The summer, or Woman's Schools, as they were called, served not only to teach the ABC's, but also as a kind of day care for busy mothers, and often as an informal work house, to which children brought sewing or straw for braiding hats.[4] Winter schools, for the older boys whose labor was needed in the fields during the summer, were kept by a master. In the 1830s and '40s in Massachusetts, however, these traditional patterns began to change, and a few women began to be listed as teachers in the *winter* district schools. The term "feminization," then, refers to the replacement of male teachers by female.

In the 1840s school committees all across Massachusetts began to comment on this displacement, and to evaluate "the experiment of hiring female teachers for the winter schools." One town remarked: "In times past, a female teacher was not to be thought of in connection with winter schools," but now four of their seven schools were successfully headed by women. In 1845, 48 of Salem's 56 teachers were women, "a large portion of whom perform the services for which but a few years since males only were deemed competent."[5] Horace Mann devoted sections of his Annual Reports of 1842, 1843, and 1845 to chronicles of the success of "the experiment" and to proselytizing for more widespread use of women for winter schools.[6]

Reading these reports, one wonders if women *did* just step into positions which were formerly male and perform the same "services" in the same ways as their male predecessors. Did the content of the role of teacher change with the gender of its occupant?

By looking at the writings of educators, we can see first whether they expected or desired any particular changes in either teacher or student roles as a result of feminization. In *The School and the Schoolmaster* (1845),[7] George B. Emerson and Alonzo Potter summarized the various arguments for hiring female teachers in winter which had been advanced up to that time:

1) Women would "give the scholars the advantage of having the same instructress throughout the year" (thus obviating the problem of

constant turnover of teachers every season);

2) "It would be a *cheap* system" (female wages being one-half to one-third those of male wages);

3) Women have a "native tact in the management of young minds, which is rarely possessed by men";

4) Women would be more devoted to teaching than men, having fewer other occupational options to attract them;

5) Teaching was "a useful as well as respectable mode of life, to any females, who are cast upon the world without property";

6) "It would conduce to the improvement of manners and morals in the schools, since females attach more importance to these than men"; and

7) Women "have a peculiar power of awakening sympathies in children and inspiring them with a desire to learn."

Not only does this list reflect a growing sensitivity to the psychological needs of children, a veiled understanding of female economic travail, and a sharp trader's sense of the economic, it augurs as well the emergence of a new understanding of teacher/student relationships. Proceeding on the assumption that women were psychologically more effective than men—better at managing children, more persuasive in promoting manners and morals, cleverer in their ability to elicit acquiescence to authority—reformers sought to transform classroom interactions by changing the gender of the teacher.

Inherent in the promotion of women as teachers were several assumptions about how children learned, female nature, and the function of schooling. First, there was the assumption (articulated and developed by Scottish Common Sense philosophers and adherents of Faculty psychology[9]) that the human mind was divided into major groups of attributes: Reason (the intellectual/rational/analytic) and Sensibility (the intuitive/emotional/spiritual). The faculties or attributes were thought to be proportionally different in the sexes. Women were the primary keepers of Sensibility, men the keepers of Reason. Men had been traditionally associated with formal education, when education was seen primarily as a mode of developing the intellect and reasoning powers. As the nineteenth century progressed, however, educators began to place more and more emphasis on the moral functions of schooling, feeling that schools were responsible for the moral as well as the intellectual development of children.[10] At this same time, theories of human development were focusing on the period of childhood as the crucial time for development of moral (or amoral) nature.[11] Children were believed to be born with innate but undeveloped faculties. The development of the two faculties, however, was not simultaneous, but sequential—Sensibility developing before Reason. A report to the New York legislature in 1844 on common school education summarized this view:

> In childhood the intellectual faculties
> are but partially developed—the affections
> more fully. At that early age the affections
> are the key to the whole being. The female
> teacher readily possesses herself of that key,
> and thus having access to the heart, the
> mind is soon reached and operated upon.[12]

In other words, since both women and children were thought to live primarily in the world of the Sensibilities, women as teachers could relate to children better than men. And since development of the Moral Sense was seen to be at least as important as intellectual development, if not more so, it is not surprising to find the Boston Board of Education asserting in 1841 that "women are incomparably better teachers for young children than males."[13] The approach of teaching children via their affections rather than their heads (or their bodies) was known as Moral Suasion, and women were thought to be its natural practitioners. In modern Freudian terms, moral suasion could be seen as an attempt to internalize the superego in the student so that he or she would in later life become self-governed.[14]

In promoting female teachers, then, educators were also proposing a major alteration in teacher/student relationships. They hoped that women teachers would shift that relationship from an intellectual to an emotional basis.

While the above arguments from educators provided justification for the view that women were preferable as teachers of young children, there was some ambivalence about the capacity of women to teach older children, especially "large and rude boys" between the ages of about 14 and 20. In fact, Emerson and Potter believed that the physical frailty of women was the only possible bar to wholesale feminization of teaching.[15]

The discipline of "large" boys in the winter schools was a major cause of concern to Horace Hann, Secretary of the Massachusetts State School Board. He reported in 1843 that over 300 schools in his state had been "broken up" in the five years preceding, and that all cases of disruption by violence were caused by boys between the ages of fifteen and twenty-one. Mann found these facts most distressing, and was "at a loss as to what measures to recommend."[16] By 1845 he had come up with one possible solution: hire female teachers to restore order in the classroom. He observed:

> Sometimes boys would be spurned on to dis-
> obedience and open rebellion against the
> authority of a master, while their generous sentiments
> would be touched with a feeling
> of chivalry towards a female; they would
> respect a request from a mistress though they
> would spurn a command from a master.[17]

Just how women might secure classroom control is illustrated in the story "Our Schoolteacher," which appeared in the *Columbian Magazine* in 1849 and was subsequently reprinted in local newspapers.[18] This tale, like other "moral prose" so popular in the mid-nineteenth century, used a fictional situation about a "real-life" event to illustrate a moral point. Essentially a fictional vehicle for arguments in favor of the feminization of teaching, "Our Schoolteacher" delineates the particular ways women elicited order in the classroom, and how their behavior contrasted with their male counterparts .

For three winters, so the story goes, the older boys in District No. 8 had rebelled against their successive schoolmasters, the last of whom was "overcome and thrust out of doors, with sundry bruises about his person, and several rents in his garments." The discipline problems had originated under "Mr. Violent," whose pedagogic skill lay in "thrashin' the larnin' in." When he applied his technique to a small girl, however, the older boys mutinied and the school closed. The district called a meeting and determined that what was needed was a stronger teacher and, accordingly, hired a master weighing over 250 pounds. Though his intellectual qualifications were debatable, nonetheless he wielded "a ruler three feet long." Unfortunately, his rule was no more successful than his predecessor's, and his career met a similar fate. At another district meeting, a Mr. Burnside, "a calm, intelligent man," offered to secure a teacher who would solve the discipline problem. The parents accepted his offer, but were appalled when they learned of his choice. "Why, the man had actually engaged a woman to teach the school!" There were grave doubts about the ability of "a little slip of a woman" to handle the school which had proved itself, "worse than a den of lions." Their apprehensions were proved groundless, however, when the graceful and serene Miss Lewis stepped in front of the classroom. The former rowdies, confronted with a woman teacher, "were somewhat at a loss as to the line of conduct they should pursue. 'If the teacher were only

a Mr. Violent,' they complained, 'we should know how to meet him.' "
But instead of the three-foot ruler, Miss Lewis greeted them with a soft
voice that asked for their respect and entreated them not to embarrass
her with disorderly conduct. The townspeople began to see the wisdom in
hiring a woman. As one man put it, "You'll never catch boys fighting a
woman." When one of the schoolboys was asked jokingly if the boys
were going to "flog the teacher and put her out of the schoolhouse," he
answered, "Put her out of the schoolhouse! If anybody has a mind to
put her out of the schoolhouse, let him come and try it while I am there!"
The tale concludes with the moral that "moral suasion" (exemplified by
the female teacher) was more effective than physical coercion.

In this story, the major difference between male and female teachers is
shown to be one of mode of discipline—males using external force and
females tapping internal motivations. The difference in modes of control, however, depended on the existence of sex-role relationships that
were part of the larger culture. A New England woman who taught in the
1840s made it clear that she understood the underlying sexual framework
of the disciplinary interaction:

[A boy]

> who would be constantly plotting mischief against
> a schoolmaster, because he was a "man of his
> size," becomes mild and gentle, considerate and
> well-behaved towards a little woman, whom he
> could take up with one hand and carry out of
> the schoolhouse, simply because she *is* a little
> woman, whose gentle voice and lady-like manners
> have fascinated him. It is the old story of Una
> and the Lion all over again.

Thus, the female teacher

> rules the turbulent boys in her school very much
> as the shrewdest and wisest of her sex rule men
> outside, by seeming not to do it.

What becomes clear here is that the disciplinary relations between both
male and female teachers and older boys are based on traditional sex-role
relationships. In the case of the male teacher and male student, the relationship is competitive and expressed physically, while the interaction
between a female teacher and a male student is based on protection and
deference, and is expressed verbally (that is, the teacher controls the student's behavior verbally). Educators in the 1840s began to realize the
potential value of sex roles learned outside the classroom for producing

desired behavior within it.

Physical violence and disruption in the common schools was becoming a cause of concern to educators. Horace Mann, for example, was especially perturbed by the boys who "broke up" district schools:

> As they are about to become members of a repub-
> lic, whose boast it is that men are capable of
> self-government, they are taking practical less-
> ons in resistance to rightful authority.[20]

The conflict between male teachers and boys, then, could be seen not only in psychological terms—as younger males asserting themselves against older ones—but in political terms as well—as part of a rhetoric which valued self-government. Self-government (or self-discipline) was thought to be essential in a democracy, which lacked the external regulations of Church and State. The burden of instilling this self-government fell to families and schools, but the particular mechanics of the process were a major subject of discussion among American educational philosophers.[21] The traditional mode of teaching, teaching with the aid of corporal punishment, ran head-on against the democratic injunction against coercion, and many mid-nineteenth century educators began to advocate "moral suasion," or appeal to the emotions, as a teaching technique which would be compatible with democratic ideals and yet, they hoped, effective in the concrete problems of school management.[22]

Educators, then, in proposing that districts hire women to teach in their winter schools, had definite goals in mind. In their promotions of female feminization upon the classroom. In their promotions of female teachers, they were advocating a radical shift in teacher/student interactions—from a relationship grounded on fear of physical punishment to one based on psychological motivation, from intellectual to moral emphases in schooling, and from external to internal modes of control.

How realistic were these educators' claims and/or expectations? Did women actually, as Horace Mann claimed, "frown into silence the slightest whisper of mutiny from the scholars"?[23] Did they exert, or attempt to exert, the advertised "moral influence"? Did they relate via the "Sensibilities"? Was sex an important factor in the nature of the student/teacher interaction?

The reports of local school committees to the Massachusetts State Board of Education in the late 1830s and early 1840s testify that, as far as the committees were concerned, women *were* making a decided difference in the classroom. A town report described the difference in 1838:

> In the South district we saw wonders done.—

> This school as you will recollect was last year
> reported in a low condition—as to government—
> in a state of insubordination—as to rise and
> progress—it had risen only in rebellion—and made
> progress only in advancing, backwards. To see
> a school of 50 or 60 in this condition, taken
> by one of the gentler sex, and brought in a
> few weeks to willing, ready, cheerful, energetic
> performance of every school duty, was indeed
> surprising, and the more so as it was done by one
> of mild and gentle spirit, and apparently of
> physical force and courage scarcely to brave a mouse.

In 1841 another town tried women teachers in two of its six winter schools and reported: "The large scholars have been more cheerfully submissive to the rules and regulations of the school than in former winters, when these schools were under male teachers."[25] Yet another town asserted: "It is frequently the case, that large and turbulent boys, whom it was quite difficult for men to govern by severe means, have been won into good behavior by the gentle treatment of a female teacher."[26] A fourth town advocated feminization because of the tendency of women "to substitute moral influence in the place of mere coercion, and to obviate the necessity of corporal punishment, especially among the larger pupils."[27] Though many Massachusetts school committees recommended female teachers only for smaller children,[28] only two in the reports from 1838-1846 directly opposed female winter teachers both on the grounds that they would not be able to handle older boys.[29] Many favored female teachers even in schools with "large boys."[30]

Although the school reports provide evidence suggesting that at least some women were successful in teaching and managing the winter schools without force, corroboration from the teachers themselves is more difficult to come by. One letter from a Massachusetts schoolmarm who went to teach on the Illinois frontier in 1849 shows how she disciplined an older boy:

> [I kept him after school, and then I]
> trembled and grew faint, for I knew not what
> to do. But God was my refuge and strength,
> When alone with him, I took him by the hand,
> and knelt down, and with one arm around him,
> carried his case and mine to God in fervent
> prayer. He was melted; and after a moment of
> conversation with him, he asked my forgiveness.
> I never had occasion to keep him after school
> again.[31]

Whether the young man was "melted" by the proximity to the teacher or the appeal for divine assistance is not clear, but it *is* clear that the woman achieved her objective by a personal and emotional appeal to the student.

A woman who had been a pupil at the first state normal school in Lexington, Massachusetts wrote a letter to the principal of that institution describing her teaching experiences since she left the Normal School:

> For the year and a half past I have been teaching
> in a private school in Fall River of twenty scholars,
> with a mixture of ages—as in other schools a barrier
> to success. The plans and modes of teaching recom-
> mended at the Normal School, I have in part adopted,
> and am satisfied a continuance would develop more
> thoroughly and awaken new fields of thought to the
> child's mind.—In disciplining schools I have not
> had satisfactory success, yet experience teaches me
> that the law of love is the first, most salutary,
> and will bestow much more good than sterner
>   measures,
> which too often methinks effect only an outward
> appearance of good order.[32]

The letter is revealing, in terms of both what her ideals were in terms of teaching, and the problems she encountered in putting them into practice. The Normal School at Lexington in the 1840s taught concepts of education—age gradation, moral suasion, and emphasis on development of the child's moral and physical aspects in addition to intellectual ones—which were probably more popular in educational journals than in classrooms at that date. The letter hints that attempts to rule by "the law of love" were more difficult, i.e., required more skill, than corporal punishment, but that its effects were more pervasive. Where corporal punishment only affected outward appearances, moral suasion (by implication) would control more completely by becoming internalized.

The recollections of students reveal a broader spectrum of female teacher behavior (and student response) than is portrayed by either educational theorists or the teachers themselves. Though we have cited evidence that some women did not resort to corporal punishment to control their charges, other evidence makes it clear that at times they did. One man, recalling his own experience, took issue with the popular image of the gentle female teacher:

> After ten or twenty years of strenuous teaching,
> a woman can become as hard-boiled as any man:
> in fact, some of them are that way when they

begin. The worst cut I ever received from a
switch in my boyhood, I took on the back of my
bare calves from a woman teacher.[33]

A man in 1853 brought suit against a woman teacher in Barnstable County, Massachusetts, for whipping his son "about the arms, back, hips,
and other parts of the body."[34]

Likewise, the "large boys" did not always respond to the "law of
love" with "cheerful submission." When Mary Abigail Dodge, a New
England schoolmistress (who later turned writer under the nom de plume
Gail Hamilton), addressed a gathering of prospective women teachers in
1853, and warned them of the dangers of taking educational rhetoric too
literally:

> We have all read any number of stories about
> hordes of ferocious boys, who have organized
> successful and successive rebellions, and ejected
> a long line of male dynasties from the professional
> chair, but who have been suddenly brought before
> you as gently as any sucking-dove, by the apparition
> of a sweet-faced, low-voiced woman. Now, I know that
> calmness and gentleness and firmness will work
> wonders, where passion and violence have been
> only abbotts of misrule—and of the
> whole circle of things, this may happen to
> you; but I would not advise you to set your
> heart upon it.[35]

What, then, are we to conclude from this mixed evidence in regard to
the behavior of female teachers? It seems that, although some did not use
corporal punishment, and others tried not to, some certainly did. Does
this completely refute the claims of educators, or their hopes that women
might change life in the classroom?

Perhaps instead of trying to make categorical statements about female
teachers behavior, it would be more fruitful to consider what the various
types of behavior indicate about the *options* that were available to
women in their role as teachers. In these terms, then, women at least had
the option of exercising physical control over their students (including
older males) in a way that they most likely would not have had outside
the classroom. When Mary Abigail Dodge first taught a classroom with
boys in it, she wrote her impressions to her sister:

> Did you ever teach boys? I cannot tell you
> how strange it seemed to me at first. Great

> burly fellows . . . . They frightened me out
> of my senses. I walked about in a dream the
> first week. They seemed so like men.[36]

Here she was outlining her perceptions of the older boys as she might
have seen them outside the classroom—as men. Yet, in the classroom,
she found that "within a few weeks the boys seemed to have diminished
very perceptibly in size and numbers,"[37] implying that her own confidence and authority had reciprocally increased.

Though corporal punishment was an option for women teachers in the
mid-nineteenth century, it should be noted here that in fact the nation-
wide trend was away from corporal punishment.[38] If one talks in terms
of trend, then, feminization correlated with a decline in corporal punishment in the schools. Whatever their *options* may have been, then, it
seems that many women chose *not* to use corporal punishment, and
educators' claims of softer modes of discipline by females cannot be entirely discounted.

But what about the students? Did the feminization of teaching change
their options, the possible ways in which they might behave in their role
as pupils? To answer this question we must ask if there were any types of
student behavior which commonly occurred with male teachers but not
with female teachers. I found just one behavior in this category—
physical abuse of the teacher by (male) students. The phrase from the
story "Our Schoolteacher," "you'll never catch boys fighting a
woman," seems to hold true. To understand more clearly the significance of this one concrete difference between male and female-run
classrooms, it would be useful to look at a specific situation in which
male students treated their male teachers with physical violence. The
"barring-out" of the schoolmaster, literally throwing the master out of
the schoolhouse, is just such a situation.

"Barring-out" had been practiced in America since at least the early
eighteenth century, but had fairly well disappeared by 1850.[39] A typical
description of a barring-out in the 1830s in Tennessee is given by a participant. On the day the boys "turned Dr. Graham out," the master

> came riding up with his dinner bucket in his
> hand, hitched his horse as usual, and started
> for the door. We all crowded around him and
> made known our request for a week's holiday.
> He flatly refused to grant it. As we persisted
> he became very angry and swore he would not give
> in. He turned away from us abruptly and started
> to enter the door. When he found it barred, he

gave it a hard kick. Abel Campbell, one of the
young men, caught him from behind and lifted him
off the doorsteps and, holding him around the
waist, said, "Now, come on boys, if you want a
holiday." The leader in the business told the
Doctor that we would take him down to the branch
and duck him if he would not grant our request.
He still declined and clawed the skin off Abel's
hand until it bled freely; but we told him
it was no use in resisting, that we did not wish
any violence, but that we were determined to
have the holiday, and that we would duck him in
the branch until he consented. After some parleying
he relented and agreed to give us the week."[40]

Another man recalled that in his boyhood in the 1840s:

It was understood throughout the country that
the boys were justifiable in barring out the
master, and if successful, were not only en-
titled to a week's recess, but the admiration
and praise of their parents.[41]

Barbara Finkelstein and others have noted the element of ritual in such
barrings-out.[42] They traditionally occurred just before Christmas. They
appeared to be a violent disruption, but represented in fact a kind of
ritualized insubordination, in which both master and students played
roles tacitly understood by all involved. Descriptions of barrings-out are
often dramatic and quasi-heroic, as when the master "assaulted the
door, pounding it with an axe until he split it in several places."[43] The
boys often plotted their defense of the schoolhouse in military fashion,
the older boys acting as generals and officers and the younger as
"troops."[44] If a master should appeal to neighbors or parents for
assistance, "they were apt to advise him to desist, and let matters take
their course."[45] The proper end of the scenario was victory for the boys.
The master would yield to their demands for a holiday, and a messenger
would be sent of "for apples and cider, and sometimes refreshments of a
more stimulating kind."[46]

A general merriment and exhilaration follows,
in which the victors and the vanquished unite
in reciting with cordial glee the comic and the
tragic of the seige. . . . And when, on next
Monday, "books" is called, each one quietly and

cheerfully resumes his position in the schoolhouse.
The master's authority is recognized as legitimate—
his instructions duly valued; the boys, late successful insurgents, have voluntarily returned
their allegiance, and continue studious and
obedient until the approach of the next Christmas.[47]

Thus, what on the surface appeared to be a violent disruption was in fact
a reinforcement of the master's authority and of community solidarity,
as well as an opportunity for the boys symbolically to defeat the teacher.

In anthropological terms, a barring-out bears many parallels to a
puberty rite, in which younger males symbolically challenge and defeat
older ones. The tacit support of the community, and especially of the
fathers, is important in this regard, and gives rise to speculations about the
possible displacement of students' aggression from their fathers (socially unac-
ceptable as targets) to schoolmasters. The ritual insubordination of the
boys served to relieve tension between the master and students without
ultimate loss of control by the master. It also served to dramatize the
boys' projection of adult male roles. A barring-out could be seen as a
kind of initiation ceremony, as interaction which foreshadowed the
status change from youth to man. On another level, it was a ceremony of
social importance, asserting social order and unity. Frank W. Young, in
Initiation Ceremonies (1965), defines the need for unity in this way: "the
dramatization of sex-role initiation is functionally neccessary for maintaining the solidarity of the man" in a given social group. Further, he
states that:

the dramatizations of status change in a group
are the most elaborate when the solidarity of
the group is great—that is, where there is a
great deal of cooperation among members for the
purpose of creating and maintaining a stable
definition of the situation.[48]

In other words, a ritual such as barring-out prevented social disruptions
by dramatizing the very conflict that could incite them. Such a ritual
would only be efficacious, however, if the entire community understood
the nature of the drama, and assented from within their own roles. According to Young's hypothesis, then, barring-out would "work" (have
the result of social order rather than disruption) in a community where
group identity and solidarity was high. (Perhaps it is not coincidental
that barring-out continued longest as a custom in the isolated communities of the Appalachian mountain states.) The reverse implication of
the hypothesis might also be considered—that where male/female rituals

were declining, so was the sense of community, harmony and integration between generations. There seems to be some evidence that many small communities were in fact disintegrating in the mid-nineteenth century. Social historians have focused on young men's assertions of independence from their families as being facilitated by expanding occupational opportunities and increased geographical mobility, and on this circumstance as a sign of disintegration of community and family identification and solidarity.[49]

Joseph Kett and others have documented the mid-nineteenth century anxiety over the lack of parental and social control over young men, and the flurry of plans and proposals for establishing such control.[50] Horace Mann's dismay at the breaking up of district schools by older boys is an example of this larger anxiety. Perhaps his worries were not unfounded. Though some of the so-called "disruptions" may in fact have been merely ritualized insubordinations, many of the schools Mann was talking about did not reopen.[51] A Worcester, Massachusetts resident claimed that "the old way of barring the master out was far less barbarous than the occasional fights, when he was carried 'will ye, nill ye' out of the door, or pitched out of the window."[51] All confrontations between master and students were not ritualized, and in some the boys asserted their dominance not only symbolically but literally. One man recalled a barring-out in which the scholars actually gored their hapless pedagogue with sharpened poles, tied him up, dropped him down a dry well, and then burnt down the schoolhouse.[53]

It must be admitted that a female teacher would not have been treated this way. (And hopefully such treatment was rare for male teachers.) But under male teachers there at least existed the option for the male students physically and even violently to express aggression and discontent. As the feminization of teaching progressed, this kind of expression became less and less an alternative. This effect was just what educators had in mind when they proposed that women take over the winter schools.

If the feminization of teaching shifted the nature of teacher/student interaction by removing the factor of physical aggression, it probably inspired the fashioning of alternate expressions of rebellion. How, then, did boys rebel against the authority of a female teacher? One way was simply to refuse to attend school. If the problem of physical violence was declining in the middle years of the nineteenth century, the problem of truancy was not. In the towns of Sheffield and Sandisfield, Massachusetts in 1839-40, enrollment in the winter schools dropped markedly after they hired women teachers: boys over the age of 15 "would not submit to be taught by a female."[54] Even in the reports of "large boys" who apparently *did* submit to being taught by women, there is the tacit assumption that the boys were *granting* deference to the female teacher from a position of superior strength "because she *is* a little woman."

The most obvious change attending the feminization of teaching, then, was in the transformation of the relationships between female teachers and male students. The role of female teacher was expanded at least potentially by the possibility of exercising control over males in a way that she would not consider outside of the classroom. Male students, however, found their repertoire diminished when women stepped into the classroom. No longer were they able to express rebellion violently, nor was the barring-out ritual appropriate with a woman teacher.

The classroom was (and is) a stage upon which new social identities are forged from old, a platform for experiments in which the experimenters participate. The schoolroom is not only an analog of society; it is that society in action. Horace Mann put it best, when he described a visit to a district school:

> This, indeed, is no mimic scene. No fiction is
> played upon this stage. The actors are real; the
> representation true;—not life-like merely, but
> life itself.[55]

FOOTNOTES

1. (New York, 1887), p. 26.
2. F.W. Hewes, "Public Schools of the United States," *Harper's Weekly Magazine,* XXIX (October, 1895), p. 1017.
3. Particularly Patricia Sexton, *The Feminized Male* (New York, 1969). The question of the influence of gender on the sex-role socialization of students has been a topic of much concern to educational sociologists. See for example: Glidwell, Kantor, Smith and Stringer, "Socialization and Social Structure in the Classroom," in *Child Development Research,* ed. L.W. Hoffman and M.L. Hoffman (New York, 1966); Stacey, Bereaud, and Daniels, eds., *And Jill Came Tumbling After: Sexism in American Education* (New York, 1974); Patrick Lee, "Male and Female Teachers in Elementary Schools: An Ecological Analysis," in *Teachers College Record,* 75(September 1973), p. 79-98. The teacher-student relationship in general is a major focus of educational sociology and psychology. Influential books are R.N. Bush, *The Teacher-Pupil Relationship* (New York, 1954), and Willard Waller, *The Sociology of Teaching* (New York, 1961). Also Talcott Parsons, "The School Class as a Social System," *Harvard Educational Review,* 29(1959), 297-318.
    While educational sociologists have focused on the impact of various social factors on the students' role and performance, there has not been much done with teachers. Historians of women and the family in the U.S., however, have been interested in the influence of the teaching experience on women. Gerda Lerner, in "The Lady and the Mill Girl: Changes in the Status of Women in the Age of Jackson," *American Studies Journal,* X (Spring, 1969), 5-15, speculates that teaching broadened womens' sphere. Barbara Finklestein, in "The Nineteenth-Century School: An Institution of Domesticity" (unpublished paper given at the Third Berkshire Conference on the History of Women, June, 1976) points out the parallels between women's domestic roles and the role of teacher.

4. See Sol Cohen, ed., *Education in the United States: A Documentary History* (New York, 1977) Vol. 1, on traditional schooling patterns in New England; also James Axtell, *The School Upon the Hill: Education in Society in Colonial New England* (New Haven: Yale University Press, 1974).

5. Massachusetts Board of Education, *Abstract of the School Returns 1845/46* (Boston, 1845), 205, 273, 37.

6. In 1838, Horace Mann first inquired about the possibilities of a policy of hiring women in the winter schools. He advocated hiring women in his 1842 and 1843 Reports as Secretary of the Massachusetts Board of Education, and by 1845, 66% of all Mass. teachers were women. The figure was over 75% by 1860. (See Massachusetts State Board of Education, *Second Annual Report* (Boston, 1838): *Third Annual Report* (Boston, 1846); and *Twenty-third Annual Report* (Boston, 1860).

7. George B. Emerson and Alonzo Potter, *The School and the Schoolmaster* (Boston, 1845).

8. *Ibid.,* p. 206.

9. For an excellent explanation of this world view, particularly as it related to women in the mid-nineteenth century, see Kathryn Kish Sklar, *Catherine Beecher: A Study in American Domesticity* (New Haven, 1973), 80-84. For more general coverage see Herbert W. Schneider, *A History of American Philosophy* (New York, 1963), 202-212; for religious and academic aspects see Daniel Walker Howe, *The Unitarian Conscience: Harvard Moral Philosophy, 1805-1861* (Cambridge, Mass., 1970). A contemporary popularized version of faculty philosophy is found in Timothy Shea Arthur's *Advice to Young Ladies on Their Duties and Conduct in Life* (Boston, 1848).

10. See Barbara Finkelstein, "Pedagogy as Intrusion: Teaching Values in Popular Primary Schools in Nineteenth Century America," *History of Childhood Quarterly* (Winter, 1975), 349-378; Timothy Smith, "Protestant Schooling and American Nationality: 1800-1850," *Journal of American History* LIII (March, 1967), 679-695. Primary sources which stress the primacy of moral education are Catherine Beecher's *Suggestions on Improvements in Education* (Boston, 1829) and *An Essay on the Education of Female Teachers* (New York, 1835).

11. See Bernard Wishy. *The Child and the Republic: The Dawn of Modern American Child Nurture* (Philadelphia, 1968). For a review of literature on the history of child rearing, see Glenn Davis' review of Mary Cable, *The Little Darlings,* in *History of Childhood Quarterly* (Winter, 1976), 438-43. See also Anne L. Kuhn, *The Mother's Role in Childhood Education: New England Concepts, 1830-1860* (New Haven, 1947) and Jay Mechling, "Advice to Historians on Advice to Mothers," *Journal of Social History* (Fall, 1975), 44-63.

12. Quoted in *New York State Educational Exhibit* (Chicago: World's Columbian Exposition, 1893), 45-46.

13. Boston Board of Education, *Annual Report* (Boston, 1841), 45-6.

14. For a Freudian interpretation of the teacher/student relationship see Wilfred Lay, *Man's Unconscious Conflict* (New York, 1920). J. H. Hardy, in the *Five Talents of Woman* (New York, 1862), included teaching as one of those talents. He asserted that in the classroom a woman "can do what no man can do...she can make her womanhood a sort of external conscience to the boys" (p.66).

15. Emerson and Potter, *The School and the Schoolmaster,* p. 206.

16. Horace Mann, *Fourth Annual Report of the Secretary of the Massachusetts Board of Education* (Boston, 1841), 87-91.

17. Mann, *Sixth Annual Report* ...(Boston, 1843), 66-67. The more general anxiety about adolescent boys and how to socially control them is documented by Joseph Kett in *Rites of Passage: Adolescence in American: 1790 to the Present* (New York, 1977), 38-61.

18. Reprinted in the Taunton, Massachusetts *Daily Gazette,* April 3 and 4, 1849.

19. Anna Callender Brackett, *Woman and Higher Education* (New York, 1893), p. 150.

20. Mann, *Fourth Annual Report...op. cit.*, 87-88.

21. For the intertwining of democratic rhetoric and educational ideology, see Rush Welter, *Popular Education and Democratic Thought in America* (New York and London, 1962).

22. The debate over the use of corporal punishment was central to educators in the mid-nineteenth century. See Donald R. Raichle, "The Abolition of Corporal Punishment in New Jersey Schools," *History of Childhood Quarterly* (Summer, 1974), 53-77; Jonathan Messerli, "Consensus and Controversy in the Reform of the Common Schools," *Teachers College Record* LXVI (May, 1965), 449-459. For general background on the trend away from corporal punishment in child rearing, see note #11, and Phillipe Aries, *Centuries of Childhood: A Social History of Family Life* (New York, 1962); Lawrence Stone, "The Rise of the Nuclear Family in Early Modern England: The Patriarchal Stage," in *The Family in History*, ed. Charles E. Rosenberg (Philadelphia, 1975), 13-57. The distinction between corporal and non-corporal control of children is the basis of Lloyd DeMause's view of changes in child rearing: see "The Evolution of Childhood" in his *History of Childhood* (New York, 1976).

23. Mann, *Fourth Annual Report...*(Boston, 1841), p. 88.

24. Massachusetts State Board of Education, *School Returns 1838/39.* (Manuscript originals of returns from town school committees, from which published abstracts were taken). Massachusetts State House, Archives Annex.

25. Massachusetts State Board of Education, *Abstract of the School Returns 1841/42* (Boston, 1842), 47.

26. _____, *Abstract of the School Returns 1842/43* (Boston, 1843), 46.

27. _____, *Abstract of the School Returns 1845/46* (Boston, 1846), 37.

28. For example, in the Massachusetts State Board of Education *Abstract of the School Returns 1839/40* (Boston, 1840), over half (17) of the 30 towns mentioning female teachers approved of them for small children.

29. In both cases (Sandisfield in 1839/40, and Peru in 1842/43), town committees felt that the large boys required a firmer disciplinary hand.

30. For example, in the Mass. State Bd. of Ed. *Abstract of the School Returns 1845/46,* (Boston, 1846), seven of seventeen mentions of female teachers favored women in schools with older boys.

31. Quoted in "Popular Education in the West," *New Englander* (1849), 598.

32. Louisa A. Stow to Mr. May, October 10, 1844. Edward S. Adams Collection, Fall River (Massachusetts) Historical Society.

33. Millard Fillmore Kennedy, *Schoolmaster of Yesterday* (New York, 1940), 93.

34. Barnstable (Massachusetts) County Court of Common Pleas Recordbook, 1853. In Clerk of Court's Office, Barnstable County Courthouse, Barnstable, Massachusetts.

35. Dodge, Mary Abigail (Gail Hamilton), *Our Common School System* (Boston, 1880), 165.

36. Mary Abigail Dodge, *Life in Letters,* I (Boston, 1869), 103.

37. *Ibid.,* 103.

38. See note #22 above and Harris Pickens, *Changing Conceptions of School Discipline* (New York, 1928).

39. The custom was probably transplanted from England. The first American mention I find is at William and Mary College in 1705 (in Edgar Knights, ed., *A Documentary History of Education in the South,* I (Chapel Hill, North Carolina: 1949), 474-488. By 1858, barring-out "could hardly be said to exist," according to George B. Emerson, in the *American Journal of Education* V(1858), 418.

40. John Massey, *Reminiscences* (Nashville, Tennessee, 1916), 51.

41. Joseph Guild, *Old Times in Tennessee* (Nashville, Tennessee, 1878), 336. Other ac-

counts of barring-out can be found in Martin Walker, "Farm Life in Ohio 60 Years Ago," *Western Reserve Historical Society Tracts,* 68(1895), 28-29; Horace Kephardt, *Pennsylvania History as Told by Contemporaries* (New York, 1925), 391-97; Clifton Johnson, *Old Time Schools and Schoolbooks* (New York, 1904), 127.

42. Barbara Finklestein, "Pedagogy as Intrusion: Teaching Values in Popular Primary Schools in Nineteenth Century America," *History Of Childhood Quarterly,* Vol. 2, #3 (Winter 1975), 359; also Joseph Kett, *Rites of Passage, (op cit.),* 47-48.

43. Kephardt, *Pennsylvania History as Told By Contemporaries, (op. cit.),* 394.

44. Guild, *Old Times...,* p. 334-5.

45. *Ibid.,* 336; see also Clifton Johnson, *Old Time Schools...,* 127.

46. Guild, *Old Times...,* 331.

47. *Ibid.,* p. 334.

48. Frank W. Young, *Initiation Ceremonies* (New York, 1965), 41.

49. Social historians have been concerned with increasing independence of young men from the paternal family in the 18th & 19th centuries in America. See Kenneth Lockridge, *A New England Town: The First Hundred Years* (New York, 1970).

50. Kett, *Rites of Passaob,* 38-61, 86-108.

51. Mann, *Fourth Annual Report of the Secretary of the Massachusetts Board of Education* (Boston, 1841), 89

52. Abijah Marvin, *History of Worcester County, Massachusetts,* 1 (Worcester, Massachusetts, 1874), 108.

53. Guild, *Old Times ...,* 334-35.

54. Massachusetts State Board of Education, *Abstract of the School Returns 1839/40* (Boston, 1840), 111, 116, 368.

55. Mann, *Tenth Annual Report of the Secretary to the Massachusetts Board of Education* (Boston, 1847), 97.

VIII

The Politics of Latency: Kindergarten Pedagogy, 1860-1930

— DOMINICK CAVALLO

INTRODUCTION

Since the Darwinian Revolution social scientists have routinely assumed that human life is punctuated by psycho-physiological stages of development such as adolescence and latency. But it is easier to give these stages names than to pinpoint where one ends and the next begins. There is, for example, no hard and fast way of determining with precision where adolescence terminates and adulthood ensues. Psychological development is not akin to ascending a staircase, in which the individual climbs a step at a time, decisively and permanently turning away from steps he has left behind. It is more like a subtly shaded continuum of light, where shadows dovetail, and past and future fade into one another.

Nor are psychological stages universal. They are inexorably intertwined with the specific "biocultural matrix within which the child grows up."[1] Developmental stages isolated by contemporary psychology did not necessarily exist in past societies. Or, if they did, they were not necessarily experienced in the same way. We cannot assume that the nature and duration of contemporary life stages apply to all societies or social classes in the past. Indeed, we can assume they do not. As Kenneth Keniston has pointed out, developmental stages, which he distinguishes from physiological maturation, are "contingent": their appearance and utility depend upon historical and cultural contingencies.[2]

All of this makes it exceedingly difficult for historians to accurately determine when, how, and why a particular psychological stage made its historical debut. The historian not only has to isolate the psychological facets assumed by the stage in a specific historical setting, but he must uncover the social, economic, and political pressures that compelled the society to recognize and actively cultivate the developmental stage. The latter problem is particularly significant because it implies that society creates social, moral, and cognitive experiences at home and in school which ensure that the psychological potential for experiencing latency or adolescence will both attain fruition and redound to what it perceives as the mutual benefit of child and society. This, of course, is another way of saying that society politicizes the life cycle for its own purposes, and that one can view psychological development from psycho-political as well as psycho-sexual and psycho-social perspectives.

In this essay I will focus on the ways in which kindergarten educators between 1860 and 1930 cultivated the period of early-latency. In particular, I shall emphasize how and why kindergartners during the Progressive Era politicized early-latency (roughly five to six years of age) by promoting compulsory, universal education for children during these years. By insisting on the need to that of remove early-latency children from the realm of family government to that of state-sponsored kindergartens, progressive kindergartners implied that children could be more effectively indoctrinated with acceptable social and political values in school. By extracting the child from family government, progressives helped give early-latency the hue and texture it has today.

A few words about latency should clarify these issues. Latency is the psychoanalytic designation[3] for the developmental stage that bridges early childhood and adolescence. Latency covers, roughly, the years between five and twelve. By contrast with the emotional lashings of the Oedipal period, latency is a period of relative emotional calm. The sexual excitations of the Oedipal period are repressed, and in their place appears a "land of fantasy and dreams," in the guise of fairy tales and culture myths, which allow the youngster to sublimate his drives by harnessing them "to the process of acquiring the traditions of culture."[4] Of course, genetic determinants allow this process to occur. The latency child must have the intellectual capacity to symbolize, the ego strength to erect defenses against sexual desires (and memories of sexual disappointments) of the preceding period, and the cognitive ability to comprehend and remember complex verbal configurations. But most of all he must possess what Charles Sarnoff calls "behavioral constancy"—the "mental ability to retain...patterns of behavior and to apply them in appropriate and varying situations to the extent expected by society."[5]

Latency, then, is a period during which the child is transformed from a being whose primitive mental organization revolves around longings for various forms of sensual gratification to one who thinks, plans, learns to read and write, and to pit his capacities against environmental expectations and opportunities. Also, the latency child incorporates what Freud called the "ethical restraints" peculiar to his culture. Indeed, moral organization proceeds hand in hand with the cognitive capacity to test reality as structured by his society.

> The setting aside of ways of remembering which include feelings and evocations of mood in favor of subtle language-oriented memory skills sharpens and increases the capacity of the child to acquire knowledge of expected behavior in disparate situations. This sets the stage for the augmentation of the superego imagoes derived from integrated parental figures which guide personal adjustment within the family, by imagoes derived from verbally subtle rules and regulations which guide the conduct of life in groups.[6]

Although the maturation of cognitive and verbal skills during latency is biologically determined, there is no physiological basis for the *promotion* of the relative emotional calm, psychological plasticity, and general educability which characterize latency in American society. These elements are promoted by society. There are "primitive societies and subcultures in which latency is not encouraged" and sexual drives are unhindered. But powerful emotional stress, sexual or otherwise, can impede cognitive and moral development, and possibly immure the child in the psychological and sexual prison of familial sexual politics. Taboos against incest and educational programs which, in their different ways, compel the child to turn away from the forbidden wishes of the Oedipal period are, in effect, means of forcing him to relinquish certain ties to the family so that he can be prepared for integration into the general society.[7] In short, the imposition of latency is a political act undertaken on the assumption that the interests of family, child, and society are served by placing the latency-aged child in community-controlled educational institutions where society, rather than the family, plays the key role (though by no means the only role), in shaping his moral and cognitive styles.[8]

When viewed from these psychological, physiological, and political perspectives, latency is hardly a modern discovery. As Philippe Aries has shown, the early-latency child who lived in Western Europe prior to the sixteenth century was quickly weaned from his family, though the focus of his activities and attachments became the general community rather than the school.[9] And according to Edmund Morgan, the daughters and sons of seventeenth-century Puritans might be "put out" with another family as early as nine years of age to learn domestic and vocational skills.[10] Thus, in both Europe and America, the five- to twelve-year-old was recognized as intellectually capable. Indeed, the Puritan child was deemed capable of moral instruction even before the age of five.[11] And, significantly, Morgan speculates that the separation of parents and children may have been caused by the parental desire to preserve peace in the immediate family "just at the time when a child begins to assert his independence. By allowing a strange master to take over the disciplining function, the parent could meet the child upon a plane of affection and friendliness."[12]

While it is not clear how extensive this practice was, how long it lasted, what social classes it affected, or the degree to which it affected early-latency children, it is probable that at least by the early nineteenth century, Americans were disinclined to remove early-latency children from the shelter of family government. Evidence for this can be found in the short American career of infant schools. Infant schools were a European innovation which catered primarily to children of the poor. They were privately sponsored and geared toward providing instruction and moral uplift to youngsters of about eighteen months to school age. In the late 1820s, attempts were made to import infant schools to the United States, particularly to urban areas blighted by industrial poverty.[13] However, as Dean May and Maris Vinovskis demonstrate in their analysis of the infant-school movement in Massachusetts, these schools failed to take hold because they were viewed as threats to the prerogatives of family government.[14] Also, the authors report that in Massachusetts during the middle decades of the nineteenth century there was a decrease in the number of children under four attending public schools. According to the authors, this indicates "dramatic" attitudinal changes about young children, and a disinclination, particularly on the part of middle- and upper-middle-class reformers, to remove even the children of the poor from the parental sphere of influence.[15]

The irony of the movement's failure in Massachusetts, as May and Vinovskis point out, is that by the 1860s and '70s another European method of educating young children, the kindergarten, enjoyed enormous popularity in Massachusetts and other industrial states. May and Vinovskis are nonplussed by the failure of the first reform and the resounding success of the second, particularly since there was "little difference in the principles or techniques of the two systems."[16]

But there was at least one central difference between the two. The first American advocates of Froebel's kindergarten, especially philosophical idealists like Elizabeth Peabody and Susan Blow, portrayed the kindergarten as an extension of home, hearth, and motherhood, whose task was to transmit the values and skills espoused by the middle-class family. Nor was the commitment of kindergarten pioneers to the family model of socialization a superficial one. It extended to the moral and cognitive training techniques employed in the kindergarten, and to the idealized, romantic image of the child championed by those who viewed home, mother, and her "immortal infant" as bulwarks against the harshness, materialism, and contingencies of the "modern" world. The kindergarten teacher was supposed to be a surrogate mother who took care of young children when natural mothers could not or would not. Not only were many of the first American kindergartens conducted in homes, but kindergarten teachers based their pedagogical techniques on what they supposed was the "normal" pattern of interaction between parents and children.[17]

During the 1890s, young kindergarten educators influenced by the "new" psychologies advanced by John Dewey, G. Stanley Hall, and Edward L. Thorndike challenged the prevailing family model of kindergarten pedagogy. Progressive kindergartners emphasized the maladaptive quality of the family model of socialization, wanted all four- to six-year-olds to attend state-sponsored kindergartens (before 1890 many kindergarten classes were financed with private funds), and advocated moral and cognitive training methods explicitly opposed to the philosophical idealism and family orientation of the orthodox Froebelians.

For nearly thirty years progressive and orthodox kindergartners struggled for control of the curriculum.[18] I will argue that the opposing methods of moral and cognitive training championed by progressives and idealists constituted far more than a disagreement about the early-latency child's nature and capabilities. Implicit in their arguments about the child's nature was a deeper struggle over whether the family or society should serve as the primary inspiration for moral and cognitive practices, and which should have the primary responsibility for socializing the early-latency child. Progressives, who by 1920 had gained control over most kindergarten curricula, wanted to politicize latency by basing moral and cognitive training techniques on a community model of social interaction, and by giving the state the responsibility for deciding what and how a child of that age could and should learn. And while it would be too much to say that progressive kindergartners created the twentieth-century version of early-latency, there can be no doubt that they did much to promote it.

Both progressive and orthodox factions agreed that the four- to six-year-old was capable of the moral and cognitive operations we associate with early-latency. The focus of what follows, then, is on the ways in which the family orientation of idealists and the social-political orientation of progressives generated distinct moral and cognitive training techniques in the kindergarten, how these differences influenced their pedagogical techniques, and how their respective pedagogies in turn created distinct moral, cognitive, and social orientations in early-latency children.

THE IDEALIST KINDERGARTEN

The kindergarten enjoyed extraordinary success in the twenty-five years following its introduction into the United States in 1855.[19] An important reason for its success was that Froebel's philosophical idealism and unabashed romanticism were shared by some of America's most influential educators, especially the transcendentalists Elizabeth Peabody, Mary Peabody Mann, and Bronson Alcott, and the Hegelian Susan Blow. More than anything else, these pioneers of the American kindergarten held in common an unshakable belief in the child's potential for spiritual—or moral—perfection. It might be true, as Alcott pointed out, that the child came into the world armed with untamed passions and appetites. But it was also true that he possessed an as yet unsullied kernel of divinity, a soul—or what Blow referred to as a God-given, hidden "something." If properly and sedulously cultivated, the divine something would develop, and allow the child to control his animal appetites and perhaps even transcend his animal nature.[20]

The divine spark within the child was irreducible. That is, it was the "germ" which contained the essential ingredients of his humanity. "The child," wrote Blow, "does not become man but he is born man."[21] According to Peabody:

A child is a living soul, from the very first; not just a mere animal force, but a person, open to God on one side by his heart, which appreciates love, and on the other side to be opened to nature, by the reaction upon his sensibility of those beauteous forms of things that are the analysis of God's creative wisdom; and which, therefore, gives him a growing understanding, whereby his mere active force shall be elevated into a rational, productive will.[22]

But such elevation did not ensue automatically. The child had to be nudged, as it were, into spiritual perfection. Froebel's American disciples, like many other mid-century members of the middle and upper classes, firmly believed that family government was the best method of promoting spiritual elevation because it was a bastion against the harshness and crude materialism of urban-industrial society. The mother in particular was endowed with an "instinctive" penchant for tenderness and love which, if blended with appropriate nurture techniques, served as a catalyst for the blossoming of the child's innate spirituality and goodness.[23] According to his American disciples, "mother-love" was the basis for Froebel's pedagogy, for only the warmth and security generated by a mother's loving heart could evoke in the child the "feeling of oneness with a loving mother" that "is the germ from which springs the feeling of union with God."[24]

The kindergarten teacher was supposed to reproduce this family model of love and nurture in her classroom, and "perform all the functions of a wise and educated mother."[25] In Peabody's opinion, the kindergarten was a necessary adjunct to family nurture because mothers with more than one young child lacked time and energy to properly care for them. The four-year-old should be handed over to matronly kindergartners who possessed both the innate feminine penchant for tender nurture and a knowledge of Froebelian pedagogy.[26] If the home was a "divine" abode and the family "eminently God's institution," which "nothing should be allowed to mar," then the kindergarten should reflect these "facts" by steadfastly fulfilling the family's divinely prescribed nurturant role.[27]

During the 1860s these concepts of kindergarten nurture were for the most part aimed at well-to-do families. The first experimental kindergartens were privately funded and patronized mostly by upper-middle-class children. But by the 1870s kindergartners became alarmed by what they viewed as a breakdown of family cohesion in the slums of American cities. Charity kindergartens were organized to "save" the children of impoverished city families. It might be true, according to Mary Peabody Mann, that only a mother could ignite the divine spark in "her little immortal." But it was also true that "nine-tenths" of mothers failed to do so. The kindergarten teacher should become the surrogate for mothers who drank, were promiscuous, or who were compelled to work. "Every good kindergartner," said Mann, "finds the motherly element in herself, and by adoption makes every child she deals with her own."[28]

The "adoption" of poor children by kindergarten "mothers" was not a particularly subtle process. Kindergartners who taught in slum schools spent half their work day in the homes of their pupils, advising mothers on matters of morality, hygiene, and diet.[29] This pedagogical version of the "friendly visitor" technique made famous by Charity Organization Societies in the 1880s and '90s provided a countermodel of "true" motherhood for students whose natural mothers were too busy, too ignorant, too poor, or too foreign to understand the importance of exposing them to prevailing middle-class perceptions of cleanliness and "good" manners. Also, given the interpenetration between home and kindergarten in the slum, kindergartners expected pupils to bring their school lessons to bear on their conduct at home. Here is how one kindergartner expressed this expectation:

Two "ragged, dirty children" bring a flower home to their dingy tenement apartment. The mother has failed to keep the house clean; the father is out drinking. Overjoyed at seeing the flower, the mother places it on a windowsill only to discover that dirt prevents any sunlight from shining through the window to the flower. With the window clean, sunlight re veals the filth of the apartment, which is then quickly cleaned, the mother is washed and dressed, and father, overcome by his new environment upon his return home, vows to give up the bottle.[30]

The idea that the home was a shelter from the "wild energies" let loose by capitalism and the quests for power and fame[31] colored the methods early kindergartners used to instill morality in their young charges. The child's moral style was supposed to be as privatized and removed from the lures of "external" corruption and temptation as his familial enclave. A "bad" mother was defined by Blow as one who instills "external standards" in her children and who emphasizes values which are "seen" rather than those that are "unseen and eternal."[32]

The ideal child adhered to the moral ideals espoused by his parents. He neither emulated the behavior or tastes of peers nor doubted the veracity of stern paternal prohibitions or tender maternal ideals. Armed with an intractable knowledge of right and wrong, the child became a self-guiding little individualist who used "constant introspection and testing to measure how well he lived up to the first principles learned from either mother or father."[33] Elizabeth Peabody advised kindergarten teachers to encourage moral autonomy in their pupils by placing the burden of moral rectitude squarely on their shoulders. If a pupil behaves discourteously the kindergarten teacher should force him to recognize his lapse:

Is that right? Would you like to have any one else do so? I would suggest that the question be asked not of the class, but of the individual culprit, whether what is being done is right or wrong.[34]

Kindergartners encouraged moral autonomy because they believed it led to social cohesion. "Self-direction" and "self-realization" were the fulcrum for social equality and unity. "Conscious individuality," wrote Peabody,

Which gives the sense of free personality, the starting point, as it were, of intelligent will, is perfectly consistent with and even dependent on the simultaneous development of the social principle in all its purity and power.[35]

From the idealist perspective, these claims were not contradictory: absolute self-direction and social harmony were not mutually exclusive. On the contrary, the idiom of philosophical idealism symbolized the harmonious balance between what Peabody called "free personality" and the "social principle."[36] The key to understanding this apparent paradox lies in the pedagogical techniques used by orthodox Froebelians: the gifts and occupations.

Froebel's eleven gifts were objects whose geometrical shapes (spheres, cubes, cylinders) were supposedly innate in the child's "sleeping thoughts."[37] According to kindergarten idealists, these mathematical forms were the metaphysical realities "behind" the sense impressions created by objects. Idealists believed that the geometrical patterns that gave spatial form to matter were alienated, objectified properties of mind. Or, to be more exact, they assumed that the spatial configurations of objects were alienated mental patterns, and that children had an innate ability to intuit this metaphysical "reality." Accordingly, the goal of kindergarten education was to help the child separate, in Alcott's words, "those outward types of itself from their sensual connection."[38] In more mundane pedagogical terms, as he worked with geometrical gifts during occupations (games and projects), the pupil learned to relate geometrical patterns to one another and to grasp the transcendent unity which was hidden behind apparent separation. As Blow put it:

> I remember well a little girl five years old who after playing for some time with her ball began to count over the different round objects she could remember, and after naming apples, grapes, cherries and peaches, suddenly exclaimed with a flash, "Why all fruits are round," and, she added after a moment's thoughtful pause, "So are all vegetables."[39]

The pedagogical uses of Froebel's first gift, the ball, demonstrates how kindergartners tried to make pupils both self-directed and socially oriented through idealist techniques. According to kindergartners, the ball had two major features: mobility and randomness. As the pupil played with it he "extracted" and personalized those characteristics. As he rolled the ball to and fro it shed its quality as an external object: its mobility symbolized to the child *his* freedom of action. And the fact that the ball remained stationary until the pupil moved it symbolized his autonomy and self-direction: he was his own mover.[40]

At the same time, the ball's sphericity and "geometrical values as germ of all other forms" symbolized an all-inclusive unity, especially when pupils sat in a circle rolling the ball to one other. Such exercises sparked a dormant "germ" in the pupil's mind, an incipient idea inherent in "pure thought" about the sphere which, in a manner never clearly explained by idealists, led him from intuitive perceptions of the ball's mathematical inclusivity to an equally intuitive recognition of it as a symbol of *social* and *moral* inclusivity and harmony.[42]

Similar attempts to harmonize self-direction and social unity characterized other gifts and occupations. The pupil who "rolled balls and cylinders on level and inclined planes," or who "whirled and spun spheres, cubes, cylinders and cones," was laying the foundation for understanding "relations between form and motion which are the fundamental facts of physics."[43] In other words, he was developing the analytical and idiosyncratic intellectual skills necessary for getting on in an advanced industrial society. Yet the ideational qualities of the objects supposedly enhanced the pupil's appreciation of the social and moral solidarity he shared with peers.

> As the divisions of the cube increase in variety and complexity, he finds he can produce more and more perfect forms, and when, through the constant association of the individual parts and the unity from which they are derived, the idea of organic connection has become the regulator of his instinctive activity (sic).[44]

In other words, the purpose of moral and cognitive training in the Froebelian kindergarten was to portray to pupils "the individual and the universal in gradation and harmony."[45] And, by imitating the movements and functions of natural and man-made objects, pupils learned that each student, though possessing utterly distinct, God-given "somethings," was an integral part in a divinely ordained "social whole."

> In the play of the bird's nest a given number of children represent trees, imitating, with arms and fingers, the branches and leaves, while others, like birds, fly in and out, build nests, and finally drop their little heads in sleep. So in the ship game, the children standing around the circle, by a rhythmical undulating movement, represent waves, while a half-dozen little children, with intertwined arms, form the ship, and with a movement corresponding to that of the waves, imitate its sailing.[46]

Their philosophical idealism allowed kindergartners to transcend, intellectually at least, the two most dangerous tendencies they perceived in capitalist society: personal greed and social conformity. By cultivating the "spiritual" dimension of the child's personality, and simultaneously honing his intuitive ability to grasp the social import of symbolic activities, kindergartners tried to harmonize moral self-direction and social unity. This synthesis was achieved by tapping the dormant metaphysical "reality" contained in the pupil's mind. In mind "the generic energy is one with its product, and hence the ideal self in one man is identical with the ideal self in every other man."[47]

Thus the creative paradox of idealism: the more the child's idiosyncratic abilities were cultivated, the more he recognized his inseparability from, and "oneness" with, his fellows. The pedagogy of the first American kindergartners was designed to develop personal skills necessary for social and economic progress while salvaging the moral sentiments necessary for social order.[48] That is to say, it provided the same service to children as the idealized mid-century middle-class family. The privatized family was supposed to foster a paternal moral autonomy and personal initiative in children while simultaneously sheltering them from a relentlessly materialistic capitalist society by providing them with a model of maternal solicitousness.[49]

TRANSITION

Both the pedagogical techniques and the social utility of the early kindergarten sprang from idealists' romantic perceptions of the privatized family and the child. Neither of these notions survived the nineteenth century, at least not intact. And to understand the pedagogy and politics of the transition from the orthodox to the progressive kindergarten we should take a brief look at what happened to these concepts during the last third of the nineteenth century.

The romantic image of the child rested on the assumption that he was divinely endowed with a permanent, irreducible spiritual and moral nature. For good or ill, the child embodied God's purpose. While external training might repress or promote specific aspects of his endowment, it could neither destroy them nor qualitatively transform his basic nature. It should be evident from our discussion of the idealist kindergarten that its advocates assumed mind and "soul" to be more or less static givens.

But the theory of evolution cut down two vital props of the idealist world-view. The very idea that mankind had evolved from "lower" creatures subverted the vision of each person as made in the image of God. More significantly, the theory of evolution suggested that initiatives for both human development and social change came from environmental pressures rather than divine or human intelligence. The purpose of life, which proponents of evolution blithely defined as "progress," was achieved by the ability of organisms to adapt to changes in the external environment. As John Dewey put it, Darwinism implied a shift away from "an intelligence that shaped things once for all to the particular intelligences which *things* are even now shaping."[50]

In other words, mind, soul, spirit, or whatever one chose to call man's irreducible "inner" reality was the result rather than the cause of history. Whatever man was, he was not necessarily the purveyor of a divine purpose, nor himself a prime mover, but an evolving physical organism whose destiny was determined by his capacity to adapt to what Dewey aptly described as "things." All this was far removed from the idealist notion that the child possessed formal mental and spiritual faculties which transcended environmental conditions.

The privatized model of family government fared no better. Some educators, most notably Dewey and G. Stanley Hall, questioned the efficacy of the family government model in an increasingly complex urban society. According to Hall, the city "shriveled" home life and rendered parental authority ineffective because many parents living in tenements could not keep an eye on their children in the streets. Nor, after 1880, could the dramatic increase in the foreign-born population be overlooked when Hall analyzed the adequacy of family government as the primary agency of socialization. In the opinions of many progressive kindergartners, neither the child's nor the country's best interests were served by leaving the immigrant child's moral training solely in the hands of his foreign-born parents.[51]

Between 1890 and 1920, the years marking the struggle between orthodox and progressive kindergartners, progressives incessantly stressed the moral and intellectual inadequacies of the privatized model of family childrearing. Progressives viewed the home less as bastion against the intrusions of materialism and more as a barrier which inhibited the child's integration into society. Luella Palmer, an outspoken progressive, asserted that the five-year-old was ready to "pass over" from family to community, and that intercourse with his "equals" in the kindergarten was more relevant to his moral and intellectual development than subservience to parental superiors at home.[52] Another progressive, Nina Vandewalker, claimed that Froebel's mother plays and nursery songs should not be included in the modern kindergarten curriculum because they embodied an antiquated "emotionalism and sentimentality" about the child and his potential. Indeed, kindergarten teachers should have more than a mother's "aggreeable disposition." They must possess knowledge of child psychology, biology, and sociology.[53] No one expressed the progressive impatience with the family government model better than Irwin Shepard in his address to the National Education Association in 1892.

(T)he very affection which has surrounded the child and guided his growth in filial love often makes difficult the exercise of that altruistic choice of the right which is alone the ethical element of an act. Beautiful as filial and fraternal love is, it may become so self-centered in the common self of the family as to become purely egoistic and hinder true ethical growth, which springs only from the soil of a broader fellowship.[54]

There were other reasons for the progressive rebellion. More than anything else, the pedagogy of progressive kindergartners like Patty Smith Hill, Alice Temple, Nina Vandewalker, and Agnes Burke was a response to a raw, unpredictable urban environment. The city, whose problems and prospects dominated discussions about the country's economic, social, political, and moral future after 1880, symbolized the differences between idealists and progressives. To idealists the kindergarten was literally a children's garden: planting the seeds of metaphysical truth generated a process whose results were as natural, orderly and predictable as seasonal changes. Progressives found little in the city which, from their point of view, was either natural or predictable, particularly its inhabitants. As Robert Wiebe has pointed out, the bustling, stimulating, impersonal tone of city life made it "difficult to untangle what an individual did and what was done to him."[55]

Given this situation, it is understandable why many kindergartners listened with interest to the criticisms of traditional kindergarten pedagogy made by Dewey and Hall during the 1890s. For example, when Dewey rejected the idealist claim that the mind contained innate universal principles for the *a priori* organization of social and moral experiences, he was articulating what many kindergartners who lived and worked in cities knew from personal experience: *their* world was more contingent, less predictable, and less "natural" than that of mid-nineteenth century idealists.[56]

It is also understandable why after 1900, progressive kindergartners looked to the stimulus-response/habit-formation psychology of Edward L. Thorndike and, to a lesser degree, to John Watson's behaviorism as major inspirations for curriculum organization. The Progressive Era was marked by efforts to create order and regularity in urban social and economic relations.[57] But the "search for order" went beyond the discovery of sophisticated administrative-bureaucratic techniques for controlling impersonal, "objective" interactions in government and industry. Thorndike's stimulus-reponse/habit-formation psychology, Watson's behaviorism, and intelligence-quotient testing—all of which influenced progressive kindergartners—attempted to calculate the "subjective" and affective human "input" into interpersonal relations.[58] To mid-nineteenth century idealists, the child's irreducible "something" made him and his moral potential immeasurable. To progressives the individual's intellect and emotions were not only measurable, but the quests for both social order and unity made calculations of human desires, drives, abilities, and potential behaviors necessary.

The ideology of progressive kindergartners emphasized the importance of biological and cultural processes and de-emphasized that of both familial and individual autonomy. These ideas had a pivotal impact on their pedagogical techniques.

THE PROGRESSIVE KINDERGARTEN

One of the hallmarks of the progressive kindergarten was the use of Dewey's concept of the school as a miniature community. Dewey criticized what he called Froebel's false notion of an "exact correspondence between the general properties of external objects and the unfolding of mind."[59] According to Dewey, pupils acquired knowledge by studying the social uses and values of objects, and young children learned most effectively by "acting out" in play and games the actual uses to which objects and social roles are put in their community.

> To do this means to make each one of our schools an embryonic community life, active with types of occupations that reflect the life of the larger society and permeated throughout with the spirit of art, history and science. When the school introduces and trains each child of society into membership within such a little community, saturating him with the spirit of service, and providing him with the instruments of effective self-direction, we shall have the deepest and best guaranty of a larger society which is worthy, lovely, and harmonious.[60]

In Dewey's experimental kindergartens in Chicago and in work done by his followers at Columbia University Teachers College, kindergarten activities revolved around "social" situations in which pupils, in effect, mimicked the occupations, domestic activities, and community episodes of the "outside" world.[61]

A mainstay of these episodes was to have children act in social dramas which demonstrated the family's interdependence with society. For example, when pupils were organized into "miniature" families they learned that the preparation of food was not done solely by mother. Someone had to procure the food from the grocer, who in turn had gotten it from a "middle man" who had purchased it from the farmer, and so on.[62]

The miniature community family was always portrayed within a communal context. Children were supposed to learn that the family unit did few things autonomously. It could neither produce food nor protect itself from fire or violence. The roads family members used to get to and from work, school, and the store were paved by others, the mail it received was delivered by others.[63] By "playing" mothers, fathers, firemen, doctors, policemen, etc., pupils learned firsthand about the "reality" of social interdependence and of the need for social cooperation across class and ethnic lines. The very idiom of the miniature *community* technique systematically disabused pupils of the notions that either the individual or the family could get on by itself in the modern world. There was no room for either moral or social autonomy in a society where everyone and everything was interrelated.[64]

Even the development of individual talents was placed in a communal context. Pupils who demonstrated exceptional abilities as singers, dancers, artists were told that it was "selfishly enervating" to cultivate these skills unless it were done to please others, enhance the general welfare, and encourage "social feeling."[65]

Ideally, the kindergarten teacher refrained from interfering with student interactions during miniature community exercises. She acted as "a guide rather than a dictator," and a "good referee" instead of a participant.[66] Whereas the matronly kindergartner, the gifts, and the model of family government dominated moral training techniques in the orthodox kindergartens, what one progressive referred to (without irony, as we shall see) as the "spontaneous and organized" peer group dominated moral training exercises in the progressive classroom.[67]

Progressives wished to instill in the pupil the notion that the peer group was the principle judge of his behavior. The pupil had to be shorn of the "egoism" and "innate selfishness" promoted by a family government which made him the center of attraction. In the classroom, if not in the home, he should be taught to "give up his own will to others.' "[68] Once the youngster "loses his little self in the greater self of the community and realizes the ethical kindergarten motto, 'Each for all, and all for each,"[69] he will understand that his aspirations and their fulfillment assume meaning only when embedded in the community's purposes and resources.

Pupils who did not learn that lesson, and who persisted in marching to their own kindergarten tune, paid the painful price of becoming isolated from their peers. One progressive kindergartner painted a rather bleak picture of how a recalcitrant pupil was brought into line by the peer group:

> If Tommy is disobedient and pulls Sally's hair, then the harmony of the circle is broken. The other children are quick to appreciate this and, when the next one is called upon to select a partner for a game, you may be sure Tommy is not chosen. Soon he begins to feel his exclusion, and it does not take him long to put cause and effect together. It is often a wise plan to keep hands off and let the boys and girls adjust their own differences.[70]

Nothing could be farther from the moral autonomy and disdain of emulation inculcated by orthodox Froebelians. Idealists tried to make the pupil feel personally responsible for his or her behavior. The pupil was taught to depend upon his "inner" parental voice when making moral judgments. This was implicit in the advice given by Elizabeth Peabody in the 1880s to aspiring kindergarten teachers:

> When she [the teacher] insists upon the children governing themselves, so far as to keep their proper places in relation to each other...she must call forth by addressing in each child the sense of personal responsibility. The reward to the children is instant in the success of the play, and therefore not thought of as reward or merit. It is a form of obedience that really elevates the little one higher in the scale of being as an individual without engendering the reaction of pride and self-conceit, for self is swallowed up in social joy.[71]

In other words, the morally autonomous individual instinctively respects the rights of others. Clearly, idealists sought to balance the needs of the individual with the requirements of social order by fortifying the pupil's moral independence vis-a-vis other pupils.

By contrast, progressives insisted that the source of both personal values and moral sanctions resided in the peer group. In their view moral autonomy was a source of social disorder. Like their idealist colleagues, progressives wanted pupils to cooperate with and understand each other. Unlike idealists, they thought the best method of attaining this goal was by fashioning a peer-group culture among early-latency children.

We cannot, of course, assume that their moral training techniques had the intended effect on the pupils. We can, however, speculate about how the pupils would have functioned if the moral training techniques worked as they were supposed to. The methods employed by orthodox Froebelians encouraged development of a guilt-prone moral style in pupils, while that promoted by progressives instilled a shame-prone moral style. A brief discussion of the psychoanalytic theory of morality and of the phenomenological differences between shame and guilt will sharpen our perceptions of the social, pedagogical, and psychological implications of the progressive rebellion.

In contemporary psychoanalytic theory,[72] the "superego," which includes the elements of conscience and moral judgment, is a system of internalized motivations. The child's moral acculturation and compliance are based on his *affective,* "understanding" of what motivates others to approve or disapprove of his behavior. That is, his compliance to authority is premised on motives which are not available for conscious examination. Parental expressions of approval or disapproval are affectively imparted to the child, and his dependence on their care and love compel him to try living up to their expectations. The parents' vocal tones, facial expressions, etc. are "expressive" vehicles through which the child perceives, and ultimately internalizes, cultural mandates about behavior.[73]

Failure to adhere to these mandates mobilizes unpleasurable feelings such as shame, guilt and remorse. Obviously, measures taken by the per-

son to avoid eruption of these unpleasant sensations affects his style of
dealing with the external world.[74]

Another significant dimension of the superego is called the "ego
ideal." The ego ideal represents the idealized persons, groups, and values
the person has chosen as models of what he would like to become. In effect, the ego ideal is a projected ethical future. Development of a significant discrepancy between what the person is and what ego-ideal standards suggest he should strive to become often results in shame affect—unpleasantness derived from exposure of a self which has failed to
live up to expectations.[75]

Among other things, ego ideals define the values the person should
cherish and help him evaluate his success in making his behavior coincide
with those values. The values and goals subsumed under the rubric "ego
ideal" may in fact be impossible to achieve realistically, or may simply
point toward an idealized future. Nonetheless, however unrealistic these
behavioral and ethical standards may be, they exert "a tremendous influence on our realistic behavior."[76]

With these aspects of conscience in mind, we can turn to the
phenomenological differences between shame and guilt. Shame and guilt
are the real or potential punishments inflicted on a person when he
violates his moral code. But whether shame or guilt is threatened depends
upon the person's superego "style." Guilt most often erupts when the
person violates a *specific* aspect of his prohibitive (thou shalt not) moral
code, while shame frequently appears when he falls short of ego ideal
aspirations. It is possible for an individual's superego to operate
predominantly (though not exclusively) along one of these routes—to use
the sanction of either shame or guilt as the principle means of compelling
the person to comply with his moral values.[77] Whether the shame or guilt
affect predominates depends upon which identifications are stirred by
the violation. Thus:

> [S]hame and guilt are highly important mechanisms to insure
> socialization of the individual. Guilt transfers the demands of
> society through the early primitive parental images. Social confor-
> mity achieved through guilt will essentially be one of submission.
> Shame can be brought to the individual more readily in the process
> of comparing and competing with the peers (siblings, schoolmates,
> gang, professional group, social class, etc.). Social conformity
> achieved through shame will essentially be one of identification.[78]

Phenomenologically, shame and guilt differ in a number of ways.
Since shame is evoked when a person fails to live up to ideals he identifies
with his "self," it threatens his self-esteem and identity. Shame affect is
a nonspecific and diffuse sensation because it is mobilized to punish the

person's failure to measure up to the idealized, projected image he has of himself, and which others have of him. In other words, shame deals with the self's generalized failure *per se* rather than with a violation of a specific, identifiable moral prohibition, such as the mandate against theft, for example. The individual threatened with shame affect is faced with the possibility of being confronted by internalized "imagos" which remind him that he has failed to become what he and "they" believed and expected he would become.[79]

> In shame, the internalized admired imago functions...as the referent "in whose eyes" shame is experienced; a "shadow" of the imago falls on the self. These "watching" thoughts may include the awareness that the person is thinking about what the other person is thinking about him. In this kind of instance, the self is both participant and watcher in its own fantasy.[80]

Another facet of shame affect is its evocation of bodily reactions like blushing, sweating, and increased heart rate. Shame has a particularly physical connotation. Potentially the shame-prone individual feels visually (that is, physically) exposed to the internalized "other's" gaze and criticism.[81] Also, shame isolates its victim. Because it exposes a deficient self, shame affect subverts the person's image of what he is and what he believes others think he is. Thus, shame tends to arouse feelings of alienation, isolation, abandonment, and self-contempt. Anxiety aroused by fear of being shamed evokes images of "social expulsion" and "ostracism."[82] Finally, shame is extremely difficult to assuage because the self *qua* self has been indicted.[83]

In contrast to the nonspecificity of shame, the experience of guilt ensues when the person has violated a specific aspect of his moral code. In guilt the act, not the self, is condemned, and expiation usually entails explicit, culturally prescribed modes of atonement. In short, guilt is a personal sensation because there is no question, as there is with shame, of the social exposure of an inadequate self. The guilty person has done *something* wrong. The shamed individual has *become* something wrong. In guilt the focus is on the transgression rather than the self.[84]

> [T]he imagery of the self *vis a vis* the "other" is absent in guilt. In the experience of guilt, the self is doing the judging; the experience is thus self-contained and self-propelled. Guilt is about something specific about which the self is critical, in contrast to shame, where criticism or disapproval seems to emanate for the "other" and to envelop the whole self. Guilt thus tends to have a more specific content, which can be put into words. It is intrinsically a more ideational experience than shame, which tends to be a wordless, acute feeling.[85]

The progressive kindergarten promoted shame-proneness by discouraging the pupil's moral and social autonomy: the peer group was the focus of moral training techniques in miniature community projects. The child who disrupted the harmony of the community "circle," who insisted on pulling Sally's hair, or who for reasons of ethnic or class background simply did not "fit in," was made to "feel the isolation of his condition."[86] As we saw from the example of recalcitrant "Tommy,"[87] teachers encouraged pupils to ostracize the disobedient student, and to make him feel as though his "bad" behavior was symptomatic of an inadequate self, rather than simply an episodic example of wrongdoing. Which is to say that humiliation, not guilt, was the weapon used to stem untoward eruptions of nonconformity. The following description by a kindergarten teacher of a miniature community episode incisively portrays the humiliation and diffuse anxiety—shame affect—experienced by the pupil who did not act in accordance with the expectations of peers and teacher:

> Let us play they [blocks] are all breakfast tables, said I; I will come around and visit each one and see what the little children have to eat. What is on your table Helen? "Oh! my children have ice-cream and cake and soda-water." Oh, dear! Oh, dear! I cried, holding up my hands, poor little things! Just think of their having such a thoughtless mamma, who didn't know how to give them good, wholesome food for their breakfast. What is on your table Frank? "My children have bread and butter, oatmeal and cream, and baked potatoes." "Oh," broke in little Helen, "my children's mamma came into the room and when she saw what they were eating she jerked the ice-cream off the table."[88]

In this example, "thoughtless" Helen was not reproached by the teacher simply for a specific wrong. On the contrary, Helen realized she had been remiss only when she was confronted by the contrary example of a fellow pupil whose behavior was both different from hers and acceptable. Helen's anxiety was generated as much by her failure to think and behave like her classmate as by her specific failure to provide her "children" with nutritious food. While the kindergartner pointed out her lapse to Helen, the youngster according to the teacher, did not react until prompted by her fellow student. Clearly, this type of reaction was the point of such exercises.

Shame-proneness is an ideal moral companion to the extreme social orientation cultivated in the progressive kindergarten. Unlike guilt, which posits awareness of wrongdoing within the person, shame makes his moral awareness a distinctly social experience. As John Dewey pointed out, the cultivation of a purely "inner personality is a sure sign of social divisions," for "what is called inner is simply that which does not connect with others."[89] In the shame-prone superego the peer group is internalized as ego ideal, thereby bridging the gap between outer mandates and inner imperatives. According to Dewey, this was the goal of progressive moral education.[90]

Also, in the shame-prone superego ideal parental prohibitions are replaced by peer-group ideals. As we have seen, the moral training practices of orthodox Froebelians clearly focused on the individual pupil's idiosyncratic awareness of his wrongdoing. Idealists assumed that the privatized family model of moral government, with its austere (paternal) prohibitions and tender (maternal) solicitousness, equipped the early-latency child with a sure feel for the differences between right and wrong. Progressives, on the other hand, made the peer group the focus of the individual's moral awareness. When Patty Smith Hill called the kindergarten a "laboratory of democracy" she was referring, among other things, to the peer group's role in easing the child's passage from the security blanket of the family enclave to the functional demands made upon him by society. As another progressive put it, parental moral training, even in the "ideal home," could not prepare the young for the strains of cooperative and "interdependent" living inflicted by modern society as effectively as "group participation" among kindergarten equals.[91]

Progressive kindergartners used the peer group as a "functional" link between family and society.[92] They viewed the stereotypical middle-class family as mired in indulgent, tender, loving nurture, which, since it reveled in "emotionalism" and "sentimentality," ill equipped the child to deal with a social reality in which the group, rather than he himself, was the center of attraction.[93] Needless to say, progressives were hardly more enthusiastic about family government within lower-class and immigrant situations. From whatever perspective, then, progressives thought the peer group more functional than the family in the area of moral acculturation. As one of them put it, in the progressive kindergarten the "child comes to value himself by what his equals think of him."[94] That is, he learns about his social roles, capabilities, limitations, and responsibilities through intercourse with peers. The implication was that he could not effectively learn these essential lessons when under the sole authority of family government.

The "projects" used by progressive kindergartners consistently emphasized the centrality of social processes and the interaction within, and between, organized groups. As we have seen, even when projects portrayed family episodes, they emphasized the influence of the "community" on the security and general well-being of the family. Most projects, regardless of their situational focuses,[95] emphasized the sensual, intellectual, and moral immediacy of animate and inanimate "reality," particularly technical, conflict-free interactions, and de-emphasized emotional and moral conflict, whether personal or familial in origin. The "airplane project" is a case in point. The project originated in a progressive kindergarten in Kansas in 1928, and the teacher's description of its progress is well worth our careful perusal.

> The children in this particular situation were for the most part from very modest homes. A large percentage were of Polish descent. As a group they were from the beginning rather passive, being content with one form of play from day to day, showing very little initiative or leadership. An activity, however, soon developed in which most of the group manifested an intense interest.

> During the summer vacation the children had heard a great deal about the trans-Atlantic fliers, and a short time before school opened Colonel Lindbergh had visited Kansas City. The subject of airplanes, therefore, was rather a common one. It also happened that one of the government air-mail routes was directly over this particular school building [and] the children could see them very well indeed.

About the second week of school several boys made what they called airplanes. They simply cut two strips of paper and pasted them together in the form of a cross. The next day more children made airplanes. The teacher and pupils made a close observation of the mail plane as it flew over the building. An interesting conversation followed concerning its construction. The next day the workbench and tools were given a prominent place in the room [by the teacher]. The children had not used them before this time.

Here the kindergartner described the pupils' enthusiasm for the tools and the project, how they constructed ever more complicated airplanes, embellished them with variations of size and color, and so on. She then described the pedagogical consequences of the project:

> They learned something of the general form of airplanes; they learned to distinguish between the monoplane and the biplane. The service of the mail plane led to an interest concerning air mail—how to stamp, where to mail, etc. Opportunity was also offered for the child to gain fluency in oral expression. A feeling of self-confidence was also developed. In the work with materials [at first] the chief interest was in the expression of an idea. After closer examination, however, and through stimulation by the proper materials, the children soon manifested a desire for a more realistic

product. Habits of neatness in the use of paint and in the proper use of the tools were established.

In this unit of activity the child was given some small notion of the interdependence of people—the service rendered by the post office department. In the construction of the planes the children felt the need of cooperation and fair play. Taking turns in the use of the tools, courtesy, and respect for others, and genuine social approval and disapproval, were social values emphasized.[96]

These pupils, as perceived by the teacher, were "passive" and lacked "initiative" when they came to the kindergarten from the family. Whether their passivity was related to family government, the kindergartner does not say. However, she is quick to point out that pupils learned to analyze complex social and technical problems in a cool, dispassionate manner. There is not a trace of personal or interpersonal conflict, no hint of moral ambiguity, self-doubt, or introspection. Indeed, one discerns no trace of affect whatever.

Perhaps this was the point of the projects. They were designed to prepare youngsters for life in a technological, bureaucratic, interdependent, and democratic society, where untoward expressions of conflict and emotion retarded development of the capacity to calmly and objectively analyze complex social processes and problems.

And if organization, bureaucratization, and administration were, as some historians have indicated, the special passions of educational and other progressives,[97] then perhaps we can discern in these passions the most cogent reason why progressive kindergartners wished to place early-latency children under the supervision of school and state. Latency is symbolic of an age of reason, an oasis of emotional calm and cognitive development sandwiched by the multiple stresses of the Oedipal and adolescent periods. The latency years, therefore, must have seemed an ideal time to drill into the child a penchant to take a cool, affectless look at his human and physical environs.

Progressive kindergartners wanted the state rather than the family to have primary responsibility for the moral and cognitive acculturation of early-latency children. If one judges their efforts solely by the proliferation of state-sponsored kindergartens after 1890, progressives were eminently successful.[98.] This is not to say they succeeded either in making the kindergarten compulsory for all four- to six-year-olds (which they did not)[99] or in socializing pupils in accordance with the prescriptions of progressive pedagogy. Children do not necessarily become what pedagogy would make of them. But if progressive kindergartners are judged by their intentions, there can be no question of their desire to make the psychological and physiological maturation of early-latency children matters of public policy. If they were less than totally successful in this quest, it was not for want of effort.

In the end, perhaps their most permanent educational legacy was their attempt to "de-privatize" the child's intellectual and emotional faculties. It was not simply that the child in the progressive kindergarten was more socially oriented than his counterpart in the idealist kindergarten. The progressive kindergarten pupil had no place to hide, no inviolate inner sanctum off-limits to intrusions by peers or superiors. His most private, inner processes were subject to the controls and measurements of peers and educational specialists. In 1919 Agnes Low Rodgers, an expert in I.Q. testing hired by the International Kindergarten Union as a consultant on measuring techniques for early-latency children, told an audience of kindergarten teachers:

> Successful teaching consists essentially in establishing certain mental associations in pupils to the required degree of strength, in the most efficient order and in minimal time, and the first stage in progress towards efficiency is knowing specifically what mental bounds are desired. The development of physical science meant the control of the material world and mental tests will ultimately mean the control of human behavior.[100]

In other other words, human beings were measurable. No sentiment more effectively conveys the differences in values and aspirations between idealist and progressive kindergartners, or between the nineteenth and twentieth centuries.

FOOTNOTES

1. Kenneth Keniston, "Psychological Development and Historical Change," in Theodore K. Rabb and Robert I. Rotberg, eds., *The Family in History* (New York, 1973), pp. 148-149.
2. *Ibid.*
3. Latency, of course, is a psychoanalytic term. But non-analysts have long recognized this age period as a watershed in moral and cognitive development. See especially the works of Jean Piaget, particularly *The Moral Judgment of the Child* (London, 1932) and *Judgment and Reasoning in the Child* (New York, 1928).
4. Charles Sarnoff, *Latency* (New York, 1976), p. 8. See also Sigmund Freud, *An Outline of Psychoanalysis* (New York, 1949), pp. 10-12, 43; *The Problem of Anxiety* (New York, 1936), p. 100; *The Ego and the Id* (New York, 1960), p. 25; Anna Freud, *The Ego and the Mechanisms of Defense* (New York, 1936), pp. 157-159.
5. Sarnoff, pp. 91-92.
6. *Ibid.,* p. 108.
7. *Ibid.,* pp. 31-32, 341-345. See also Arthur Hippler, "Cultural Evolution: Some Hypotheses Concerning the Significance of Cognitive and Affective Interpenetration during Latency," *Journal of Psychohistory,* 4 (Spring, 1977), pp. 419-39.

8. Of course this does not mean that parents have no influence on the child's moral and intellectual development after he enters school.

9. Philippe Aries, *Centuries of Childhood* (New York, 1962), pp. 405-415.

10. Edmund Morgan, *The Puritan Family* (New York, 1966), pp. 72-79. See also James Axtell, *The School Upon a Hill* (New Haven, 1974), *passim*.

11. Morgan, pp. 96-97.

12. *Ibid.,* p. 79.

13. Dean May and Maris Vinovskis, "A Ray of Millennial Light: Early Education and Social Reform in the Infant School Movement in Massachusetts, 1826-1840," in Tamara K. Hareven, ed., *Family and Kin in Urban Communities, 1700-1930* (New York, 1977), p. 62.

14. *Ibid.,* pp. 82-83.

15. *Ibid.,* pp. 89-90.

16. *Ibid.,* p. 94.

17. Marvin Lazerson, "Urban Reform and the Schools: Kindergartens in Massachusetts, 1870-1915," in Michael Katz, ed., *Education in American History* (New York, 1973), pp. 224-228.

18. For an excellent analysis of this struggle see Evelyn Weber, *The Kindergarten: Its Encounter with Educational Thought in America* (New York, 1969), pp. 65-97.

19. In 1870 there were fewer than twelve kindergartens in the country and only one teacher-training school. By 1880 over four hundred kindergartens in thirty states were being supplied with professionally trained kindergartners by ten training schools. See Nina Vandewalker, *The Kindergarten in American Education* (New York, 1908) p. 23; Weber, p. 36; Elizabeth Dale Ross, *The Kindergarten Crusade* (Athens, Ohio, 1976), chapters one and two.

20. Charles Strickland, "A Transcendentalist Father: The Child-Rearing Practices of Bronson Alcott," *History of Childhood Quarterly,* 1 (Summer, 1973), pp. 7-12; Susan Blow, "The Mother Plays and Nursery Songs," in Henry Barnard, ed., *Kindergarten and Child Culture Papers* (Hartford, Conn., 1884), p. 578.

21. *Ibid.,* p. 575.

22. Elizabeth Peabody, "Froebel's Principles and Methods in the Nursery," in Barnard, p. 562.

23. On maternal nurture during this period see Anne Kuhn, *The Mother's Role in Childhood Education: New England Concepts, 1830-1860* (New Haven, 1947), *passim;* Bernard Wishy, *The Child and the Republic* (Philadelphia, 1968), *passim*.

24. Blow in Barnard, p. 586.

25. Thomas Hunter, "The Kindergarten in Normal Training," in Barnard, p. 535.

26. Peabody in Barnard, p. 567.

27. Mary P. Mann, "The Kindergarten and Homes," in Barnard, p. 654.

28. *Ibid.,* pp. 654-655.

29. Robert L. Church, *Education in the United States: An Interpretive History* New York, 1976), p. 324; see aslo Lazerson in Katz, pp. 324-327.

30. Church, pp. 324-325.

31. Elizabeth Peabody, "The Necessity of Kindergarten Culture," in Barnard, p. 623.

32. Blow in Barnard, p. 588.

33. *Ibid.,* p. 588; Wishy, p. 56; see also Strickland, *History of Childhood Quarterly,* pp. 9-15.

34. Peabody, "Froebel's Principles," in Barnard, p. 571.

35. *Ibid.,* p. 566.

36. On Froebel's idealism see William H. Kilpatrick, *Froebel's Kindergarten Principles Critically Examined* (New York, 1917), *passim;* Weber, pp. 11-36; Dom Cavallo, "From Perfection to Habit: Moral Training in the American Kindergarten, 1860-1920," *History of Education Quarterly,* 16 (Summer, 1976), pp. 148-152.

37. Susan Blow, "Some Aspects of the Kindergarten," in Barnard, pp. 604-613.
38. Alcott quoted in Perry Miller, Ed., *The Transcendentalists* (Cambridge, Mass., 1967), p. 141.
39. Blow, "Some Aspects," in Barnard, p. 605.
40. Kilpatrick, *Froebel,* pp. 1-4, 119.
41. *Ibid.,* p. 112.
42. *Ibid.*
43. Susan Blow, *Educational Issues in the Kindergarten* (New York, 1908), pp. 42-43.
44. Blow, "Some Aspects," in Barnard, p. 606.
45. Kilpatrick, *Froebel,* pp. 160-161.
46. Blow, "Some Aspects," in Barnard, p. 598.
47. Susan Blow, *Symbolic Education* (New York, 1894), p. 34.
48. *Ibid.,* pp. 40-41.
49. Kuhn, pp. 22, 99, 182; Strickland, pp. 7-15.
50. John Dewey, *The Influence of Darwin on Philosophy and Other Essays in Contemporary Thought* (New York, 1910), p. 15.
51. G. Stanley Hall, *Life And Confessions of a Psychologist* (New York, 1925), p. 379; Lazerson in Katz, pp. 234-236.
52. Luella Palmer, "The Place of the Kindergarten as an Institution," *Pedagogical Seminary,* 14 (Dec., 1909), pp. 558-560.
53. Nina Vandewalker, "The Mother Plays in Kindergarten Training," *Kindergarten Magazine,* 19 (June 1907), pp. 632, 637.
54. Irwin Shepard, "Ethical Culture in the Kindergarten," *National Education Association Proceedings* (1892), p. 92.
55. Robert Wiebe, *The Search for Order* (New York, 1967), p. 133.
56. John Dewey, *The School and Society* (Chicago, 1899), pp. 113-115; *Democracy and Education* (New York, 1916), pp. 68-69; with Evelyn Dewey, *Schools of Tomorrow* (New York, 1915), pp. 105-120; G. Stanley Hall, *Educational Problems,* 2 vols. (New York, 1911), chapter one.
57. In addition to Wiebe see Jerry Isreal, ed., *Building the Organizational Society* (New York, 1972); Samuel Haber, *Efficiency and Uplift* (Chicago, 1964).
58. By 1919 there were 84 standardized educational tests to measure the intellectual progress of kindergarten and primary-school students. See Agnes Low Rodgers, "The Scope and Significance of Measurement in Early Elementary Education," *International Kindergarten Union Proceedings* (1918), p. 180.
59. Dewey and Dewey, *Tomorrow,* p. 104.
60. Dewey, *School and Society,* pp. 27-28.
61. Dewey, *Democracy,* pp. 39-48.
62. "The Kindergarten Curriculum," *Bureau of Education Bulletin,* 16 (1919), pp. 2-12.
63. *Ibid.,* p. 17.
64. *Ibid.,* pp. 11-15.
65. *Ibid.,* pp. 62-63; Elizabeth Harrison, *A Study of Child Nature* (Chicago, 1905), p. 57.
66. Patty Smith Hill, "Introduction," in Agnes Burke et al., *A Conduct Curriculum for the Kindergarten and First Grade* (New York, 1923), xi-xii.
67. *Ibid.*
68. Harrison, p. 81.
69. Shepard, pp. 97-98.
70. Emily V. Hammond, "Team Work for Children," *Kindergarten Magazine,* 32 (Jan., 1920), p. 135.
71. Peabody, "Froebel's Principles," in Barnard, p. 569.

72. Roy Schafer, *Aspects of Internalization* (New York, 1968); Edith Jacobson, *The Self and the Object World* (New York, 1964).
73. Talcott Parsons, *Personality and the Social Structure* (New York, 1962), pp. 55-64.
74. Jeanne Lampl-DeGroot, "Ego Ideal and Superego," *Psychoanalytic Study of the Child,* 17 (1962), pp. 99-100; Peter Blos, *On Adolescence* (New York, 1962), p. 184; Jacobson, pp. 146-149.
75. Roy Schafer, "Ideals, Ego Ideal, and Ideal Self," *Psychological Issues,* 18/19 (New York, 1967), pp. 129-174.
76. Jacobson, p. 111; M. Laufer, "Ego Ideal and Pseudo Ego Ideal in Adolescence," *Psychoanalytic Study of the Child,* 19 (1964), pp. 200-201.
77. Helen Lewis, *Shame and Guilt in Neurosis* (New York, 1971), pp. 21-26, 82.
78. Milton Piers and Gerhard Singer, *Shame and Guilt* (Chicago, 1953), p. 36.
79. Lewis, *Shame,* pp. 30-31; Helen Lynd, *Shame and The Search for Identity* (New York, 1958), p. 236.
80. Lewis, *Shame,* pp. 23-24.
81. *Ibid.,* p. 34.
82. Piers and Singer, *Shame,* p. 16: Lynd, *Shame,* pp. 34-43, 67.
83. Lewis, *Shame,* pp. 25, 507.
84. *Ibid.,* pp 30-34. It should be emphasized that shame and guilt are not mutually exclusive experiences. For example, it is possible for a person to feel ashamed for violating a moral prohibition. In speaking of a "shame-prone" moral style I am referring to a general tendency, a predilection, as it were, rather than an absolute state.
85. *Ibid.,* p. 251.
86. Harrison, p. 115.
87. See this test, page 172.
88. Harrison, pp. 53-54.
89. Dewey, *Democracy,* p. 143.
90. *Ibid.,* p. 418.
91. Palmer, pp. 557-559; Hill, xi.
92. On the functional role of the peer group see S. N. Eisanstadt, "Archetypal Patterns of Youth," in Erik H. Erikson, ed., *The Challenge of Youth* (New York, 1964), pp. 29-50.
93. Shepard, p. 97; Vandewalker, *Kindergarten Magazine,* 19, p. 632.
94. Palmer, p. 560.
95. For an outstanding collection of kindergarten miniature community projects see Lucy Weller Clouser and Ethel Milliken, *Kindergarten-Primary Activities Based on Community Life* (New York, 1929).
96. *Ibid.,* pp. 34-46.
97. David Tyack, *The One Best System* (Cambridge, Mass., 1974); Wiebe, *The Search for Order;* Michael Katz, *Class, Bureaucracy and the School* (New York, 1975).
98. Vandewalker, *Kindergarten,* pp. 184-208.
99. Lazerson in Katz, pp. 230-231.
100. Rodgers, p. 183.

IX

In the Name of the Prevention of Neurosis: The Search for a Psychoanalytic Pedagogy in Europe 1905-1938

— SOL COHEN

Looking back, then, over the patchwork of my life's labours, I can say that I have made many beginnings and thrown out many suggestions. Something will come of them in the future, though I cannot myself tell whether it will be much or little. I can, however, express a hope that I have opened up a pathway for an important advance in our knowledge. (Sigmund Freud, *An Autobiographical Study, 1925)*

This study began in the winter of 1976 as a seemingly straightforward inquiry into the connection between psychoanalysis and permissivist aspects of American education. My hunch was that psychoanalysis provided a major theoretical underpinning for the permissivist thrust in American *progressive* education, and from there entered into the American educational atmosphere more pervasively. My original plan was first to investigate the link between psychoanalysis and education in its European setting (briefly, I thought), and then move on to the American phase, the major phase, of the investigation. I began with an inquiry into the question: What did the pioneer psychoanalysts have to say about education? To my surprise, the answer was: Plenty. As I burrowed into the literature, developments in Europe began to seem more important than the general problem of the influences of psychoanalysis on American education. The historical record disclosed a close and surprisingly direct connection between psychoanalytic theory and education in Europe, and opened up a hitherto largely unknown chapter in the history of education as well as in the history of psychoanalysis.

The connection between psychoanalysis and education dates back to Vienna in the first decade of this century, to 1905 and Freud's classic *Three Essays on the Theory of Sexuality* and the discussions of the fledgling Vienna Psychoanalytic Society. Freud and his early circle were fascinated by the meliorative potential of a new education informed by psychoanalysis, what Freud called "the princely education along psychoanalytic lines." But it was in the 1920s, under the leadership of the newest branch of psychoanalysis, child analysis, that a movement to create a "psychoanalytic pedagogy" emerged in Vienna. Psychoanalytic pedagogy had as its goal the prevention of neurosis. To anticipate one of our findings, many of the principles and practices involved in these early applications of psychoanalysis to education are now well known in progressive education. For almost a generation before its demise in the late 1930s, psychoanalytic pedagogy enjoyed great favor among the psychoanalytic community on the Continent. If only because there may be some lessons to be learned from it, the history of the rise and fall of the movement to create a psychoanalytic pedagogy is too important to be allowed to sink into oblivion.

Some scholars are unaware of or seem to be anxious to deny any direct connection between Freudian concepts and doctrines of permissiveness in education and child rearing.[1] Others exaggerate the liberationist orientation of Freud's educational prescriptions, ignoring their complexity.[2] Here, a closer familiarity with the whole of the historical development of Freud's work is indispensable.

There are two sides, or two different, somewhat contradictory moral philosophies in Freud. One side is Freud the liberator. Freud once claimed that psychoanalysis "stands in opposition to everything that is conventionally restricted, well-established, and generally accepted."[3] It is well known, writes Anna Freud, that "when psychoanalysis came on the scene, it did so in a revolutionary spirit."[4] Freud's writings, observes Peter Gay, are pervaded with invitations to be more wicked, to accept eccentric behavior as normal, to give up punitive attitudes toward "the perversions," to accept, in short, the instinctive life. "He was...a moral liberator," writes Gay.[5] Freud, as we shall see, pleaded eloquently at one time on behalf of more freedom and indulgence for children. But there is another, darker side to Freud that deserves equal acknowledgment, one more pessimistic and controlling. This is the Freud who confronted narcissistic humanity with harsh truths: civilization imposes sacrifices; life is hard and unremitting; blows are inevitable; we all are scarred. There is no way out of our predicament, "The ego of man is not master in its own house."[6] This is the Freud of the '20s and '30s who teaches that

childhood is no golden age of innocence and happiness, but a time of extraordinarily intense sexual and aggressive feelings. This is the Freud
who teaches that children cannot simply be let free, without adult
guidance and discipline. Usually one side of Freud, the liberating Freud
in the case of education and childrearing, is emphasized at the expense of
the other. The result has been a distorted emphasis on partial aspects of
Freudian theory; the rest is ignored or denied. The vastness of Freud's
theoretical construction, its technical complexities, and his repeated
modifications of it, made his work peculiarly vulnerable to distortion
even by psychoanalysts, as we shall see.

Some critical phases in the evolution of Freudian theory may be
followed in the vicissitudes of the movement to create a psychoanalytic
pedagogy in Europe. If earlier developments in Freudian theory helped
give birth to the movement to create a psychoanalytic pedagogy, later
developments in theory helped to hasten its demise—a point of no small
theoretical, as well as historical significance.

The tie between psychoanalysis and education can best be explored in
its native habitat—central Europe. What did the pioneers of
psychoanalysis have to say about education?

In *An Autobiographical Study,* Freud writes, "I myself have contributed nothing to the application of analysis to education." But it was
natural, he continued, "...that analytic discoveries about the sexual life
and mental development of children should attract the attention of
educators and make them see their problems in a new light." Freud is too
modest. True, his work was generally concerned with theoretical issues
and not applied ones. But Freud, in more places than one, compared
psychoanalytic treatment to a kind of educational process—*Nacherziehung,* a form of post-education, or second education; "a kind of
after-education (sic)," or a "late re-education in the conquering of the
remnants of childhood." Psychoanalytic treatment, Freud said, "acts as
a second education of the adult, as a corrective to his education as a
child."[8] If psychoanalytic treatment could be considered a form of re-
education, then it inevitably had to open up the question of the possibility of devising a new or reformed *first* education that would do away with
the need for therapy. In any event, despite his disclaimer, Freud did indeed contribute something to the application of psychoanalysis to the
education and upbringing of children, and that something is important.

The genesis of psychoanalytic pedagogy can be directly traced to 1905
and one of the most fundamental of Freud's books, his *Three Essays on
the Theory of Sexuality.*[9] Briefly, in Freud's view, the child has its sexual
instincts and activities from the first; "it comes into the world with
them." The child's sexual instincts must undergo a highly complicated

development, passing through many stages until about the age of four or five and the establishment of the primacy of the genitals and the resolution of the Oedipus complex, after which no further progress toward sexual maturity is made until pre-adolescence. Freud located the causative factors of neurosis in early childhood, and found them originating in disturbances in the child's sexual development. But were these disturbances due essentially to heredity or innate constitution, or to experience or education? If certain deviations from the normal pattern of development were due not so much to constitution but to experience, and were therefore modifiable, then it opened up the question of the prevention of neuroses through early intervention in the child's development. In the *Three Essays* Freud leaned toward constitution. But he hedged, leaving room "for the modifying effects of accidental events experienced in childhood and later." And, Freud added, critically, if "accidental events," i.e., experience or education, do count, "...we shall be in...closer harmony with psychoanalytic research if we give a place of preference among the accidental factors to the experiences of early childhood."[10]

With its theories of infantile sexuality, the developmental stages, and, especially, the significance of early childhood experiences, the *Three Essays* seemed to lay the groundwork for a new scientific pedagogy of early childhood. At this time Freud stressed the part of parents in mental illness. In 1909, at a meeting of the Vienna Psychoanalytic Society, Freud observed how "enormous a role is played by education"; in fact, the illness "is often only the echoing voice of parents and educators."[11] Freud's thinking suggested that parents and educators harmed children in two ways: by a too strict upbringing that led to "pathogenic repression" of sexual instinct, and by misleading children in matters of sex.

Freud, by the mid-1890s, had isolated repression as the chief factor in the aetiology of the neuroses—the most prominent and the most pathogenic factor.[12] Repression, wrote Freud, "is the essential condition for the development of symptoms." The repressed instinct is withdrawn from conscious influence, but it becomes more potent for that. "It ramifies like a fungus...in the dark and takes on extreme forms of expression...." Neurotic symptoms, says Freud, can be fairly described as "the return of the repressed."[13]

For Freud there was always something positive and therapeutic about venting the emotions; one of the aims of psychoanalytic treatment was to allow the patient an expression of feelings that had been repressed. In any event, analysis would "replace repression by healthy suppression." What was more, analysis facilitated "sublimation, the deflection of instinct to more social ends"—an important new concept that appears first in *Three Essays on the Theory of Sexuality*.[14] Since decisive repressions take place in childhood, the solution seemed obvious—a freer, more lenient, indulgent, and permissive upbringing. Only in the '20s, however, did permissiveness emerge as the major theme of the new psychoanalytic pedagogy. In these first attempts to apply psychoanalytic findings to education and childrearing, the priority went to sex education.

The matter of sexual education or sexual enlightenment was thoroughly aired between 1907 and 1909 at meetings of the Vienna Psychoanalytic Society. Freud insisted on the advisability of the sexual enlightenment of children. At one meeting, during a discussion devoted to "Sexual Traumata and Sexual Enlightenment," Freud raised the question of whether early sexual enlightenment might not serve as a protection against neurosis, as "a kind of protective inoculation against traumata."[15] Freud thought it probably could. Sexual life must "from the start be treated without secretiveness in the presence of children." The main damage done by the failure to enlighten children "lies in the fact that for the rest of the child's life, sexuality is afflicted with the character of the forbidden." This stigma, concluded Freud, "...above all, should be removed from sexuality."[16] Freud was convinced that sexual prohibitions helped to create stupidity in children: "If it is the purpose of educators to stifle the child's power of independent thought as early as possible, in favor of the 'goodness' which they think so much of, they cannot set about this better than deceiving him in sexual matters."[17] Still, in making recommendations regarding education and childrearing, Freud was inclined to caution. In general, he advised that it is better to delay making direct proposals until more was known about the child.[18]

In 1909, Freud published the first account of the analysis of a child—"A Phobia in a Five-Year-Old Boy," the famous Little Hans case, one of the classics of psychoanalytic literature.[19]

The Little Hans case confirmed Freud's speculations regarding the importance of early childhood, the existence of infantile sexuality, the role of parents in the aetiology of neurosis, and the therapeutic effects of sexual enlightenment. He also explicitly raised the issue of permissiveness versus strictness in upbringing. "It is, to say the least of it, extremely probable that a child's upbringing can exercise a powerful influence for good or for evil upon the predisposition [to mental disease], but what that upbringing is to aim at and at what point it is to be brought to bear seem at present to be very doubtful questions."[20] Freud recognized the enormity of the child's problem "when in the course of his cultural training he is called upon to overcome the innate instinctual components of his mind." Though cautious about making recommendations, Freud was more critical of education than he had ever been before. In bringing up children, Freud noted, adults aim to train up a model child. In the process they pay little attention to whether such a course of development is for the child's good as well. In the name of Little Hans, Freud introduced a liberationist slogan: "Hitherto education has set itself the task of controlling, or it would often be more proper to say, of suppressing the instincts. The results have been by no means gratifying.... Nor has anyone enquired by what means and at what cost the suppression of the inconvenient instincts has been achieved." Supposing, Freud continues, "....that we substitute another task for this one, and aim instead at making the individual capable of becoming a civilized and useful member of society with the least possible sacrifice of his own [instinctual] activity; in that case the information gained by psychoanalysis upon the origin of pathogenic complexes and upon the nucleus of every nervous affection can claim with justice that it deserves to be regarded by educators as an invaluable guide in their conduct toward children."[21]

In the period before World War I, as we have seen, Freud had arrived at a set of hypotheses regarding the aetiology of the neuroses which rested on two pillars: disposition or innate constitution, and experience or education. In theory, Freud may have been convinced that "disposition and experience are linked up in an indissoluble aetiological unity," but in practice at this time, the emphasis was on the latter. Childhood experiences constituted the key aetiological factor in neurotic symptom formation in the adult.[22] If the experiences of early childhood were basic, when environment and education still counted for much, then early childhood was a strategic time for intervention. But on the question of what sort of early education was best, strict or lenient, Freud wavered, or tried to keep these basic attitudes toward child rearing in tension, or balance. There was implied in the Little Hans case an eloquent plea for more freedom for the child, for an end to punishment or threats of maiming, for a new sympathy and indulgence for the child's instinctual life, and a warning against the dangers of repression. But soon Freud was warning against the dangers of indulgence and spoiling in childrearing and education. In 1911, in his famous paper on the two principles of mental functioning (the "reality principle" and the "pleasure principle"), Freud succinctly defined education as "an incitement to the conquest of the pleasure principle, and to its replacement by the reality principle." That is, Freud continues, education seeks "to lend its help to the developmental process which affects the ego. To this end it makes use of an offer of love as a reward from the educators; and it therefore fails if a spoilt child thinks that it possesses that love in any case and cannot lose it whatever happens."[23] Freud seems definite and clear enough here.

A few years later, however, in 1913, commenting on the relevance of psychoanalysis to education and the upbringing of children, during the course of a general review of the status of psychoanalysis, Freud's view tilted once more towards indulgence.[24] Freud noted that psychoanalysis takes seriously the old saying that the child is father to the man; especially does psychoanalysis observe "the extraordinarily important influence exerted by the impressions of childhood...on the whole course of later development." Freud's point was that only when adults become familiar with the findings of psychoanalysis would they become capable of educating children. When educators become familiar with the findings of psychoanalysis, it will be much easier for them to reconcile themselves to the phases of infantile development. "They will refrain from any attempt at forcibly suppressing the children's instinctual impulses."[25] Furthermore, psychoanalysis could also show what precious contributions to the formation of character are made by the "asocial and perverse instincts" of children, if they are not subjected to repression "but are diverted from their original aims to more valuable ones by the process known as 'subimation.' " Education, Freud advises, should "scrupulously refrain from burying these precious springs of action, and should restrict itself to encouraging the processes by which these energies are led along safe paths." Freud concludes: "Whatever we can expect in the way of prophylaxis against neurosis in the individual lies in the hands of a psychoanalytically enlightened education."[26] Freud's call for a certain relaxation of restrictions and controls could hardly be called radically permissive: note the emphasis on "sublimation." Nevertheless, a second generation of psychoanalysts, and even some in the first, would be, as we shall see, less circumspect and prudent.

In the pre-World War I period, many other psychoanalysts in Freud's early circle had become deeply interested in the problems of education. During the early years of its existence, the application of psychoanalysis to the upbringing and education of children was a staple of the discussions of the Vienna Psychoanalytic Society. The discussions among the regulars—Freud, Muller, and Tausk—are exciting to read even today. Sandor Ferenczi, one of Freud's inner circle, addressed the First Psychoanalytic Congress in Salzburg in 1908 on the subject of psychoanalysis and education. Some of the pioneers in the psychoanalytic movement—Adler in Vienna, Ferenczi in Hungary, Carl Jung and Oskar Pfister in Switzerland, and Ernest Joncs, first in Canada, then in England—were already publishing for a lay audience on the subject of education.[27] In 1913, Otto Rank and Hanns Sachs, in their *The Significance of Psychoanalysis for the Mental Sciences,* summarized the mainstream position of psychoanalysis in Europe in the pre-World War I period so far as education was concerned. On the negative side, they warned against imposing a too demanding repression of instinct. "So far as possible, one should leave the child alone, with as complete withholding of direct injurious influences as possible, and inhibit him as little as possible in his natural development." On the positive side, he advocated sexual education and enlightenment.[28]

There was, then, in the pre-World War I period among European psychoanalysts widespread agreement on the importance of early childhood, widespread interest in the problems of education, widespread isolation of and focus upon environmental over constitutional or intra-psychic influences in the aetiology of the neuroses, and a shared conviction that sex education and a more indulgent attitude toward the child's actions would provide prophylaxis. The essential ingredients of a psychoanalytic pedagogy were already present.[29] Nevertheless, the attempted fusion of psychoanalysis and education had to wait for the post-war period and the emergence of a new branch of applied psychoanalysis—child analysis.

The emergence of child psychoanalysis was almost exclusively the work of a small group of women, many of them former school teachers—Hermine von Hug-Hellmuth, Berta Bornstein, and Anna Freud, in Vienna, Alice Balint in Budapest, Steff Bornstein in Prague, Ada Mueller-Braunschweig, and Melanie Klein in Berlin, then after 1926 in London—aided by a smaller group of men—Siegfried Bernfeld, Willi Hoffer, and August Aichhorn in Vienna, Ferenczi in Budapest, and Karl Abraham in Berlin.[30] By the mid-1920s, child analysis seemed to be well on the way to becoming the most promising branch of psychoanalysis. Child analysis served as the bridge between psychoanalysis and education. It was from the child analysts that the movement to create a psychoanalytic pedagogy started.

In the post-World War I period, everywhere in Europe, there seemed to be a new interest in the child, in child problems, in child saving, in the mental life of the child. Ellen Key's hopefully titled *The Century of the Child* was published in 1909. Now, thanks to Binet, Montessori, Decroly, Claparede, Stern, and Freud, among others, Key's prophecy seemed to be coming true. The child was becoming a social issue. Parents and teachers were expecting expert advice on the rearing and education of children. The first generation of psychoanalysts, however, was slow to respond. Given, for example, their environmentalist leanings, it seemed inevitable that Freud and his followers would stress child analysis. But they did not. Freud and the first generation of psychoanalysts—all of them male, it might be noted—were not eager to pursue child analysis; they simply could not work with children.[31] The field was left to a group with first-hand experience with children and with their language and mentality—the teaching profession. Teachers, most of them women, most of them originally kindergarten, nursery , elementary, or high school teachers, became the first child analysts.

Obviously, children couldn't be treated in the same way as adults. The psychoanalysis of children had to be a modified form of adult psychoanalysis. The process of verbal free-association, especially, had to be considerably supplemented by methods more appropriate to the child's age and typical forms of expression. As early as 1911, Hug-Hellmuth, the first woman member of the Vienna Psychoanalytic Society, was experimenting with a form of psychoanalytic treatment combining education and play therapy for emotionally disturbed children.[32] She apparently intended to establish child analysis as a branch of special education.[33] With her premature death in 1924, it fell largely to Anna Freud in central Europe and to Melanie Klein in London to create child analysis as a branch of psychoanalysis. It was Anna Freud and her central European circle—the Vienna-Prague-Budapest circle of analysts—who subsequently attempted to combine psychoanalysis and education into a psychoanalytic pedagogy for children which, by preventing neurosis, might do away with the need for treatment. It is doubtful that we can understand these developments, however, without some fuller understanding of the social and intellectual milieu in Vienna.

In the 1920s, the Vienna municipal administration was controlled by Socialists, i.e., the Social Democrats. The immediate concern of the Socialists was to save the children. Under the regime of Mayor Karl Seitz, Vienna became the rallying point for reforms in social welfare, housing, public health, and education.[34] In 1920, under Otto Glockel, president of the Vienna School Board, a glorious epoch of school reform was inaugurated. A "new education, a form of *"Arbeitsschule"* or "Activity School," usually called simply "the school reform," was aggressively promoted by the Vienna school board.[35] The post-war period in Europe witnessed the greatest educational ferment of modern times. Progressive education and the Activity School were everywhere gaining enthusiastic converts.[36] But Vienna was an inspiration. Roberts Dottrens of the Institute Jean Jacques Rousseau in Geneva reported at the conclusion of a tour through England, France, Belgium, Czechoslovakia, Germany, and Austria that Vienna was "...ahead of all the other cities of Europe from the point of view of educational progress." It was to Vienna, "the pedagogical Mecca...that the new pilgrims of the modern school must go to find the realization of their dreams and hopes."[37]

In Vienna the mood among those concerned with education was one of almost utopian optimism. The war had administered a profound shock to comfortable dogmas. The redrawing of frontiers was not enough. Only the reconstruction of humanity itself, through a "new education," could prevent further catastrophe.[38] Many of the idealistic, talented Viennese youth of the new generation were swept up in the 1920s in the enthusiasm for "the school reform" and went into the teaching profession. Anna Freud and Willi Hoffer saw in these school teachers promising material from which to create not so much a corps of child analysts, but a corps of psychoanalytic pedagogues.[39]

As a "service of child experts," child analysts could only reach a few children. But the child analysts seemed to be in a strategic position to do more. After all, if psychological problems were in fact due to nurture, to faulty education rather than to nature, heredity, or constitution, then potentially, through a new education, neuroses might be ameliorated or even prevented en masse. At this time psychoanalytic opinion reflected a belief that the origins of neurosis lay in the environment, in the experiences of childhood. The Little Hans case was exemplary. What visions were opened up! Child analysis, Anna Freud declared in 1926, "furnishes a transition to a sphere of application which, as many think, should in the future be one of the most important for psychoanalysis: to pedagogics, or the science of upbringing and education."[40]

The child analysts were swept up in enthusiasm for a new education. An elite group of teachers would be recruited, given training, and persuaded to undergo analysis, and then they would return to the schools as the revolutionary vanguard. At the Vienna Psychoanalytic Society, in the Mid-'20s, Anna Freud, Hoffer, and August Aichhorn gave special courses and lectures and organized discussion groups for teachers. A small number of school teachers on the Continent were introduced to psychoanalytic theories in Miss Freud's seminars on child analysis, beginning in 1926-1927. Besides the lectures, courses, and seminars, especially important in diffusing psychoanalytic views of pedagogy among educationists was the inauguration in the winter of 1926 under psychoanalysts Heinrich Meng and Ernst Schneider of the *Zeitschrift für Psychoanalytische Pädagogik,* the *Journal of Psychoanalytic Pedagogy.* In the winter of 1931, Hoffer finally organized a formal, three-year training course in psychoanalytic pedagogy, the "Lehrgang für Psychoanalytische Pädagogen," at the Vienna Psychoanalytic Institute.[41] The child analysts were convinced that they were on the threshold of a new historical epoch. The psychoanalysts talked then of psychoanalytic therapy as *Nacherziehung;* as a kind of post-education, or re-education. If, as they said, psychoanalytic therapy was a form of re-education, then it was possible to think in terms of a progressive pedagogy that would eliminate or minimize the need for a second education.[42] The first issue of the *Zeitschrift für Psychoanalytische Pädagogik* announced as its aim to lay the foundation of a psychoanalytic pedagogy that would prevent neurosis or extirpate it from human life.[43] Psychoanalyst Heinz Hartmann recalls the time when the prevention of neurosis was considered to be the heart of the psychoanalytic contribution to education.[44]

But the prevention of neuroses en masse through a new education was not in the 1920s and 1930s just the utopian dogma of the child analysts. Inspired by the hope of the prevention of neurosis through a new education, Wilhelm Reich in the late 1920s took practical steps to launch a mental-hygiene movement, first in Vienna, then in Berlin.[45] Perhaps Reich, as Anna Freud put it, was "the most uncompromising exponent" of the view that neurosis could be extirpated through new methods of education and upbringing, but there were many psychoanalysts who shared Reich's opinion, including Meng, Schneider, Ferenczi, Paul

Federn, Wilhelm Stekel, Fritz Wittels, and many more.[46] Even Freud himself was sometimes swept up in the enthusiasm and tempted to become a healer to humanity. Freud not only gave his sanction to child analysis, but also encouraged the child analysts in their efforts to apply psychoanalysis to education. "None of the applications of psychoanalysis," Freud wrote in 1925, "has excited so many hopes, and none consequently has attracted so many capable workers, as its use in the theory and practice of education.[47] In 1928, in *The Question of Lay Analysis,* Freud forcefully came out in support of the application of psychoanalysis to the education of young children. A treatment that combines analytic influence with educational measures, he said, carried out by people who are not ashamed to concern themselves with the affairs of a child's world, and who understand how to find their way into a child's mental life, could bring about two things at once—the removal of neurotic symptoms, and the reversal of any change for the worse in character which might already have begun. Analysis still had "enemies," Freud concluded, but he did not think they had the means at their command for stopping the activities of "these educational analysts or analytic educationalists."[48]

"Freud himself, from the very beginning," writes Willi Hoffer, "encouraged us to think not only of cure but of how to minimize or prevent the 'traumatic effects of education on children.' "[49] The earliest conclusions drawn for education and parental guidance, even by Freud, as we have seen, called for more freedom and indulgence for the child and emphasized the faults of parents and teachers and the cost of the repression of the child's instincts. In 1923, in *The Ego and the Id,* Freud again called attention to the potentially pathogenic effects of unenlightened upbringing. Freud emphasized the weakness of the ego in relation to the superego, reformulating the "echoing voice of parents and teachers," and illuminating its harsh and punitive nature. Freud then believed that the severity of the superego reflected the severity of one's upbringing. Freud's point was that psychoanalysts were obliged to do battle with the superego and work to *moderate* its demands.[50] But it was easy to jump to the conclusion that the less superego the better. To Berlin psychoanalyst Franz Alexander the superego was "an anachronism of the mind." It was not enough to modify the superego. Alexander in 1925 confidently proclaimed: "The dissolution of the superego is and will continue to be the task of all future psychoanalytic therapy."[51] It was this notion of the superego as the root of all evil which helped inspire among the child analysts such high hopes of a prophylaxis of neurosis through a more permissive education.

During a period lasting until at least into the early '30s on the Continent, was considered to contribute most to psychopathology the tyranny of a too strict superego. "Much of the psychoanalytic writing of the, 1920s stressed the faults of parents and teachers—overly strict, Victorian, traumatizing. To the psychoanalysts, the parents were the adversaries. Ferenczi used to say, "There are no bad children. There are only bad parents."[52] An influential 1923 effort to summarize the state of psychoanalysis looked forward to the time when every family would have its own psychoanalyst, "a doctor of souls."[53]

The child analysts followed their elders and mentors. Thinking that they would please or impress Freud, they took it upon themselves to devise a new education which would prevent the development of nervous disorders. For their theory, they went back to Freud's early work. In their youthful exuberance, optimism, and social zeal, they could not, as Freud had done, hold in tension the polarities of indulgence and restriction, expression and suppression, freedom and restraint. Inevitably, the new education had as its main plank the liberation of the child's instinctual drives and the abolition of repression, the "liberation of the instincts and the crusade against the faults of parents and educators."[54] The object was to minimize the frustration of instinctual demands. It was assumed that pathogenic repression of the instincts would thus be avoided. Psychoanalyst Rudolf Ekstein, a former Viennese school teacher who was swept up in the movement, labels this new education "progressive education," and defined it: "Progressive education was seen as the liberation of the instincts, as a struggle against trauma, as favoring laissez-faire, with a minimum of intervention on the part of educators and parents."[55] Ekstein's succinct definition can serve as an introduction to the early work of Anna Freud, the guiding spirit behind the movement for a psychoanalytic pedagogy.

Anna Freud, the youngest of Freud's six children, became active in psychoanalysis in 1918 at the age of 23. She came into psychoanalytic work from the teaching profession, having served for five years as a teacher in a primary school in Vienna. She became a member of the Vienna Psychoanalytic Society in that same year. In 1923 she began to practice child analysis. Beginning in that year, with the discovery of Freud's cancer, she became his spokesperson and heir apparent as leader of the psychoanalytic movement. By 1926 Miss Freud was secretary of the International Pscyhoanalytical Association. With Hug-Hellmuth's death in 1924, and Melanie Klein's move from Berlin to London in 1926, she quickly assumed the role of leadership in child analysis on the Continent.[56] It was Anna Freud who most explicitly attempted to define the relationship between psychoanalysis and education. She staked out her position in 1929 in a series of lectures delivered to teachers of the *Hort,* the children's day-care centers in Vienna.[57] The reformist note of hope, enthusiasm and prevention is the dominant one. Miss Freud pinned her hopes on a permissive pedagogy; she proved herself a diligent interpreter of her father's early teachings on education and childrearing. Education, she admonished her audience, does not begin with the child's entrance into school: *"The education of a child begins with his first day of life* (sic)."[58] Miss Freud refers to the "definite danger arising from education," and the demands of the adult world and the prohibitions imposed on children. Education "struggles with the nature of the child or—as the grown-up usually calls it—with his naughtiness." But, she stated, psychoanalysis discovers this so-called "naughtiness" to be an inevitable consequence of events in accordance with the stages of development, such as we have long recognized in the development of the physical body. In the interests of the child's development, educators push through these stages, afraid to let the child pause on the way—anxious to get the child to the last stage, the quicker the better.

Too often, Miss Freud continued, parents secure obedience by threatening children with punishment, in terms that to the child imply bodily damage. Less brutal, but equally harmful in the long run, is the parental threat to withdraw their love. Now the child enters school. The parents have every right to be proud. But what has happened to the child's shrewdness and originality? Their disciplinary techniques have helped the parent change the "crying troublesome and dirty infant" into the well-behaved school child, but often at a price. The "originality of the child, together with a great deal of his energy and talents, are sacrificed to being 'good.' " Obviously, Miss Freud observed, "to bring up 'good' children is not without its dangers."[59] Psychoanalysis, whenever it has come into contact with pedagogy, Miss Freud says, has always expressed the wish to limit education; it has stressed the definite dangers arising from education. Miss Freud spoke of the psychoanalyst as one who "certainly learns to know education from its worst side." The analyst, she continued, resolves to leave his own children free rather than to educate them in this way. The analyst would rather "risk the chance of their being somewhat uncontrolled in the end instead of forcing on them from the outset such a crippling of their individuality."[60] In fact, Miss Freud continued, "the question remains unanswered as to what would happen if the adults around a child refrained from interfering in any way."[61] This was the conventional wisdom of psychoanalytic pedagogy in the late 1920s. The apogee of permissiveness in education is reached in Wittel's *The Liberation of the Child,* whose title can stand as the slogan of the new psychoanalytic pedagogy.[62]

The theory of psychoanalytic pedagogy pertained, in the main, to early education within the home circle. Some psychoanalysts in Europe, working independently, at different times and in different places, and with various degrees of eclecticism, tried to demonstrate the practical corollaries of psychoanalytic doctrine in the education of children in

groups—in institutional or school settings. There were a handful of experiments in psychoanalytic pedagogy on the Continent—most of which
have been neglected or forgotten—such as those by Siegfried Bernfeld,
Lili Roubiczek-Peller, Anna Freud and Dorothy Burlingham in Vienna,
and Vera Schmidt in Moscow.

In the fall of 1919, Siegfried Bernfeld, a young social worker,
Socialist, Zionist, and leader in the Jewish youth movement in Vienna,
deeply immersed in psychoanalysis, opened the Kinderheim Baumgarten,
a co-educational, residential school for Jewish refugee children displaced
by the war. The school, five cottages in a former army barracks on the
outskirts of Vienna, was established under the auspices of the Austrian
branch of the "Joint Distribution Committee for Relief of Jewish War
Sufferers" (soon to be renamed the American Joint Distribution Committee).[63] The Kinderheim, the "Children's Home," opened with almost
300 children, aged 3-16. Bernfeld was the director; his collaborators included his wife Anne, Willi Hoffer, Gerhard Fuchs, Greta Obernik, and
Hella Rosenblum, all active in "the school reform" in Vienna.

Bernfeld was convinced that any "new education" must be founded
on psychoanalytic principles. Anna Freud calls Kinderheim Baumgarten
"a first experiment to apply psychoanalytic principles to education."[64]
Bernfeld, however, was influenced not only by Freud and
psychoanalysis, but also by some contemporary progressive educators:
Maria Montessori, Paul Geheeb, Berthold Otto, and Gustav Wyneken,
especially Wyneken and his self-governing, co-educational, residential
school, the "Freie Schulgemeinde" (the Free School Community), at
Wickersdorf, Germany. Of course, Bernfeld was concerned with the
children's maximal psychological development. But Bernfeld also hoped
to develop in the children at the kinderheim the kind of character and
personality that would prepare them for life in a Socialist, Zionist state
of Palestine.

Bernfeld and his co-workers at the Kinderheim were especially influenced by Freud in their approach to the psychosexual problems of the
children. They tried to help the children therapeutically, through a permissive milieu rather than to control the children through restraint,
punishment or coercion. The children's psychological problems were explored, not suppressed. In his fascinating account of the experiment,
Bernfeld described the children as being, at first, selfish and always com-
plaining, distrustful of adults, and brutal towards those younger than
themselves, and as habitually lying and stealing. Their outlook on life
was one of *"hemmungsloser Egoismus"* i.e. unbounded egoism. In
specific reference to their sexual behavior, Bernfeld described many of
the children as lacking in anal inhibitions, with the adolescent boys in-
dulging in frequent masturbation practices, especially in mutual masturbation. In psychoanalytic terminology, Bernfeld observed that the

libidos of most of the children were fixated at a narcissistic level, and that most of the children were still at the anal and sado-masochistic stages of development, which, at their ages, they should have outgrown.[65]

During the first few months of its existence, the Kinderheim Baumgarten was characterized by chaos, or, in Bernfield's term, *"schöpferisches chaos,"* creative chaos. There were no rules. The children were free from all restraints; they received no punishment. The results were as unanticipated as they now appear to us to be predictable.The youngsters fought, broke furniture, clattered with plates and utensils, and shouted loudly for food; the buildings of the Kinderheim were quickly covered with graffiti. But Bernfeld encouraged the children to speak and write freely and to express their grievances and desires, and what soon emerged was a form of student self-government in a family atmosphere. There was a general legislature, or meeting of the whole body of the Kinderheim the "Schulgemeinde," or the school community—presided over by a small elected board, which formulated the rules and regulations. There was a student court which dealt with disciplinary offenses. The oldest boys were organized into a sort of monitor force to help police the Kinderheim. Most of the children responded positively. In Bernfeld's words, the youngsters began to sublimate their anal and sado-masochistic tendencies, diverting them toward higher, more social ends.[66]

The abandonment of discipline and compulsion in the Kinderheim implied a compensatory emphasis on the children's special interests. At first, Bernfeld's idea was to offer no formal instruction at all. It soon became clear that this policy was impractical or imprudent. Many of the 18 teachers wanted more formal instruction, the Joint Distribution Committee demanded it and the Austrian authorities prescribed it. The teachers, however, were encouraged to experiment with more permissive disciplines and to develop their own courses. There were no exams or grades. Unfortunately, there is no account of precisely what subjects were taught. Bernfeld mentions math, history, civics, and Bible-reading. We know that there was a Montessori-type kindergarten for the infants. We know too that youngsters were encouraged to participate in activities like gardening, handiwork, sewing, and bookbinding. And we also know that the adolescents took formal classes and participated in interest groups gathered around an adult, and in peer-led groups which usually met once a week to read books, discuss politics and social issues, or study Hebrew. Bernfeld hoped that the Kinderheim would become a model for other residential schools for "special" children in Austria. It was not to be. The Kinderheim was short-lived, remaining open for only about nine months in all. Bernfeld fell seriously ill in December of 1919. Because of his illness, insuperable problems with the Joint Distribution Committee and with some of the teaching staff for whom the permissive atmosphere was anathema, the experiment was terminated on April 15, 1920.[67]

In 1922, Lili Roubiczek-Peller, with the assistance of four other young women—part of that pioneer group of young Viennese teachers attracted to the school reform and organized into an *Arbeitsgemeinschaft*—founded the Haus der Kinder, a Montessori School in a working-class district of Vienna.[68] Peller, who before undergoing Montessori training in London had studied psychology under Karl Buhler at the University of Vienna, soon came under the influence of the charismatic Bernfeld and became interested in psychoanalysis. Since both Freud and Montessori emphasized the critical importance of early childhood, it seemed feasible for Peller and her co-workers to attempt a synthesis of the two. The Hans der Kinder tried to incorporate Montessori's stress on the rational side of personality with the psychoanalyts' stress on the instinctual, combining Montessori's conception of the child's "sensitive periods" with Freud's theory of the child's developmental stages. With the psychoanalysts, Peller believed that "permissiveness should be the keynote of early education." She wanted to allow children the free expression of their instincts. Prohibitions and restrictions at the Haus der Kinder were minimal; punishments were forbidden on principle. With the Montessorians, Peller was concerned with the child's moral and social education. The infant's social education was to be steered by the "transference," that powerful leverage of attachment to the mother or mother-figure (the teacher), as well as by the "reality" factors inherent in the Montessori didactic apparatus and in the group life of the school.[69]

The Haus der Kinder began with 25 children, boys and girls between the ages of two and four. It quickly earned a reputation. By 1928 the school enrolled 50 children, aged 2½ to 10, and had moved into a handsome new building designed by architect Franz Schuster of the Bauhaus. By that time most of the teachers at the Haus der Kinder, as well as Peller, were attending Anna Freud's seminars in child analysis and other courses at the Vienna Psychoanalytic Institute. Subsequently most of them enrolled in Hoffer's special training course for teachers at the Institute and some of the child analysts had become interested in the Montessori method, viz., Anna Freud, Robert Waelder, and Erik Homburger Erikson.[70] Madame Montessori, ever sensitive to changes in her "method," was not flattered by Peller's interest in psychoanalysis and withdrew her blessings from the Haus der Kinder. In any event, Peller gradually become more interested in child analysis than pedagogy, became a psychoanalyst, and in the early 1930s gradually withdrew from active Montessori work.[71] In February, 1934 as the Nazi darkness descended on the Continent, Peller and her husband Sigismund, a physican, emigrated to Palestine, but the Haus der Kinder continued until the Nazis closed it in 1938.[72]

In 1927, Anna Freud, along with her good friend and sister child analyst Dorothy Burlingham, collaborated in the establishment of a school for children.[73] There were about twenty children enrolled in the school. Many of them were in analysis as were many of the parents who intended to become analysts themselves. The teachers, Eric Homburger Erikson and Peter Blos, two fledgling child analysts, soon joined by Erikson's wife, Joan, were given full freedom to organize the curriculum and teach it any way they chose. Erikson's biographer, Robert Coles, describes the school. The children were not graded. They were taught as individuals. They were encouraged to share in planning the day's activities and choosing the subject matter. But the children were exposed to science, history, geography, and English, Blos' specialties. Naturally, with Erikson on the staff, artistic self-expression, drawing, painting, and poetry were also emphasized. Blos and Erikson "wanted the children to feel 'free,' that is, unafraid of school, and in many respects their own masters." The result, says Coles, was "what could be called a progressive school, similar in some respects to some American experimental schools.[74] The school closed in 1933, as Blos and the Eriksons emigrated to America.[75]

The experiments in applied psychoanalysis in schools and other institutional settings are obviously not of a piece. They have their different moods and emphases and degrees of orthodoxy. In a place by itself in the literature of educational history is the experiment of Vera Schmidt in Moscow.

In revolutionary Russia in the early '20s, psychoanalysis was for a time held in favor by the State. In the summer of 1921, Vera Schmidt, a psychoanalyst probably trained by Ferenczi, was given permission by Dr. Ivan Ermakov, director of the State Institute of Neuropsychology in Moscow and the leader of the psychoanalytic movement in Russia, to organize a residential school for infants, to be run "exclusively" on psychoanalytic principles.[76] The Moscow Children's Home and Psychological Laboratory, as it was called, began with 30 children, boys and girls, aged 1 to 5 and from families, we are told, from diverse social classes. The children were divided into three groups: there were six children aged 1 to 1½, nine children aged 2 to 3 and 15 children aged 3 to 5. There were four women teachers or leaders, "directresses," for each group.

At the Children's Home and Psychological Laboratory the teachers refrained as much as possible from interfering with the children's spontaneous process of development. The children's instinctual manifestations were permitted free expression. It was not until the end of the second year and only "at certain intervals" that children were put on the toilet. But the children were never forced to attend to their needs in precisely this manner. The attitude of the teachers toward the children's excretory processes was entirely relaxed. Our method, writes Schmidt, "seems likely to save children from the severe traumatic experiences usually connected with sphincter control."[77] No moral judgments were made regarding the children's sexual activities. Masturbation was not condemned. Children were free to satisfy their sexual curiosity among themselves. Nudity was the rule in warm weather. Children's questions about sexual matters received clear and truthful answers. Punishments of any kind on the part of the teachers were forbidden. There was no praise or blame; neither was there overt display of love or affection. Since there was no need on the children's part for secrecy or shyness, Schmidt writes, teachers had every opportunity to observe the sexual development of the children step-by-step. By such means, Schmidt hoped, it would be established whether the various phases of infantile sexuality postulated by Freud arise spontaneously and then disappear without any educational influence. However, there were abundant toys and games fitted to the needs, interests, and abilities of the children, and the children's surroundings were made as agreeable as possible. "When necessary" the child was aided progressively to master and surmount the "pleasure principle" and replace it with the "reality principle."[78]

The Moscow Children's Home never had it easy. Even for Moscow in the early '20s the experiment was radical. In April, 1922, after a public outcry and a series of investigations having to do with accusations that the school was encouraging sexual precociousness in the infants, the Institute of Neuropsychology withdrew support for the experiment. Subsequently, The Children's Home was saved by the joint effort of a group of German and Russian workers—miners, in fact—and the newly organized Russian Psychoanalytic Society. But now the experiment, re-named the International Solidarity Children's Home, was cut down to twelve children—five boys and seven girls, ages 3 to 5—four of whom remained from the original group.[79] Schmidt reported on the experiment in the winter of 1923 in a series of talks to the psychoanalytic community in Vienna and Berlin. She reported favorable results in the children's sexual and personality development, and on the relationships between the children and their parents. She also observed the unsettling effect of this free education on the emotional lives of the teachers who had not been psychoanalyzed.[80] (Similar results had been observed by Bernfeld at the Kinderheim Baumgarten.)

Schmidt was forced to terminate the experiment in about 1929, as the Russian authorities withdrew their favor from psychoanalysis. Wilhelm Reich met Schmidt in Moscow in 1929. He was disappointed to learn that she encouraged the children to learn to control their instincts. But on the whole he was favorably impressed. Schmidt's experiment, he wrote, "was the first attempt in the history of education to give practical content to the theory of infantile sexuality."[81] In an all-too-brief reference written in 1929, Anna Freud observed that Schmidt's experiment was short-lived, and the question of the relative influence of predisposition and education, "except in the case of one child," remained unsolved.[82]

The demise in the 1930s of the movement to create a psychoanalytic pedagogy was almost as sudden and rapid as its efflorescence in the 1920s. Anna Freud and her circle had at one time believed that they were ushering in a historical epoch; it was only a historical moment. By the early 1930s, among the child analysts and the psychoanalytic pedagogues the mood had begun to shift from one of optimism to one of pessimism. The shift in mood was, in psychoanalytic terms, overdetermined. There were many problems—some having to do with theory, others having to do with the relation between theory and practice, some having to do with status, others having to do with politics. Even in the Soviet Union, by the late '20s, as is well known, the authorities absolutely halted the growth of psychoanalysis.

In central Europe, there was hardly fair sailing. Some child analysts were M.D.'s, but many were former teachers or lay persons. The psychoanalytic movement was embroiled in the late '20s in the issue of "lay analysis." Freud's own wishes in this matter had been overridden. Many of the older generation of psychoanalysts never accepted child analysis as a legitimate brand of psychoanalysis, and looked on its practitioners with suspicion, if not contempt.[83] This was hardly an atmosphere conducive to continued exploration of the possible connections between psychoanalysis and education. There were other problems. For example, incidents of cooperation between analysts and educationists remained few and far between. The movement to create a psychoanalytic pedagogy was confined to a small circle of enthusiasts, and hardly affected the public-school sector or rank-and-file educators. As we noted earlier, the post-war period in England, France and Germany coincided with the efflorescence of a vigorous and progressive school reform movement. It was pan-european in scope and represented by the New Education Fellowship. A distinguishing mark of "the new education" was a much greater interest in the early years of childhood. Among its watchwords were "freedom," "self-expression," and "activity." There were also in the New Education Fellowship emphases on the social—"education for service" and "democracy through education"—and even the spiritual—"the life force" and "the God within"—which were absent from psychoanalytic pedagogy. Thus the latter found itself placed not outside of the new education, but on its left wing. But the Central European circle of child analysts around Anna Freud, who had led the effort to create a psychoanalytic pedagogy, rarely made any direct effort to cooperate with or propagate their views among the progressives in European education, let alone the educational Establishment.[84] Furthermore, there was among the child analysts and those seeking to create a psychoanalytic pedagogy an increasing tendency toward orthodoxy, a tendency to seek some precedent in Freud's own writing for any theory that was advanced, a tendency which hardened in the late '20s and early '30s. Thus few attempts were made to explore any possible connection between child analysis and psychoanalytic pedagogy, on the one hand, and the history of educational thought on the other.

From the perspective of the history of education, the movement to create a psychoanalytic pedagogy was but the logical continuation of the Romantic tradition in pedagogy. From this vantage point, the movement to create a psychoanalytic pedagogy was simply a new phase of a venerable movement that we can date back to Rousseau in the 18th century, and which was carried forward in the 19th century by Pestalozzi and Froebel. To Austrian and German teachers who had studied Rousseau, Pestalozzi, or Froebel, the emphasis in psychoanalytic pedagogy on the years of infancy, the critical role of parents, the merits of permissiveness, the educational value of play, the concept of "sublimation" and even infantile sexuality would not have been novel or bewildering. Anna Freud and her circle sought links neither with their contemporaries nor with their precursors in education. Most of the child analysts repressed their previous awareness that some analytic concepts might have some connection with the history of educational ideas. They wanted to be "scientific" and original.[85] The *Lehrgang fur Psychoanalytische Pädagogen* was a major effort on the part of the movement to break out of isolation, but it reached relatively few teachers. Then, those who were recruited from teaching to be trained at Vienna, who were supposed to have become the vanguard of psychoanalytic pedagogy and the bearers of the new pedagogy to the schools, instead of returning to the schools, preferred to remain and become child analysts.[86]

Most significant, there was the growing weight of evidence that between principle and practice there was a huge lacuna, through which many a theory, and many a child, could fall. Take the key area of sexual enlightenment. It was clear by the late 1920s that this innovation was not delivering the hoped-for results. Erik Homburger Erikson warned in 1930 that sexual enlightenment of children, through the simple process of imparting information, was no panacea. It applies, he said, too much to the child's intellect, but does not connect enough with the child's "affects," i.e., the child's unconscious fantasies, and is therefore of little use. The "formation of anxieties, fantasies, and unconscious theories continues," Erikson said, regardless of sexual enlightenment.[87] Freud himself became increasingly disillusioned with what was at one time the major plank of his liberating pedagogy. In one of his last works, Freud declared of sexual education that "the prophylactic effect of this liberal measure has been greatly overestimated." We come to see, he said, that children make no use of the new knowledge that has been presented to them. "For a long time after they have been given sexual enlightenment they behave like primitive races who have had Christianity thrust upon them and who continue to worship their old idols in secret."[88]

Nor did disillusion strike only at this plank of psychoanalytic pedagogy. At least the European psychoanalysts in general and the child analysts in particular were able and willing to learn from failure or partial failure. The experiments in psychoanalytic pedagogy at the Kinderheim Baumgarten, the Haus der Kinder, and the Children's Home and Laboratory School may have been short-lived and inconclusive, but the first-hand experience of a generation of effort in education and child rearing, by the analysts, their friends, and patients, provided an across-the-board corrective to the Utopian hopes of a psychoanalytic pedagogy that would prevent neurosis. Over and over again it appeared that even with the most enlightened pedagogical attitudes the same problems and difficulties made themselves manifest. Willi Hoffer speaks with authority on this subject. The psychoanalysts, he observed, attempted to turn the course of upbringing and education toward abolishing repression and giving way to the child's instinctual drives. Much stress was naturally laid on the management of the Oedipus situation. Sexual curiosity was satisfied, and sexual information was willingly given. Masturbation was unrestricted and parents' naked bodies were revealed to their children's sight. Expressions of jealousy, hate, and discontent "were never disapproved of." In general, "there was a tendency to avoid any form of prohibition." Unquestioned parental authority was replaced by the explanation of all demands and constant appeals to the child's insight and affection. "Authoritative demands were condemned as they were considered sadistic and likely to cause castration fear."[89] It was thought, Hoffer says, that, if the child's development were left to itself, it would automatically follow the course of Freud's psychosexual stages. Thumb-sucking, pleasure in dirt, smearing, exhibitionism and scopophilia, and masturbation were expected to give way step by step to the normal processes of the latency period. When children reached school age they would settle down to normal intellectual and social activities, less hampered by repression and more inclined to sublimation.

To the surprise of those who advocated it, Hoffer continues, a psychoanalytically-based education did not yield satisfactory results. Children from an "enlightened environment" had been spared overly strict prohibitions and traumatic restrictions. Yet many cases of character disturbance and behavior disorder in children brought up along these lines became known. It is true that in comparison with children reared in the conventional way, these children appeared less inhibited, "but they were often less curious about the more complicated world of objects, they had no perseverance, and they easily relapsed into daydreaming." They clung to many infantile habits. Periodically some showed lack of control of bodily functions in enuresis or encopresis. They readily gave vent to emotions that vanished as quickly as they appeared. Thus the expected changes during the latency period did not occur: only a limited reduction of instinctual expression could be observed. Normal school life put a great strain on these children. Even in "modern" schools they showed comparatively little spontaneity, and their concentration was easily disturbed. "They seemed egocentric; group demands affected them little. They were extremely intolerant of the demands of adults: ... time tables, mealtimes, table manners, routine hygienic measures, even if leniently handled, became sources of conflict." To the psychoanalytically trained observer, Hoffer concludes, these children "showed an unexpected degree of irritability, a tendency to obsessions and depression, and ... anxiety." When these children reached the period of latency, "development could not be revoked; psychoanalysis had to be called in to deal with the threatened deterioration of character."[90] In the end, the child psychoanalysts and the psychoanalytic pedagogues had to accept the insight to which experience as well as clinical work had increasingly led. Their picture of the child, who had only to be spared mishandling to grow into untroubled and joyous adulthood, was a Froebelian dream. A child's life is a drama of division and conflicting forces. No outward adjustment can avail to save children completely from the succession of inward crises inherent in the very nature of their development. This leads us finally to Freud's new theoretical formulations, which in retrospect, help explain why things went wrong in practice.

The psychoanalytic pedagogy which emerged in Europe in the '20s and '30s was for the most part composed of strands from theories formulated by Freud prior to World War I, a partial selection at that, emphasizing the earlier, liberationist aspect of his work. But few of Freud's concepts were static, enunciated in final and finished form; they changed and developed during the course of almost half a century of work. By the mid 1920s, Freud had published *Beyond the Pleasure Principle* (1920), *The Ego and the Id* (1923), and *Inhibitions, Symptoms and Anxiety* (1926). By 1926 he had made thorough revisions of the psychoanalytic edifice. One of the effects of Freud's new theoretical speculations was a pronounced shift in emphasis from the role of the environment in the aetiology of neuroses, to the instincts and their vicissitudes. By the late 1920s, Freud had come around to the view that little could be done to mitigate the force of infantile conflict. The instinctual drives alone, which the child cannot satisfy and which he is not old enough to master, are enough. The child lives in a world of frustration, goaded by unappeasable desires and envies. Conflict and hence anxiety are bound up with growth. Childhood neurosis is not the exception but the rule; it is unavoidable.[91] Freud had also concluded that aggression is man's basic problem—an expression of an innate destructive urge. In the latter part of the 1920s Freud was increasingly preoccupied with the violent, destructive side of man. In two books, *The Future of an Illusion* (1927), and especially in his landmark *Civilization and Its Discontents* (1930), Freud clarified his position. If civilization is to be maintained, not only sexuality but also aggression must be repressed. Repression, restraint, social controls serve necessary functions. Men exchange happiness, i.e., instinctual satisfaction, for security. "Civilization has been attained through the renunciation of instinctual satisfaction." The super-ego, said Freud, "represents the ethical standards of mankind."[92]

There may be an ebb and flow to Freud's sentiments, but from at least the time of the end of World War I Freud's thinking developed in a direction that was stoical, even pessimistic, and certainly anti-utopian and anti-liberationist. Freud anticipated no salvation. He understood the ego to be unremittingly buffeted and burdened: "...driven by the id, confined by the super-ego, and repulsed by reality, ... and thus we can understand how it is that so often we cannot suppress a cry: 'Life Is Not Easy.' "[93] "I bring no consolation," Freud said at the end of *Future of an Illusion*. In *Civilization and Its Discontents,* he wrote, "I have not the courage to rise up before my fellow men as a prophet; and I bow to the reproach that I can offer them no consolation, for at bottom that is what they are all demanding—the wildest revolutionaries no less passionately than the most virtuous believers."[94] Psychoanalysis could offer only the healing power of self-knowledge. "Where id was," Freud said, "there ego shall be."

Whatever anarchistic or hedonistic tendencies there might have been within classical psychoanalytic theory, they were short-lived. Freud, writes William Kessen, revived "a demonic view of the child." Freud's newer formulations concerning the psychology of the aggressive drives and of anxiety clearly showed that gratification of the instincts, irrespective of their nature or of the child's age, cannot lead to mental health. Freud wrote no briefs for the pleasure principle; rather he exhibited its futility. Freud refers to the hope of inducing patients to "adopt our conviction ... of the impossibility of conducting life on the pleasure principle."[95] We must, says Freud, abandon the infantile world of the pleasure principle: "Infantilism is destined to be surmounted. Men cannot remain children forever; they must in the end go out into hostile life. We may call this 'education to reality.' "[96] Freud's pre-World War I warnings regarding the dangers of overindulgence were not heeded. He repeated them with more success in the late '20s. Spoiling, wrote Freud, encourages the individual to remain in the state of childhood, "the period of life characterized by ... helplessness."[97] Freud's revised formulations on aggression demolished one of the main pillars of the permissivist bias in psychoanalytic pedagogy: "The severity of the superego which a child develops in no way corresponds to the severity of treatment which he has himself met with." A child, Freud wrote, who has been very leniently brought up can acquire as strict a conscience as one who has been strictly brought up. Leniency may cause children to form an overly strict conscience because, under the love they receive, they have no other outlet for their aggressiveness than turning it inwards.[98] What it amounts to is an admission that the parent-blaming doctrine was misguided. In the formation of the superego, innate constitutional factors and influences from the real environment act in combination and in unpredictable ways.

In 1933, in *The New Introductory Lectures on Psychoanalysis,* Freud returned, for the last time, to the theme of the possible role of education as a prophylaxis against neurosis, and concluded that the problems involved were almost insurmountable. Let us make ourselves clear, Freud wrote, as to what the first task of education is: "The child must learn to control his instincts .... education must inhibit, forbid and suppress." But psychoanalysis teaches that precisely this suppression of the instincts involves the risk of neurotic illness. Thus, education has to find its way "between the Scylla of noninterference and the Charybdis of frustration." An optimum must be discovered which will enable education to achieve the most and damage the least."[99]

By the early 1930s child analysts and others concerned with psychoanalytic pedagogy began to realize that it was impossible to rear children nonjudgmentally. They were beginning to appreciate the fact that both parents and teachers had to play an active role in curbing the strength of the instinctual drives that most children possess. The child's poorly developed ego needs help in controlling the powerful aggressive and sexual instincts; the child's ego needs to be encouraged or compelled to set up repressions. Reformulation of the concept of aggression by Freud, and Melanie Klein, very important here, indicated clearly that gratification of the aggressive instincts and absence of guidance by the parent or teacher cannot lead to mental health.[100] Nor can the sexual drive be simply freed. It too must be curbed or controlled. We want the child, wrote Anna Freud in 1935, to have control over his sexual drives, "for if they are constantly breaking through, there is a danger that his development will be retarded or interrupted, that he will rest content with gratification instead of sublimating, with masturbation instead of learning; that he will confine his desire for knowledge to sexual matters instead of extending it to the whole wide world. This we want to prevent."[101]

Finally, there was the belated acknowledgment that the prevention of neurosis could no longer realistically be a goal of pedagogy. Two pathbreaking books which appeared in the late '30s, Anna Freud's *The Ego and the Mechanisms of Defense* (1939) and Heinz Hartmann's *Ego Psychology and the Problem of Adaptation* (1939), made this point pellucidly clear. Miss Freud puts it this way: "I do not believe that even the most revolutionary changes in infant care can do away with the tendency to ambivalence or with the division of the human personality into an *id and ego* with conflicting aims." Mental distress, concludes Miss Freud, "has to be accepted as a normal by-product of the child's dependency, his exposure to frustrations, and the inevitable strains and stresses of development." The emergence of neurotic conflicts is the price paid for the complexity of the human personality. "The hope of extirpating neurosis from human life is found...to be illusory."[102]

In mid May of 1937, "Four Countries Conference," in Budapest marked the final closing of an epoch. One of the main topics was "A Review of Psychoanalytic Pedagogy." Present were many of the European analysts from Italy, Germany, Hungary, Austria, France, and Czechoslovakia who had not yet fled into exile, including child analysts Anna Freud, Dorothy Burlingham, Alice Balint, Berta and Steff Bornstein, Greta Bibring, Sophie Morgenstern, and others. There were revisionist papers by Burlingham, Steff Bornstein, Balint, and Anna Freud. It was fitting that Miss Freud read the epitaph for psychoanalytic pedagogy. "After years of intensive work by some of the best psychoanalytical research workers, we are certain only that there still exists no practicable psychoanalytical pedagogy," and a long period of time was anticipated before psychoanalytic theory and educational practice might be united usefully.[103] The movement for a psychoanalytic pedagogy was almost over. In March, 1938, Austria was invaded by the Nazis. The Vienna Psychoanalytic Society was disbanded; the Lehrgang fur Psychoanalytische Pädagogen gave its last courses in the winter of 1937-38.[104] The last issue of the *Zeitschrift Fur Psychoanalytische Pädagogik,* ironically containing the articles from the Budapest conference, came out in the winter of 1938. Freud with his daughter Anna, fled to England that June. He died on the night of September 23, 1939.

For a long time, nothing was heard about the movement to create a psychoanalytic pedagogy. The child psychoanalysts who were involved in the movement—most of them now in the U.S.—wrote about education in the 1940s and 1950s, theirs were mostly criticisms of American progressive or permissive education for its overindulgence of children, its lack of structure, authority, and limits, and its misuse or its misinterpretation of Freud. They carefully detached psychoanalysis from permissive attitudes or practices in childrearing and education. They preferred to forget that there had been at one time, and not that long ago, a very intimate connection between psychoanalysis and permissive pedagogy. Then in 1965 Anna Freud published her *Normality and Pathology in Children.*[105] In her introductory section, a truly extraordinary document, Miss Freud summarizes the efforts of the 1920s and 1930s to achieve a psychoanalytic education for children. Looking back over their history, after a period of more than 40 years, she writes, "We see these efforts as a long series of trials and errors." Analysts applied, she writes, the new knowledge of the upbringing of children to observations of neurotic adult patients they saw in their offices. The analyses of adult patients left no doubt about the detrimental influence of many parental and environmental attitudes and actions, such as dishonesty in sexual matters, unrealistically high moral standards, overstrictness, frustrations, punishments. It seemed a feasible task to remove some of these threats from the next generation of children by enlightening parents and educators and by altering the conditions of upbringing, thus creating, hopefully, "a psychoanalytic education serving the prevention of neurosis."

The body of psychoanalytic knowledge grew gradually, Miss Freud noted, one small finding being added to the next. The application of psychoanalytic theory to pedagogy and childrearing also proceeded gradually, by a sequence of extrapolations from clinical work and theory. Miss Freud takes note of the great hope and faith that was involved in all this: "In the unceasing search for pathogenic agents and preventive measures, it seemed always the latest analytic discovery which promised a better and more final solution of the problem." Some of the pieces of advice given to parents over the years, she continued, "were consistent with each other: others were contradictory and mutually exclusive." Some proved beneficial. On the other hand, there was no lack of disappointment. Above all, to rid the child of anxiety proved an impossible task. Parents did their best to reduce their childrens' fear of them, merely to find that they were increasing guilt feelings—i.e., the child's fear of his own conscience. Where in its turn the severity of the superego was reduced, children experienced the deepest of all anxieties—the frightening sense of being unprotected against the pressure of their drives. In short, Miss Freud continues, "in spite of many partial advances, psychoanalytic education did not succeed in becoming the preventive measure that it had set out to be. It is true that the children who grew up under its influence were in some respects different from earlier generations, but they were not free from anxiety or from conflicts, and therefore not less exposed to neurotic or other mental illnesses." Miss Freud concluded that this need not have come as a surprise "if optimism and enthusiasm for preventive work had not triumphed with some persons over the strict application of psychoanalytic tenets. There is, according to the latter, no wholesale 'prevention of neurosis.' "[106]

Whether the same tight relationship between psychoanalysis and education existed in the United States as in Europe, and whether there was any interconnection between psychoanalytic pedagogy in Europe and American progressive education, remain agenda for future research. In the meantime, this study may have some theoretical as well as historical significance. That is, this study may have some significance for educators and parents as well as for historians and psychoanalysts. There may be a lesson of primary importance to be learned from the European experience.

The Freudian revolution is, in Ricouer's phrase, "one of diagnosis, lucid coldness, and hard-won truths."[107] For Freud, truth and courage were everything. "The great ethical element in psychoanalysis," Freud explained to American psychiatrist James J. Putnam, who sought to inflate the ethical meaning of psychoanalysis, "is truth and again truth, and this should suffice for most people."[108] We might emulate Freud's example and try to follow the evidence wherever it leads. We may ask now, what is, so to speak, the future of a disillusion?

The psychoanalytic experience in Europe has something very important to tell us about childrearing and education. History, as John Lukacs observes, does not teach us what to expect or what to do, but it does suggest what is not likely to happen, what not to expect, what not to do. In this sense we can learn from the past. It is fairly evident that Freud's later revisions of psychoanalytic theory, no less than the history of the movement to create a psychoanalytic pedagogy, add up to the most trenchant and devastating critique of permissiveness extant.[109]

Permissiveness in American education has characteristically had, as one of its major goals, the prevention of neuroses, i.e., "mental hygiene," or "mental health." But, at least from the perspective revealed by the history of psychoanalytic pedagogy, this goal may certainly be in need of serious reappraisal. We really know very little about how to raise or educate children and make them mentally "healthy," however mental health is defined. Then, too, the myth of American culture is one of confidence and hope, of unlimited optimism. It is widely assumed in America that the child is born with infinite potentialities which can be adduced by a tractable environment. Any defects which subsequently appear are due to the ignorance or malice of teachers or parents who mar what would otherwise be a perfect, or at least well-adjusted, human being. American education, Francis Keppel writes, rests on two assumptions from which all else derives: "The idea that man is potentially good, and that this good can be brought about by education....The American educational system renews each day its faith in this principle of the perfectability of man."[110] This conviction is far too simple on the one hand, and far too idealized on the other. From the perspective of this study, it is an illusion to hold these Utopian beliefs. And, as Freud put it, good cannot be done in the name of illusion. If we could give up our tendency to think of the task of education in idealized and grandiose terms, then a step toward demystification will have been taken, and a step away from demoralization as well.

An early version of this paper was read at the Div. F (history and historiography of education) section of the Annual Meeting of the American Educational Research Association in San Francisco, April 22, 1976. Several friends and colleagues have made incisive and constructive comments on various drafts: Nathan G. Hale, Jr., C. H. Edson, N. Ray Hiner, Fred Matthews, Michael McGuire, Emma Plank, and Peter Paret. I'm especially indebted to Rudolf Ekstein and Louise Tyler, who persuaded me of the significance of reopening the issue of psychoanalysis and its meaning for education.

FOOTNOTES

1. See, for example, Gerald M. Platt and Fred Weinstein, *The Wish to Be Free: Society, Psyche and Value Change* (Berkeley, 1969), 299-300. See also Ernst Kris, "On Psychoanalysis and Education," *American Journal of Orthopsychiatry,* 18 (October 1948), 625; and Wolfgang Lederer, "Dragons, Delinquents and Destiny (New York, 1964), pp. 72-73.
2. Caroline B. Zachary, "The Influence of Psychoanalysis in Education," *Psychoanalytic Quarterly,* X (1941), 434.
3. "Psychoanalysis and Telepathy" (1921), S.E. *18,* 178. See also Freud's earlier " 'Civilized' Sexual Morality and Modern Nervous Illness" (1908), S.E. *9,* 177-204, and "The Further Prospects of Psychoanalytic Therapy" (1910), S.E. *11,* 145-151.
4. "Child-Analysis as a Sub-Specialty of Psychoanalysis," *International Journal of Psycho-Analysis,* 53 (1972), II.
5. *Freud, Jews and Other Germans* (New York, 1978), 66-69. See also Paul Roazen, *Freud: Political and Social Thought* (New York, 1968), 247-48, 252 ff.; and Philip Rieff, *Freud: The Mind of the Moralist* (New York, 1961), 163 ff.
6. "A Difficulty in the Path of Psychoanalysis" (1917), S.E. *17,* 143. Some cautionary notes may be permitted here. Freud wrote beautifully, but his oeuvre is vast. And he continually developed and modified his ideas. And since this study is also a chapter in the history of the psychoanalytic movement, it would be well to remember that we lack a detailed and objective history of that movement.
7. "An Autobiographical Study" (1925), in *The Standard Edition (S.E.) of the Complete Psychological Works of Sigmund Freud,* trans. and ed. by James Strachey in collaboration with Anna Freud (London, 1953), vol. 18, p. 69.
8. "On Psychotherapy" (1905), S.E. *7,* 266-67; "Five Lectures on Psychoanalysis," S.E. *11,* 48; *Introductory Lectures* (1916-17), S.E. *16,* 451; "Psychoanalysis" (1926), S.E. *20,* 268.
9. *Three Essays on the Theory of Sexuality* (1905), trans, and ed. by James Strachey (New York, 1962). There is a good summary in Freud's "Five Lectures on Psychoanalysis" (1910), S.E. *11,* 42-48.
10. *Three Essays on the Theory of Sexuality,* 71-72, 145-46.
11. "We are obliged," Freud wrote in another place in 1905, "to pay as much attention in our case histories to the purely human and social circumstances of our patients as to the somatic data and the symptoms of the disorder. Above all, our interests will be directed towards their family circumstances...and not only for the purpose of inquiring into their heredity." "Fragment of an Analysis of a Case of Hysteria"

(1905), S.E. *7,* 18. *See aslo* Heman Nunberg and Ernst Federn, eds., *Minutes of the Vienna Psychoanalytic Society (Minutes),* 4 vols. (New York, 1962), Vol. II (Dec. 15, 1909), 359.

12. Here we should be well to recall the earlier *Studies on Hysteria* by Freud and Josef Breuer, in which mental disturbances are traced back to traumatic experiences in childhood. The dangers of repression are depicted, and the treatment, catharsis, and "abreaction," a form of discharge or release of "strangulated" affects, are described. "Hysterics," Freud wrote, "suffer mainly from reminiscences." And "it appears that...these memories correspond to traumas that have not sufficiently been abreacted," i.e., discharged in appropriate signs of emotion, words, or action. *Studies on Hysteria* (1895), trans. and ed. by James Strachey (New York, 1966), 42-44. See also Freud's "Five Lectures on Psychoanalysis" (1910), S.E. *11,* 16-20, and his "An Autobiographical Study," 21-2.

13. *A General Introduction to Psychoanalysis* (1916-17), trans. by Joan Riviere (New York, 1920), 259: "Repression" (1915), *Collected Papers of Sigmund Freud,* IV, 87, 92-93. Through all the extensions and modification of Freud's thought, repression remained a potentially pathogenic method of defense against the instincts. Charles Brenner, "The Nature and Development of the Concept of Repression in Freud's Writings," *Psychoanalytic Study of the Child,* 12 (1957), 19-46.

14. *Minutes of the Vienna Psychoanalytic Society,* I, May 15, 1907, 200. See also "Five Lectures on Psychoanalysis," 53-54; *Three Essays, on the Theory of Sexuality,* pp. 143-44.

15. Discussion of Dec. 18, 1907 in *Minutes,* Vol. I, 272-4; "On the Sexual Theories of Children" (1908), *Collected Papers of Sigmund Freud,* II, 61.

16. Discussion of May 12, 1909, *Minutes,* Vol. II, 236. The entire meeting was devoted to the issue of "Sexual Enlightenment." See also the meeting of Dec. 15, 1909 in *Minutes,* Vol. II, 353-364.

17. "The Sexual Enlightenment of Children" (1907), S.E., *9,* 136-37.

18. *Minutes,* Vol. II, Dec. 15, 1909, 359.

19. "The Little Hans Case" (1909), S.E. *10,* 3-149.

20. *Ibid., 146.*

21. *Ibid.,* 146-47.

22. In 1914, in the preface to the third edition of *The Three Essays on Sexuality,* Freud wrote, "Preference is given to the accidental factors, while disposition is left in the background...For it is the accidental factors that play the principal part in analysis; they are almost entirely subject to its influence." XVI.

23. "Formulations on the Two Principles of Mental Functioning" (1911), S.E. *21,* 224; "Introduction to Oskar Pfister's *The Psychoanalytic Method"* (1913), S.E. *12,* 331.

24. "Scientific Interest in Psychoanalysis" (1913), S.E., *13,* 189-90.

25. It seems self-evident that the "educator" or "parent" to whom Freud refers has to be the mother, though Freud, strangely enough, never uses the word. And, so far as I have been able to discover, this is nowhere explicitly stated in his writings.

26. *Ibid.,* 190. And, that same year: "Let us hope that the application of psychoanalysis to the service of education will quickly fulfill the hopes which educators and doctors may rightly attach to it. A book such as this..., which seeks to acquaint educators with analysis, will then be able to count on the gratitude of later generations." "Introduction to Oskar Pfister's *The Psycho-Analytic Method"* (1913), S.E., *12,* 331.

27. Alfred Adler, "Das Zartlichkeitsbedurfnis des Kindes" (The Child's Need for Tenderness), *Monatshefte fur Pedagogik und Schulpolitik,* I, (1908), cited in *Imago,* I (1912), 95-96; Carl Jung, "The Association Method," *American Journal of Psychology,* 21 (April, 1910), 246-251; Ernest Jones, "Psychoanalysis and Education," *Journal of Educational Psychology,* I (1910), 497-520; Oskar Pfister, *Die Psychoanalytische Method* (Zurich, 1913), trans. into English first as *The*

Psychoanalytic Method (London, 1915), then as *Psycho-analysis in the Service of Education* (London, 1922); and Sandor Ferenczi, "Education and Psychoanalysis," a paper delivered in 1908 and published posthumously in *International Journal of Psychoanalysis,* 30 (1949), 220-24.

28. Otto Rank and Hans Sachs, *The Significance of Psychoanalysis for the Mental Sciences,* (New York, 1916), 121.

29. Among the psychoanalysts, there was so much interest in education that in 1913 German psychologist William Stern was moved to publish a *Protest-Pamphlet* against those whom he described as those enthusiastic followers of Freud who were recommending the psychoanalysis of children as the general foundation of education reforms! Cited in Stern's *Psychology of Early Childhood,* 2nd ed. (New York, 1930), 31-32.

30. See the following by Anna Freud: "Child Analysis as a Sub-Specialty of Psychoanalysis," *International Journal of Psychoanalysis, 53 (1972), 152; and "A Short History of Child Analysis," The Psychoanalytic Study of the Child,* 21 (1966), 7-8.

31. Freud, "Sexuality in the Aetiology of the Neuroses" (1898). *Collected Papers of Sigmund Freud,* 5 vols. (London, 1957), I, 245-46. "If mankind had been able to learn from a direct observation of children," wrote Freud in 1920, in the preface to the fourth edition of *The Three Essays on Sexuality,* "these three essays could have remained unwritten." XVIII. See also Ernest Jones, *The Life and Works of Sigmund Freud,* 3 vols. (New York, 1955), II, 260-61; Ferenczi, "A Little Chanticleer" (1913), in his *Sex in Psychoanalysis: Contributions to Psycho-Analysis,* trans. by Ernest Jones (Boston, 1916), 244.

32. Extremely little information about Hug-Hellmuth has come to light. In a will made a few days before her death "she expressed a desire that no account of her life and work should appear, even in psychoanalytical publications." *International Journal of Psychoanalysis,* 6 (1925), 106. Her wish has been honored to this day. Hug-Hellmuth published two books, *A Study of the Mental Life of the Child,* trans. by James J. Putnam (Wash., DC, 1919), and *Neue Wege Zum Verstaendnis der Jugend* (Vienna, 1924), which has not been translated into English. She also published one major article: "On the Technique of Child Analysis," *International Journal of Psychoanalysis,* 2 (1921), 287-305.

33. Willi Hoffer states that Hug-Hellmuth intended "to be the first psychoanalyst to establish child analysis as a special branch of education." "Psychoanalytic Education," *Psychoanalytic Study of the Child,* 1 (1945), 296. Hoffer may have meant that Hug-Hellmuth intended to establish child analysis as a branch of "special education." It is interesting that at this time "Heilpadagogik," a broadly based and eclectic movement in the field of special education, was making its appearance among a group of German, Austrian, and Swiss educators led by Theodor Heller in Austria and Heinrich Hanselmann in Switzerland. Alexander Walk, "The Pre-History of Child Psychiatry," *British Journal of Psychiatry,* 110 (1964), 765; Leo Kanner, *Child Psychiatry, 3rd. ed. (New York, 1957), 10;* and Henri Ellenberger, "The Scope of Swiss Psychology," in H.P. David and H. von Bracken, eds., *Perspectives in Personality Theory* (New York, 1957), 49-50.

34. William M. Johnston, *The Austrian Mind: An Intellectual and Social History, 1848-1938* (Berkeley, Calif., 1972); Alfred Schick, "The Vienna of Sigmund Freud," *The Psychoanalytic Review,* 55 (1968-1969), 545; Allan Janik and Stephen Toulmin, *Wittgenstein's Vienna* (New York, 1973), 241 ff. See H. Stuart Hughes, *Consciousness and Society: Reorientation of European Social Thought, 1890-1930* (New York, 1958) for a broader context.

35. Ernst Papanek, *The Austrian School Reform: Its Bases, Principles and Development in the Twenty Years Between the Two World Wars* (New York, 1962); Charles

A. Gulick, *Austria from Hapsburg to Hitler,* 2 vols. (Chicago, 1948), Vol. 1, Chaps. XV and XVI; Beryl Parker, *The Austrian Educational Institutes* (Vienna, 1931); May Hollis Siegl, *Reform of Elementary Education in Austria* (New York, 1933).

36. Recall the organization in 1920 of the New Education Fellowship, with its branches in Europe in England, France, and Germany. See William Boyd and Wyatt Rawson, *The Story of the New Education* (London, 1965); W.A.C. Stewart, *The Educational Innovators,* 2 vols., Vol. II, *Progressive Schools 1881-1967* (London, 1968); Adolph E. Meyer, *Modern European Educators* (New York, 1934).

37. Robert Dottrens, *The New Education in Austria* (New York, 1930), 202.

38. Paul Dengler, "Creative Personality and the New Education," *Progressive Education,* 6 (1929), 134.

39. Rudolf Ekstein, a Viennese schoolteacher who became a child analyst in the 1930s, summarizes this development: "Psychoanalytic pedagogy and child analysis, sociologically speaking, derived from the same social matrix...the teaching profession." Rudolf Ekstein and Rocco L. Motta, "Psychoanalysis and Education—An Historical Account," in Rudolf Ekstein and Rocco L. Motta, eds., *From Learning for Love to Love of Learning* (New York, 1969), 8; Margaret S. Mahler, "Child Analysis," in Nolan D. C. Lewis and Bernard L. Pacella, eds., *Modern Trends in Child Psychiatry* (New York, 1945), 265-66.

40. "The Theory of Children's Analysis," *International Journal of Psychoanalysis,* 8 (1927), 65.

41. *International Journal of Psychoanalysis,* 20 (1939), 212; Anna Freud, "Willie Hoffer, M.D., Ph.D.," *Psychoanalytic Study of the Child,* 23 (1968), 7-8; Rudolf Ekstein, "Willie Hoffer's Contribution to Teaching and Education," *Reiss-Davis Clinic Bulletin,* 5 (Spring, 1968), 4-10.

42. In fact, reminisces Ekstein, "it was almost possible to think of analysis...as a kind of progressive pedagogy." "Psychoanalysis and Education—An Historical Account," 16.

43. Ernst Schneider, "Geltingsbereich der Psychoanalyse für die Pädagogik," *Zeitschrift für Psychoanalytische Pädagogik,* 1 (1926-27), 2-6.

44. Heinz Hartmann, *Ego Psychology and the Problem of Adaptation,* (1939), trans. by David Rapaport (New York, 1958), 12-13.

45. See *Reich Speaks of Freud,* ed. by Mary Higgins and Chester M. Raphael (New York, 1967), 24, 32-33. See also David Boadella, *Wilhelm Reich: The Evolution of His Work* (London, 1973), 68 ff.

46. Philip R. Lehrman, "Fritz Wittels, 1880-1950," *Psychoanalytic Quarterly,* 20 (1951), 97; Fritz Wittels, *Freud and His Times,* (New York, 1931), 323-24; Franz Alexander, *The Western Mind in Transition: An Eye-Witness Story* (New York, 1960), 81, 99-100, 110-111; Anna Freud, "Changes in Psychoanalytic Practice and Experience," *International Journal of Psychoanalysis,* 57 (1976), 257.

47. "Introduction to Aichhorn's *Wayward Youth*" (1925), S.E., *19* 273.

48. Freud went on to speculate that it might be the destiny of psychoanalysis to train "a band of helpers for combatting the neuroses of civilization...'a new kind of Salvation Army!' " "The Question of Lay Analysis" (1928), S.E., *20,*249; "An Autobiographical Study," S.E., *20,* 70; see also Freud to Pfister in Heinrich Meng and Ernst L. Freud, *Psychoanalysis and Faith: The Letters of Sigmund Freud and Oskar Pfister,* trans. by Erich Mosbacher (London, 1963), 126.

49. "Psychoanalytic Education," *The Psychoanalytic Study of the Child,* I (1945), 299.

50. The superego, Freud writes, "can be super-moral and then become cruel." Later, Freud continues, it may become a burden on the ego in the form of an unconscious and complusive sense of guilt. *The Ego and the Id* (1923), trans. by Joan Riviere, revised and ed. by James Strachey (New York, 1960), 18, 24-25.

51. "A Metapsychological Description of the Process of Cure" (1925), in Franz Alex-

ander, *The Scope of Psychoanalysis, 1921-1961: Selected Papers* (New York, 1961), 223.

52. Quoted in Maurice R. Green, ed., *Interpersonal Psychoanalysis: The Selected Papers of Clara M. Thompson* (New York, 1964), 74. Dr. Thompson was a friend and former analysand of Ferenczi. See Also Ferenczi and Otto Rank, *The Development of Psychoanalysis,* trans. by Caroline Newton (New York, 1925), 64-65.

53. Reich, *The Sexual Revolution,* trans. by Therese Pol (New York, 1970), XIV.

54. Ekstein, "Psychoanalysis and Education—An Historical Account," 16.

55. *Ibid.*

56. We still know very little about Miss Freud. Ernest Jones in his biography of Freud is most reticent about Anna, and, as I have reason to know from our correspondence, Miss Freud is reticent about herself. Informative is Paul Roazen, *Freud and His Followers* (New York, 1975), 436 ff. See also Robert Coles, "The Achievement of Anna Freud," *Massachusetts Review* 7 (Spring 1966), 203-220. Miss Freud's position on child analysis was explicated in 1926 before the Vienna Psychoanalytic Society. Anna Freud, *Introduction to the Technic (sic) of Child Psychoanalysis,* trans. by L. Pierce Clark (New York, 1928). This slim volume comprises the series of four lectures delivered in 1926 before the Vienna Psychoanalytic Institute, and first published in German in 1927. It has subsequently been republished, together with "The Theory of Children's Analysis," a paper read at the Tenth International Psychoanalytical Congress in 1927, and a 1945 paper "On the Theory of Child Analysis," as *The Psychoanalytical Treatment of Children* (New York, 1946). Like Hug-Hellmuth before her, Anna Freud stood for a more interventionist, active form of therapy, combined with restraint in respect of interpretation of unconscious material. Anna Freud was more concerned with the conscious than the unconscious, the influence of the environment than with intrapsychic conflict—a form of therapy hard to distinguish from educational intervention. Although Sigmund Freud was usually skeptical about analytic innovations, he took a father's pride in Anna's work. Freud to Oskar Pfister, Nov. 21, 1926, in *Psycho-analysis and Faith: The Letters of Sigmund Freud and Oskar Pfister,* 106. The most judicious comparison of the two major schools of child analysis—that of Anna Freud and that of Melanie Klein is in Victor Smirnoff, *The Scope of Child Analysis* (New York, 1971).

57. This volume was originally published in 1929 as *Einfurung in die Psycho analyse für Pädagogen.* It was first published in England in 1931 as *Introduction to Psychoanalysis for Teachers* (with a trans. by Barbara Low), and then in the U.S. in 1935 as *Psychoanalysis for Teachers and Parents.* The following discussion is from the 1931 edition.

58. *Introduction to Psychoanalysis for Teachers,* 39.

59. *Ibid.,* 45-6.

60. *Ibid.,* 76-7.

61. *Ibid.,* 99-100. It would be better, Miss Freud concludes, if teachers and parents underwent analysis before they started to teach and raise children; "the teacher or educator should have learnt to know and to control his own conflicts before he begins his educational work."

62. The fundamental idea, writes Wittels, is "leave your children to themselves. Do not educate them, for you cannot educate them." "We hear much," Wittels continues, "about 'the century of the child.' But that century will not begin until grown-ups realize that children have less to learn from them than they have to learn from children." *The Liberation of the Child,* trans. by Eden and Cedar Paul (New York, 1927), 242. This volume was first published in German as *Die Befreing des Kindes* (Set the Children Free) in 1925. See also Wittels, *Freud and His Time Time* (New York, 1931), 354 ff.

63. Siegfried Bernfeld, *Kinderheim Baumgarten: Bericht Ober Einen Ernsthaften Versuch Mit Neuer Erziehung* (Berlin, 1921). This volume has unfortunately not yet been translated into English. A student of mine, Doris Klubitschko, helped me with the translation. There are brief descriptions of the Kinderheim in Willi Hoffer "Siegfried Bernfeld and Jerubbaal," Publications of the Leo Baeck Institute, *Yearbook,* 10 (1965), 159-166. See also Peter Paret's Introduction to Bernfeld's *Sisyphus, or the Limits of Education,* trans. by Frederic Lilge (Berkeley, California, 1973). Originally published in 1925 as *Sisyphus: oder die Grenzen der Erziehung.*

64. "Willi Hoffer," 7.

65. Bernfeld, *Kinderheim Baumgarten,* 30, 74.

66. *Ibid.,* 74.

67. The final blow-up is described by Hoffer in "Siegfried Bernfeld and Jeruubaal," 165-66. Bernfeld, deeply hurt by this denouement, considered the experiment a failure. But Hoffer reports that anybody who met the Kinderheim children after the first few months "would have agreed that these children were not 'institutional children.' " Quoted in Paret's Introduction to Bernfeld's *Sisyphus,* XX. August Aichhorn also built a reputation in Austria at about this same time as a "re-educator" of adolescents, especially delinquent boys, in two reformatories; first at Ober-Hollabrun, then at St. Andras. But this was before Aichhorn had become interested in psychoanalysis. His well-known *Wayward Youth* (1925) was written after he'd become a psychoanalyst.

68. The following is based largely on information given in Emma Plank's eulogy of Lili R. Peller, "In Memory of Lili Peller," December 17, 1966, mimeo copy in my possession. Also Emma N. Plank, "Reflections on the Revival of the Montessori Method," *Journal of Nursery Education,* 17 (1961-62), 131; and Rita Kramer, *Maria Montessori: A Biography* (New York, 1976), 285-91.

69. Mrs. Peller published three articles describing the theoretical aspects of the experiment in the *Zeitschrift fur Psychoanalytische Pädagogik* in 1929, 1932, and 1933 respectively. They are "Die Grundsaetze der Montessori-Erziehung" (The Principles of Montessori Education); "Die Wichtigsten Theorien des Spieles" (The Most Important Theories of Play), and "Gruppenerziehung des Kleinkindes" (Group Education of the Young Child). Two of her articles published later, in English, are also informative: "Incentives to Development and Means of Early Education," *The Psychoanalytic Study of the Child,* 2 (1946), 397-415; "The School's Role in Promoting Sublimation," *ibid.,* 11 (1956), 437-49. See also Rudolf Ekstein "Lili E. Peller's Psychoanalytic Contributions to Teaching," *Reiss-Davis Clinic Bulletin,* 4 (Spring, 1967), 6-8. And, in general, Emma N. Plank, ed., Lili E. Peller, *On the Development and Education of Young Children: Selected Papers* (New York, 1978).

70. Kramer, *Maria Montessori: A Biography,* 289.

71. *Ibid.,* 319-321.

72. The spirit of the late '20s is communicated by a former pupil of the Haus der Kinder. On learning of Lili's death, he wrote to one of the survivors of the old *Gemeinschaft,* Mrs. Emma Plank, as follows: "...you all laid the foundation in me, as in the other children, for our attitude towards life. You educated us with the hope that we would grow up to be honest people, who could grasp the spirit of Internationalism, understand democracy, and carry the banner and propagate the responsibility for others and for an ideal socialism. I think you really gave us that." Plank, "In Memory of Lili Peller," 10.

73. Robert Coles, *Erik H. Erikson: The Growth of His Work* (Boston, 1970), 16-20.

74. *Ibid.,* 20. An American psychoanalyst who trained in Vienna in the '30s makes an almost identical observation. He refers to the school as "the nearest thing to the American progressive schools" with which he was familiar. Edward Liss, "The

Vicissitudes of a Hybrid," *Journal of the American Academy of Child Psychiatry,* 3 (1964), 765.

75. In 1937, in Vienna, Anna Freud, in conjunction with Dorothy Burlingham and Dr. Edith Jackson, organized an experimental day-nursery for infants between one and two years of age. This experiment was terminated in 1938, with the onset of the Nazi occupation of Vienna. Subsequently, the organizers of the Vienna Nursery, now in London, founded the famous Hampstead Nurseries and Training Course for Children's Nurses and Teachers, in which Anna Freud is still very active.

76. Vera Schmidt, *Psycho-analytische Erziehung in Sowjetrussland, Bericht uber das Moskauer Kinderheim Laboratorium* (Vienna, 1924). This is a series of lectures delivered by Schmidt in November, 1923 before the Vienna and Berlin Psychoanalytic Societies, and published by the official psychoanalytic publishing house, the Psychoanalytische Verlag. I've been unable to locate this pamphlet; it has never been translated into English. There is available, however, a briefer, French version of the original: "Education Psychanalytique en Russie Sovietique," *Partisans,* 46 (Febrier-Mars, 1969), 58-71. There is a brief account of the early years of the Children's Home and Laboratory School in *International Journal of Psychoanalysis,* 5 (1924), 258-66.

77. "Education Psychanalytique en Russia Sovietique," 66.

78. *Ibid.,* 69-70.

79. *International Journal of Psychoanalysis,* 5 (1924), 259.

80. "Education Psychoanalytique en Russia Sovietique," 70.

81. *The Sexual Revolution,* 259-60.

82. *Psychoanalysis for Teachers,* 79-80.

83. As late as 1972 Anna Freud could refer to "the problematic subject of child-analysis and the question whether to consider it a sub-specialty of psychoanalysis." There was at one time, says Miss Freud, every reason to expect that all analysts would be interested in child analysis. But this did not happen. Child analysis did not have the triumphant career we had envisaged for it. The analyst of adults, she sadly observes, "remained more or less aloof from child analysis, almost as if it were an inferior type of professional occupation." "Most analysts," Miss Freud continues, "preferred the childhood images which emerged from their interpretations to the real children in whom they remained uninterested." "Child-Analysis as a Sub-Specialty of Psychoanalysis," *International Journal of Psychoanalysis,* 53 (1972), 153.

84. I'm aware of only one effort in which those interested in psychoanalytic pedagogy in Europe attempted to directly build a bridge to educational progressives. This was at the Fifth International New Education Fellowship Conference, at Elsinore, Denmark, in August, 1929. In attendance were Oskar Pfister, Ernst Schneider, and Hans Zulliger from Switzerland, Carl Muller-Braunschweig and Nelly Wolfheim from Berlin, Rene Laforgue from Paris, Lili Peller and Emma Plank from Vienna. William Boyd, ed., *Towards a New Education* (New York, 1930), Appendix.

85. There was a further inhibition in the development of a psychoanalytic pedagogy—the internecine quarrels that took their toll. There was especially an interdiction of ideas which might be reminiscent of the deviations of Adler, Jung, or Otto Rank. See Erik H. Erikson, *Life History and the Historical Moment* (New York, 1975), 38: Paul Roazen, *Erik H. Erikson: The Power and Limits of a Vision* (New York, 1976), 6-7.

86. Firtz Redl "Psychoanalysis and Education," in his *When We Deal with Children* (New York, 1969), 147-149.

87. "Psychoanalysis and the Future of Education," *The Psychoanalytic Quarterly,* 4 (1935), 50-68. This paper was originally read before the Vienna Psychoanalytic Society in April, 1930.

88. "Analysis Terminable and Interminable" (1937), S.E., *23* 223-224.

89. "Psychoanalytic Education," 301.

90. *Ibid.,* 302-303. Similar comments are made by Dorothy Burlingham, "Problems Confronting the Psychoanalytic Educator," in her *Psychoanalytic Studies of the Sighted and the Blind* (New York, 1972), 76-78. The children portrayed by Hoffer and Burlingham show symptoms of what has been called "pathological narcissism." They "become so spoiled through the easy achievement of a high degree of fore-pleasure, that they lose the capacity for real and complete achievement." Paul Federn, *Ego Psychology and the Psychoses* (New York, 1952), 346.

91. "An Outline of Psycho-analysis" (1940), 41-42.

92. "An Autobiographical Study," 59.

93. "New Introductory Lectures on Psychoanalysis" (1933), S.E., *22,* 78-79.

94. S.E., *21,* 145. Of *Civilization and Its Discontents,* Lionel Trilling wrote: "For social thought in our time its significance is unique. It may be thought to stand like a lion in the path of all hopes of achieving happiness through the radical revision of social life." *Sincerity and Authenticity* (Cambridge, Mass., 1971), 151. But there was some hope. Freud said, "The voice of the intellect is a soft one, but it does not rest until it has gained a hearing. Finally... it succeeds....A point of no small importance." "The Future of an Illusion" (1927), S.E., *21,* 49. Freud once described himself as an optimistic pessimist.

95. "Lines of Advance in Psychoanalytic Therapy" (1919), S.E., *17,* 157.

96. "The Future of an Illusion," (1927), S.E., *21,* 49.

97. "Inhibitions, Symptoms, and Anxiety," (1926), S.E., *20,* 167.

98. "Civilization and Its Disccontents" (1930), S.E., 21, 171-72.

99. *New Introductory Lectures,* 149, 150.

100. See Melanie Klein and Joan Riviere, *Love, Hate, and Reparation* (London, 1937).

101. Anna Freud, "Notes on Aggression," *Bulletin of The Menninger Clinic,* 13 (1949), 65-70; "The Bearing of the Psychoanalytic Theory of Instinctual Drives on Certain Aspects of Human Behavior" in R. M. Lowenstein, *Drives, Affects, Behavior,* I (New York, 1953), 261-64; and "Psychoanalysis and the Training of the Young Child," *Psychoanalytic Quarterly,* 4 (1935), 20.

102. *The Ego and the Mechanisms of Defense,* 54 ff.; "Psychoanalysis and Education," *The Psychoanalytic Study of the Child,* 9 (1954), 14-15; "The Significance of the Evolution of Psychoanalytic Child Psychology" (1950), in *The Writings of Anna Freud,* IV, 616 ff.; and her "The Contributions of Psychoanalysis to Genetic Psychology," *American Journal of Orthopsychiatry,* 21 (July 1951), 488. See also, Heinz Hartmann, *Ego Psychology and the Problem of Adaptation,* 80-82 and "Psychoanalysis and the Concept of Health," *International Journal of Psychoanalysis,* 20 (Jan.-Oct., 1939), 308-15 Bernfeld's "Psychoanalytic Psychology of the Young Child," *Psychoanalytic Quarterly,* 4 (1935), 6-7. Reich alone remained unconvinced. The development of psychoanalytic pedagogy, he wrote in 1934, is inhibited by two ideological limitations of "the bourgeois analysts": their refusal to cope with the contradictions between the removal of sexual repression and bourgeois sexual inhibitions in children and adolescents, and their biological view of the child-parent conflict. *Sex-Pol; Essays, 1929-1934,* trans. and ed. by Lee Baxandall (New York, 1960), 48, 58.

103. Quoted in Michael Balint, "Ego Strength, Ego-Education and Learning" (1938), in his *Primary Love and Psychoanalytic Technique* (London, 1952), 197. Steff Bornstein's paper "Misunderstandings in the Application of Psychoanalysis to Education" was published in the last issue of the *Zeitschrift fur Psychoanalytische Padagogik,* II (1937-38). Dorothy Burlingham's paper "Problems Confronting the Psychoanalytic Educator" was also published in the same edition of the *Zeitschrift,*

and subsequently republished in English as chapter 5 of her *Psychoanalytic Studies of the Sighted and the Blind*. Alice Balint's paper likewise appeared in the *Zeitschrift* for 1937-38, is translated into English as "Fundamentals of Our Education," and appears as an appendix to her *The Early Years of Life* (New York, 1954). There is a brief account of the symposium in *International Journal of Psychoanalysis*, 19 (1938), 170-71.

104. In all, the teacher-training course at the Vienna Psychoanalytic Institute had been attended by some 180 teachers; the number of analyzed teachers had reached "more than forty." "Report of the International Training Commission," *International Journal of Psychoanalysis*, 20 (1939), 212-213. For the last course listings see p. 218.

105. New York, 1965, 4-8. See also Miss Freud's "Psychoanalytic Knowledge Applied to the Rearing of Children" (1956), in *The Writings of Anna Freud*, II, 268 ff.

106. Erik Erikson provides an interesting sidelight. "In psychoanalytic circles," he writes, "we have witnessed a little private history of tentative child training systems dedicated to instinct indulgence, or to the avoidance of anxiety in our children. We know that not infrequently a new system of 'scientific' superstitions has resulted." *Childhood and Society*, 2nd ed., revised and enlarged (New York, 1963), 414.

107. Paul Ricoeur, *The Conflict of Interpretations: Essays in Hermeneutics*, trans. and ed. by Don Ihde (Evanston, Ill., 1974), 154.

108. Freud to James Jackson Putnam, March 30, 1914, in Nathan G. Hale, Jr., ed., *James Jackson Putnam and Psychoanalysis* (Cambridge, Mass., 1971), 171.

109. The recent advent of psychoanalytic ego psychology has not affected this critique of permissiveness, only rephrased it. See especially Heinz Hartmann's "Comments on the Psychoanalytic Theory of the Ego," *The Psychoanalytic Study of the Child*, V (1950), 78, and his "Notes on the Reality Principle," *ibid.*, XI (1956), 35, 36, 39. See also Ernst Kris, "Notes on the Development and Problems of Child Psychoanalysis," *ibid.*, V (1950), 36, 37; and Robert M. White, *Ego and Reality in Psychoanalytic Theory* (New York, 1963).

110. *The Necessary Revolution in American Education* (New York, 1966). 11.

Index